Soccer Coaching:
Principles of Technical and Tactical Development

Andrew Caruso

Reedswain Publishing
Spring City, PA
www.reedswainsoccer.com

**Library of Congress
Cataloging - in - Publication Data**

Soccer Coaching: Principles of Technical and Tactical Development
by Andrew Caruso

ISBN-13: 978-1-59164-184-1
ISBN-10: 1-59164-184-5
© 2013

Editing, Layout, Cover Design and Diagrams
Bryan R. Beaver

Diagrams created with the following software:
Easy Sports Graphics - www.sports-graphics.com
Session Planner - www.soccerspecific.com

Cover photo: © Michael Krinke

Reedswain Publishing
88 Wells Road
Spring City, PA 19475
www. reedswain.com
orders@reedswain.com

Table of Contents

Acknowledgements v

Foreword vii

Preface ix

Introduction 1

Chapter 1 - Principles of Player Roles in Soccer 7

Chapter 2 - Dribbling Development of First Attacker 17

Chapter 3 - First and Second Attacker Passing/Receiving
Combination Play 31

Chapter 4 - Creating Space and Development of Third Attacker 53

Chapter 5 - Principles of Defense 65

Chapter 6 - Functional Training in Defensive Third 87

Chapter 7 - Functional Training in Midfield 99

Chapter 8 - The Strike, Functional Training in Attacking Third 111

Chapter 9 - Shooting, Strictly Shooting 129

Chapter 10 - Possession Prototypes 155

Chapter 11 - Keeper Techniques and Decision Making 173

Chapter 12 - Special Situations 209

Chapter 13 - Team Tactics Coaching 221

Chapter 14 - Shortsided Games and Training 229

Chapter 15 - Pedagogical Soccer Techniques 237

Chapter 16 - Warm-up, Stretching, Cool Down 249

Chapter 17 - Continuing Growth in US Soccer 255

Appendix I - The Prepared Coach 263

Appendix II - Giving Players Ownership 267

Appendix III - Fun Skill Soccer Games 273

Bibliography 279

Acknowledgments

Thanks are in order to my wife, Eva who has endured my passion for the game for more than 45 years. Thanks also to my son, Troy, and my daughter, Janine, who brought me into the realm of youth sports mainly in their respective sports of basketball and soccer.

Thanks to the National Soccer Coaches Association courses, USSF Licensing courses and Wiel Coerver and no less than 350 plus clinics that I attended as President and Founder of Kwik Goal. This unbelievable opportunity helped to form the foundation concepts.

Thanks to the many unmentioned contributors who have also been infected with The Great Game.

Also thanks to Long Island Junior Soccer League and the chance to be on the state staffs of Pennsylvania and Florida. Teaching coaching licensing courses definitely fostered my growth. I would be remiss if I didn't mention my 10 years of high school coaching and my several years spent as Coaching Director for various youth soccer clubs. But the training and coaching of some 30+ teams was the ultimate education. While U-15 thru U-17 boys was a minor challenge, the major challenge was the many demonstration clinics for coaches with U-6 players.

My most recent experience as a consultant to a large soccer club has been very revealing. I never realized how much you can learn when you do not have to prepare and train teams yourself. Furthermore, it is much easier to see the areas that others can improve in as opposed to seeing your own areas that could be improved.

There is no intention to compare to Sir Isaac Newton, but my version is: "It is not I, but the soccer leaders' shoulders that I have stood upon that allows me to see a bit of the Great Game."

Foreword - The Great Game

Over twenty million Americans are playing the great game of soccer. This guide is for their coaches; it will help both the new and the experienced youth and high school coaches develop complete players, those who master the three fundamental elements of technique, tactics, and function. There are many technique books on the market, and a few tactical books, but none which attempt to integrate technique, tactics, and function with accompanying game activities. As in state-of-the-art coaching for all sports, this integration is best developed through a system of progressions. Building upon a logical progression of exercises, activities, and shortsided games, this guide will help the coach to apply the principles of play to the game of soccer and the development of soccer players. Too often these principles are overlooked by coaches; yet they are the very foundation of the game! Once a coach can view game action from this point of view he is capable of making important/relevant suggestions that relate to training and general principles. This facilitates player growth and game results.

This book is the culmination of a lifetime of soccer experience as player, fan, coach, author, clinician, licensing instructor, and designer of equipment. While it remains true that the game itself is the best teacher, the best coaches also learn from licensing courses, clinics, videotapes, books, observation, the internet and conversation. This book owes something to each of these sources. It shares the vision of American soccer as seen by the United States Soccer Federation, the National Soccer Coaches Association of America, the United States Youth Soccer Association, and top youth, high school and college coaches across the nation, whose contributions to the game and to this book are invaluable.

If you think it is all about correction, guess again. Tony DiCicco says it best: "Catch them being good". Of course, correction is sometimes in order, but 50%+ had better be about the good decisions and execution of technique. While not all will subscribe to integrating sports psychology techniques, at the bare minimum, positive coaching is imperative if one hopes to have successful player development and results. Players without confidence will never be able to assert themselves to perform their best. The added benefit is that the confidence you help your players develop will carry over to their other life activities.

May your love of the great game of soccer ever increase, and may this journey contribute to your knowledge and enjoyment.

Preface

This book is a reference to the advanced fundamental principles of soccer. This is particularly so for the first several chapters in regard to the structure of the game and true for the whole book as the activities enumerated later on will also be something that many will want to refer to as *how* to accomplish certain goals with their team.

It is nearly impossible to coach well, employing generalizations that apply to virtually all aspects of the game, without a clear understanding of the responsibilities of **first, second and third attackers and defenders**. In order for players to be able to grow continuously, they must understand these basic principles. Without these principles the communication and cumulative growth necessary to understanding is extremely difficult, if not impossible. Without this knowledge there are innumerable isolated facts that prohibit growth and understanding of the many offensive and defensive solutions available for the various game situations. The ability to build one idea upon another without this generalized understanding would leave one with a huge task that with these understandings becomes much easier. On the other hand, anyone who understands the basic offensive principles of **penetration, support and mobility; and pressure, cover and balance** on defense can grow very rapidly. It also allows them to make valid game adjustments consistently in order to help their team.

Avoiding this learning merely makes understanding the game at a high level a long and arduous journey. Fans often understand **what** is wrong. It is the coach who must have a general understanding of **why** a team is doing well or poorly. Furthermore, a coach must know **how** to provide some valid game-like (motivating) activities at subsequent training sessions for further growth and fixing the problems. This *why* and *how* is greatly assisted by understanding the general principles of offense and defense.

Probably much of what is said to help a team win at halftime talks and in developing game plans is not clear enough to help a team play better unless these foundation concepts are understood. Mixed in with the great insights players offer at halftime and for game plans, there usually is a preponderance of thoughts that were not applicable to assisting your team. One very high level player starting out as a young coach would discuss and even demonstrate techniques in regard to playing, with no realization that technique can only be changed by abundant repetition in training with the ball. It has little or nothing to do with talk, and certainly is not what will help the team in the second half of the game! Unfortunately, almost all recommendations that were not trained for in practice will be ineffective. Thus, training is where the "coach", manager or trainer really makes the biggest difference.

It is with these few thoughts that this book focuses on the basic responsibilities of attack and defense, but goes much further by sharing many useful **activities** for the development of those foundations of the game. In the interest of clarity, there is a very careful design to avoid using the word support for defense. It is much clearer and less confusing, especially when communicating with players, to have the second attacker referred to as a **support** player and the second defender as a **cover** player. By the same token the third attacker and defender become much clearer through the use of the terms mobility for offense and balance for defense.

In the end, a clear understanding of the roles with appropriate activities for developing these attributes in your players leads to rapid and long-term development of players. Naturally, the when and where on the field of how these responsibilities are developed is a process that a player from the youngest age to the professional level is constantly developing, hopefully efficiently, due to the intelligent grasp by the coach. As a general rule we always try to develop the offensive responsibilities before the corresponding defensive responsibility. There can be no serious defense until players have reasonable control of the ball.

Shortsided games with greatly reduced numbers are often the most efficient means of accomplishing these understandings.

Finally, it is my hope that this text will greatly help all readers in reaching a basic understanding of these principles with players of all ages. Naturally, there will be different degrees according to age and ability of the players. Certainly, mobility and balance might not be understood before age eleven or older. Still, the basic mobility resulting from combination play is introduced early on (well before age 10) in assisting the development of young players.

Every coach, including the professional coach, needs reminders to return to the basic techniques and tactics of the game. In fact, professional coaches often warn all others that fundamentals are critical.

I hope you enjoy this book is as much as I enjoyed writing and sharing it with you.

Introduction

Principles of Coaching

A coach should weigh the relative importance of four main objectives for any soccer program: player development, fun, participation, and sportsmanship. A sound program should allow for all four objectives. The key word for practice sessions is...FUN! If your players had fun, chances are you ran a good training session. If they did not have fun, you may have covered too much, taken some short cuts, or coached above or below their level. Competitive practice games are usually fun, and can embody anything you want to teach. With variety, full participation, and positive reinforcement, you can maintain motivation and fun. Not to be confused with silly behavior, fun comes from an involvement in learning which depends on a level of activity appropriate to the players' needs; fun also comes from accomplishment, as in a progression to higher levels of play.

Participation directly relates to fun. Most kids would rather be actively playing on a team that goes 3 and 7 than sitting on the bench for a team that goes 7 and 3. But participation is even more important in practice! Good coaches ensure participation by avoiding inactive waiting lines in drills, and by insisting that each player have a ball of his own whenever appropriate, especially during the warm up. The regular use of 1 v 1 and shortsided games, with 2 to 6 players per side, dramatically increases player involvement as well as development; therefore smallsided games are absolutely essential for all levels, but especially the younger players. **No soccer country in the entire world starts its youth players with 11-a-side games before age 12!**

Development is an aspect of coaching that is often misunderstood by well-intentioned coaches. Development is concerned with the emotional growth and physical skill of the individual player, rather than the record of the team. We would do well to remember that not every team and not every kid is capable of world class levels of play. Our task is to help players become as good as they can be, and want to be. Your players will respect you for the person you are long after they have forgotten the season's won-lost numbers. A sound program adjusts these objec-

tives according to the needs of the players, not the coaches! The younger the player, the greater the emphasis on fun. But even high school
players and above need a certain amount of enjoyment. Good coaches
find the balance that keeps a healthy perspective on fun, participation,
development and sportsmanship.

Good coaches also must find the balance in all four components of any
game, which must be adjusted according to the player's individuality.
The first is psychological, which does not need to be all that complex.
Suffice it to say that players need fun, variety, and encouragement. They
do not need to be criticized nor told what to do every time they get the
ball. The second component is fitness; players can develop fitness by
working with a ball, developing skill alone or in small groups instead
of running laps. The activities in this book will develop fitness for your
youth players. The third component is technique; this refers to the basic
skills of soccer: shooting, dribbling, heading, passing, receiving, and
tackling. Development of technique requires time and repetition. The
fourth component is tactics; these are the thinking and decision-making
aspects of the game, such as what to do and where to go with and without the ball. Shooting is a technique; deciding when, where, and how to
shoot is a tactic.

How does the coach deal with all these components within the con-
fines of a single practice session? First, the psychological aspect is best
handled by being positive, and by asking rather than telling, i.e. "Where
should the standing foot be when passing?" Fitness, technique, and
tactics can be incorporated into a system called "Economical Training,"
which incorporates two or more of these components into a single
activity. With the activities and smallsided games outlined in this guide,
players can develop any skill at the same time they are learning tactics
and/or improving fitness. Good coaching, however, predominantly
concentrates on only one aspect of the game per practice, though techniques and tactics are integrated.

Teaching the basic skills in soccer requires time, patience, long range
planning, and imagination. To get the maximum number of touches
on the ball, each player must have a ball. Each skill is best taught using
the established progression of fundamental, game-related, and game
condition exercises. Teach only one skill per session. At the fundamental
stage, the skill is demonstrated, key points are briefly explained, and

time allowed for sufficient practice and correction. There is no pressure on the players, no defender, and little movement. When players can execute the skill, the coach can progress to the match-related stage; that is, some movement and defensive pressure is added. As soon as the skill can be successfully executed at this level, move on to the match condition stage; gradually increase the speed and defensive pressure to actual game conditions. Make up a game that will allow the players to repeatedly perform the selected skill and score it so that use of the skill is rewarded. This approach will incorporate the given skill into real game conditions, as well as motivate the players more than drills. The following chapters will suggest progressions that are fun, practical, and proven successful with players of widely varying ages and abilities. The activities in this book use the progression concept not only to develop technique, but also to develop tactics. Many coaches believe that no amount of tactical knowledge will make up for poor technique. Therefore, they neglect to develop their players' tactical knowledge. We need to teach both technique and tactics in an integrated fashion!

While there is some truth to the idea there are no tactics without technique, a better statement is we can never separate technique from decisions - - playing soccer involves both, OR IT IS NOT SOCCER! Once a player thinks the game is played only at his feet, and not in his mind, he is damaged.

In good practice sessions and smallsided games, technique, tactics, and functional roles are developed simultaneously; however, coaching involves a logical order of instruction in focusing on a single aspect at a time. When we teach players, we must integrate technique with tactics, and then move on to function, which refers to either a particular position or an area of a field (i.e., defender in defensive third). Under the pressures of time and the winning ethic, many coaches make the mistake of advancing from technical training directly to functional training, thus by-passing the tactical stage. This strangles both technical and tactical development because it limits the all important stage of making and carrying out decisions. The result is a deadly game where defenders often stand idle, occasionally clearing the ball with aimless kicks. To develop young players, we need to concentrate on technique and related basic individual and small group tactics. Simply stated, teach your players how to play soccer; then, and only then, teach them how to play specific positions! Even if you never get to functional training, you will have set the proper foundation.

Of course, the priorities for young players are ball control, collecting, dribbling, shooting, basic passing and receiving, and shortsided work requiring much ball contact and decision-making. But before there is any concern for positioning, team arrangements, or team tactics, the coach should teach the PRINCIPLES OF PLAYER ROLES in soccer, upon which all tactics must be understood! Discussions of formations (5-3-2, 4-4-2, etc.) are academic and futile without the basic knowledge of first, second, and third attackers and defenders and their roles in the game. Once a player has a reasonable feel for the ball so that she can receive, dribble, pass, and shoot, she is ready to learn these basic principles of player roles. Even average players as young as seven years can begin to implement these concepts, which can be refined over an entire playing and coaching career. Players need not know the names of roles, nor be able to explain them; but they do need to use these concepts, though their knowledge may be mostly reactive.

Young players will not learn roles in 11v11, so we must play much 1v1, 2v1, 3v3, 4v4, etc., in order for players to master penetration, support, mobility, pressure, cover and balance. Without this knowledge no team arrangement is effective and with players who understand these basics of soccer any system will have an excellent chance of success.

The principles of player roles can be demonstrated using six players, three attackers and three defenders. Any team on attack must have:
1. a first attacker (player about to receive or in possession of the ball) whose job it is to penetrate or at least draw a defender;
2. a second attacker who gives support; behind the ball, usually diago- nally.
3. third attackers (there should be more than one) who provide mobil- ity, penetration.
Any team defense must have:
1. a first defender whose job is to apply pressure to the ball and delay the attack when cover is absent;
2. a second defender who offers cover (help for the first defender in case he gets beat);
3. third defenders who balance and concentrate the defense.

Please recall, this book will always identify the second attacker as the support player and the second defender as the <u>cover</u> player to avoid needless confusion.

Note a simple example of all three attacking and defensive roles in the diagram that follows:

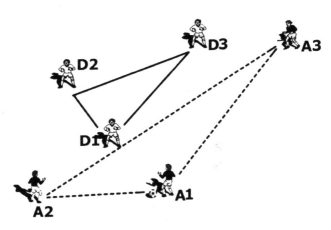

Diagram #1:
D1 - First Defender - DELAY or PRESSURE on the ball
D2 - Second Defender - COVER
D3 - Third Defender - BALANCE

A1 - First Attacker - PENETRATION
A2 - Second Attacker - SUPPORT
A3 - Third Attacker - MOBILITY

These principles will be developed throughout this book to enable the coach to build a working knowledge of basic soccer, to foster quality player development and to devise intelligent individual and team tactics. The first chapter will fill out the skeletal diagram with the vital information about the principles of play, which are simple to understand, to teach and to apply to every aspect of the great game of soccer!

1

Principles of
Player Roles in Soccer

The basic principles of soccer deal with the contrast between attack and defense. Attack begins the instant a team is about to or has gained possession of the ball. The responsibilities of the attacking team involve three major roles, which we call first, second, and third attacker. The FIRST ATTACKER (A1) is the player in possession of the ball or about to receive the ball, regardless of his position on the field. A1's main responsibility is PENETRATION; that is, to get the ball forward and possibly behind the defenders. If within scoring range, the first objective is to score a goal. Otherwise he will try to move the ball forward with dribbling or a penetrating pass. A1 attempts to get the ball safely to the most dangerous location possible. The mental responsibility of A1 may be the easiest, but penetration is the single most difficult skill in soccer, requiring excellent technique. Imaginative, skillful dribbling and shielding, accompanied by deft passing, are difficult and important. Passing and moving and/or combination play always facilitates penetration.

Obviously possession is primary. Turning the ball over to the other team is always a calculated risk that should be taken if there is somewhat of a realistic chance of completion, especially when a scoring opportunity can be materialized. If a turnover is inevitable, one needs to consider the possession alternative, which frequently involves a square pass, diagonal backward pass, layoff or dribbling in those directions. The word negative pass was not used because any pass that preserves possession instead of turnover cannot be called negative in the context of this book. At advanced levels quick counter attack, breakout options, risky long ball service all need to be taught. This should only be after some consistent rudimentary notions of possession are achieved. Once a player thinks that soccer is kicking a ball instead of passing among teammates, great harm to player development has occurred! Obviously, in defensive areas of the field safety is paramount.

The first attacker becomes much more dangerous when a SECOND AT-TACKER (A2) creates quality SUPPORT, thus giving the attack the width and options it needs to be effective. This gives A1 more options. A2 can generate penetration by receiving a pass (thereby becoming A1), or by drawing a defender away. A2 is most effective when she forces a defender to commit either to marking her or covering a space, but not accomplishing both. A2's main responsibility is to ensure possession, by always being ready to receive A1's pass, either to the feet or to space. Generally supporting from a position diagonally behind the first attacker, A2 offers quality support. She must always be ready to become the first defender if the ball is lost.

There may be several THIRD ATTACKERS (A3), whose job is to create MOBILITY by disturbing the defense through positioning and running forward, diagonally or across the field. These movements are designed to get behind and spread the defense. Often working with other third attackers, A3 draws the defenses attention and disturbs its balance. This creates openings or passing lanes for the first attacker. In youth soccer, third attackers may tend to be stationary because they seldom realize they are involved in the play, especially in 11 aside. At higher levels, third attackers make many runs which do not reward them with the ball, yet they help the attack immensely by creating space and forcing difficult, or even inadequate defensive decisions upon the defense. The role of the third attacker is the most complex of the attacking roles and the most difficult to achieve.

Obviously more mature players must learn how to draw defenders away from the ball. In professional matches invariably we see a player at full width, near the opposite touchline from the ball. Naturally when the attacking team loses possession or is about to lose possession this wide player must immediately pinch in to assist the defense. This simply follows the first law of offense and defense; when in possession of the ball "open up", create width and depth and when on defense remain compacted in order to regain possession of the ball. Compacting creates many tackling situations and reduces or closes passing lanes in order for the defense to win possession and begin their own attack.

A sophisticated offense requires a worthy defense if it is to develop further. Therefore, once players have developed confidence in individual and small group usage of the ball, then we begin teaching defensive roles. Like the attacking roles, there are three roles of defense, which begins the moment possession of the ball is lost. Often it begins when a player anticipates possession will be lost.

The FIRST DEFENDER (D1) is the player who pressures the first attacker. The major responsibility of the first defender is to DELAY the attack and put pressure on the ball. It is important to note that D1's first priority is not to immediately attempt to win the ball through aggressive play or tackling. The essence is to slow down or stop penetration, whether by pass, dribble or shot. The first defender protects the goal by staying goal side of A1. He must be patient; once there is cover (a second defender to assist him), he attempts to win the ball. He may try to steer opponents away from a dangerous area or toward numbers up of his teammates, or he may force A1 to make a square or backward pass. D1 is successful when he prevents penetration in any form; that is:

1. He delays A1 until defensive cover (D2) arrives;
2. He wins the ball;
3. He prevents A1 from turning towards goal or looking up;
4. He forces A1 to make a poor pass;
5. He forces A1 to make a square or backwards pass;
6. He forces A1 to shield or dribble across the field or backwards

The #1 fault for first attackers, especially when 30 to 50 yards from the goal is they are too far away from the attacker and thereby allow many forward passing options to other attackers. There is a strong tendency for players to play 1v1 defense, not realizing that ever important element of **TEAM DEFENSE!** The defender thinks that because he was not beaten by the dribble he has done his job, when in fact he did not because he allowed a penetrating forward pass. As coaches we must constantly be vigilant of this tendency by players because it is a serious bad habit which is difficult to correct once a player has done this for a number of years without proper correction. This does not mean diving in, but it does mean that if you are beaten immediate chase must be given with great effort.

Alternatively, D1 is unsuccessful when he allows A1 to penetrate in any way (dribble forward, pass forward, or shoot). Where D1 is defending against two attackers, he is successful when the defense recovers to a two-versus two, or preferably numbers up.

The SECOND DEFENDER (D2) is usually the next closest to the ball and at least slightly behind D1. The role of second defender involves several responsibilities, but foremost is to offer COVER for D1. This means his first job is to assist D1 by positioning himself at a correct angle and distance behind D1 and communicating with him (such as telling him when to tackle). This provides depth for the defense, and forces A1 to deal with two defenders. D2's second role is to mark A2, but he cannot mark him so closely as to deny cover for D1. In fact, he may invite a pass from A1 to A2, but if this is a square or backwards pass, D2 is successfully doing his job. The second defender must play a space, a man and the ball simultaneously, as well as use the off-side law to his advantage. D2 is successful when he provides good cover for the first defender. If A1 beats D1 or passes to A2, D2 must be ready to become the first defender.

As in the attacking roles, there may be several THIRD DEFENDERS (D3), who add CONCENTRATION and BALANCE to the defense. They accomplish this by staying goal side of the player they mark, restricting space, providing tight marking in the vital area, and communicating. All defenders must work hard when the ball is moving. Third defenders may mark an attacker, cover a space, or both. Thus this role can become too complex for the beginner. The youth player needs to know only the basics of this role: mark a man or cover a space to keep the attack from entering a dangerous area. Note a more detailed example of all three offensive and defensive roles is shown here.

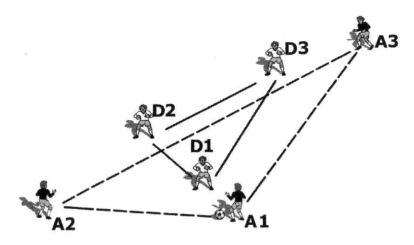

Diagram #2: This is the foundation for understanding 11v11 team play. Note offense is more spread out, while the defense is more compact.

A1 will try to penetrate. Note A2 has excellent opportunity to receive the ball. A3 is allowing for a long pass (mobility), but definitely keeping D3 from A1.

A1 = First Attacker
(player about to receive or in possession of ball)
PENETRATION
(Main responsibility is to get behind defenders, maintain possession and only take calculated risks)
- Score if possible
- Forward movement preferred
- Get ball to most dangerous location possible
- Take chances to score
- Becomes much more dangerous when a 2nd attacker offers quality support and 3rd attacker truly provides mobility (width, depth)
- Confident ball handlers with excellent dribbling skills make very dangerous first attackers creating enormous problems for the defense, especially when they shoot well from distance.
- Maintains possession

A2 = Second Attacker
(Try to insure possession)
SUPPORT
(Focus is possession)
- Generally behind ball and open to receive ball
- Confuse second defender, do not allow him to cover and mark
- Always ready to receive-at feet or in space
- Be ready to be first defender if ball is lost
- Communicate to first attacker (talking, pointing, body language, etc.)

A3 = Third Attacker
(Disturb defense through positioning)
MOBILITY
(Width and depth)
- Get open to receive ball (constantly check away & to ball)
- Draw defender's attention
- Work with other third attackers
- Get behind and spread defense

- Maintain eye contact and accelerate to receive
- There can be several third attackers
- Diagonal runs, overloads, occupy dangerous locations, overlap, blind-side runs, etc.

D1 = First Defender
(Covers first attacker)
PRESSURE ON THE BALL: DELAY if last defender
- Be patient; once there is cover, more aggressive moves to win ball are made
- Attempt to steer player to sideline or a helping teammate
- Protect goal, stay goal side
- Force square or back passes
- Win ball, go for ball or tackle when you have cover
- Keep attacker from turning and looking up

D2 = Second Defender
(Helping first defender)
COVER
(Focus is double coverage)
- Cover precedes man coverage, do both as best as possible, but cover is first priority
- All players who have an immediate shot if they get the ball must always be marked
- Provide DEPTH
- Attempt to cut out passes
- Be ready to be first defender, stop shots and dangerous passes
- Maintain a space; see ball and man
- If the ball is won do something constructive

D3 = Third Defender
BALANCE
(Concentration)
- Restrict space; squeeze attacking space
- Cut out passes when attempt is safe
- Stay goal side and talk (communicate)
- Recover to the near post or penalty spot unless behind it
- Always attempt to see ball and man
- There can be several third defenders

The defense steps up when the ball is won or the offense passes backwards, first and foremost to support teammates and move the attack away from the goal. Often, youth coaches teach this as an offside trap, which may work against poorly prepared coaches and teams, but against reasonably sophisticated teams this is likely to be a losing behavior. For a highly trained coach it is easier to teach methods to beat an offside trap than it is to set one, especially with youth players. The sad fact that it often works because teams are so poorly trained for beating the trap, this often hurts the development of players when they progress to higher levels.

In diagram 3 there is still support (A2) and mobility (A3), but the total posture is more aggressive in terms of penetration, since both receivers are in front of the ball. Following the first law of attack, the team in possession is spreading out and therefore using a larger area. The defense, on the other hand, follows its first law, which is concentration. They therefore occupy a smaller area.

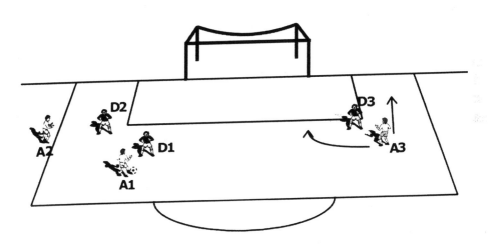

Diagram #3: Aggressive support

It would be nice if the roles were static, but in fact they are constantly changing rapidly. Thus players must move from one role to another at lightning speed, which requires anticipatory thinking which can best be learned by game and game condition experiences. The transition from one role in offense or in defense must be extremely quick, but the changes in role from offense to defense or vice versa are equally important. Thus, one begins to see the extremely dynamic forces in soccer, but this is one of the attributes of the game that make it so exciting. Virtually no one on the field either close to the action and ball or far away is ever not involved in an integral manner when the game is played at higher levels. Higher levels does not necessarily mean professional level, it also includes a U12 match that is being conducted at a high level of competency commensurate with the age level.

Teaching the responsibilities of these player roles might be done in a 3v3 activity, but 4v4 might be better for experienced players. In a 20 by 30 yard grid, the coach can walk the players through a demonstration, briefly explaining how the roles change as the ball is passed. Focus on only one role at a time. Bear in mind that development of a single role may take two to five sessions. Furthermore, only 20 minutes a session can be devoted to direct teaching of these roles, because all teachings must be placed into a progression leading up to match condition. Explanation and demonstration must take less than three minutes. After the walk through demonstration, the coach may have a 3v3, 4v3, or 4v4 shortsided game in the grid. The coach would use `freeze' commands: at the command "Freeze!" or the whistle, all players immediately stop where they are. The coach explains where selected players are supposed to be and why. Play continues. Even though errors may occur every 15 seconds, the coach usually allows continuity of play to develop, and only stops play every two minutes or more. Only during the freeze does the coach talk to the group. Coaching points for individuals can be made as play continues, but talk is not continuous.

From here this exercise could progress in any of several directions, depending upon the coach's objective for the practice. (Each practice should focus on a single skill and related tactic, and always progress through the fundamental, match related, and match condition stages to as realistic a game as possible, adapted to the particular skill and tactic of that session). For example, goalkeepers and/or goals could be added to afford realistic shooting and goalkeeping practice (you might need to enlarge the grid). Another approach would be to impose specific limitations on the players, such as not allowing A1 to try to penetrate unless she has good support from A2. These adaptations would focus on each of the offensive and defensive roles, one role per session. Other limitations could focus on technique, such as left foot only, or two touch only. The possibilities are endless, and the coach will soon be able to devise her own adaptations to achieve the desired result. The next chapters will show you how to use these principles in specific progressions to develop your players in various aspects of the game.

2

Dribbling Development
of First Attacker

The youth coach should focus on player development which is greatly dependent upon the ability to dribble the ball. Of course, there is a place for one touch soccer; but there is a greater need for players developing confidence with the ball prior to one touch. In order not to kick the ball away mindlessly when there is no available pass, first attackers must be able to dribble and shield. Since every player becomes the first attacker as soon as she receives the ball, every player, even the keeper, needs to develop dribbling skill. Exciting dribbling, such as a series of 1v1's, is a highlight of the game.

Great players are able to penetrate with the ball or possess when either is required. While nearly all the immortals of the game were excellent dribblers, most relied on one or two good moves which they used repeatedly. However, the way to develop good dribblers varies greatly from being one. Developing good dribblers is not simply teaching one or two moves; teaching dribbling involves training players to perform many moves; then, and only then, can they choose the few that work best for them. Besides, when you teach dribbling there is much ball contact which automatically enhances total ball control.

Dribbling is the most individual, creative, and expressive skill in soccer. There may be no "wrong" way to dribble, but there are general characteristics of good dribbling. These include keeping the ball under close control, even to the point where the ball is sometimes under the player (Cruyff move); touching the ball with almost every step taken; using both feet, and also the various surfaces of each foot, including the inside, outside, sole, rear, and instep; going in either direction with a particular move; keeping the head up enough to see both the ball and the field; changing direction sharply, quickly, and frequently; also changing speed, with stops, slow deliberate movements, rapid acceleration from dribble to drive (when driving, the ball is pushed way out ahead, but at a safe distance for the situation) and rapid deceleration from drive to dribble, as well as being able to stop; and most important, using a variety of well-executed feints.

Dribbling development helps players build confidence and poise. The physical requirements are flexibility, fast footwork and thousands (even millions) of touches on the ball in practice and game conditions. While flexibility varies from player to player, it can be maximized through proper stretching at the end of practice and practice with the ball. Flexibility allows the player to get very low and explode away with speed using a power move. The power move begins with a low crouch or boxer's stance over the ball, with the player gradually rising to an upright position as speed is attained. Fast footwork is developed when good technique is combined with rapid and numerous repetition, which calls for literally hundreds of touches per practice session. This is not nearly as difficult as it may sound! In fact, good training sessions often have as many as a thousand touches per session. Of course, line drills and excessive talking will prohibit this.

There are dozens of moves, which can be joined together in innumerable ways, thus creating a dribbler's unique style. Although many of these moves can be named (scissors, sole roll, pulling the V, swivel hips, Charlton), players need not learn them by name. Over the course of a season, the coach should introduce many moves to the players; if he cannot demonstrate, he should find someone who can. Often players can teach each other their favorite moves. Bear in mind that every player will not make use of every move; it is enough that each player find the two or three moves that work for her. As the coach, teach players to go both ways from a given move, and to gain some "ambifootedness" from the exercises. Require flexibility and an explosive getaway. To do this, players should bend their knees to lower their center of gravity. Here then is a workable progression for teaching the technique of dribbling. First of all, dribbling can be an integral part of the warm-up. For the youngest players, juggling helps develop coordination and touch. It develops control and is a good warm-up component. Allowing the ball to bounce between juggles is another helpful step before full-scale juggling, and is especially helpful in loosening the hips. The inside and the outside of the foot can be used more easily when a bounce is employed. Competent jugglers should work from left to right and right to left, high to low and low to high body parts, then add movement and change of direction. Instead of stopping whenever the ball hits the ground, players should explode away and change direction with the ball the instant it touches the ground. Collection and lifts can be developed at the same time. These approaches are much more valuable than simply trying to keep the ball in the air with random touches or a single body part used repeatedly. Group juggling in threes in a triangle is very economical. Control the ball on the first touch, followed by a change of direction pass to a teammate. The two touch restriction makes it very functional; first touch is *control*, second touch is *pass* or *shot*. Groups of three is excellent for incorporating heading, especially the turning of the ball skill of heading for passing and shooting. The demand should be to hit it to a teammate's feet and have them collect the ball. This allows for some excellent collection skill development. Such variations make it game related and challenging fun. Consider having groups do their own scoring. To maintain high interest, briefly ask who had the high score in each group.

The next activity for all age players is dribbling in a confined area, which forces them to look up in order to avoid collisions. The basic tactic involved here is to slow down in traffic, and speed up in open space. Beginners often do the opposite. The coach can then add specific demands - left foot only, outside of foot, change direction or speed on whistle, shielding whenever close to another player. The coach can evaluate his players during this time, so he knows what to emphasize in the instruction. Meanwhile, the players are getting a warm up and valuable ball control work. Now they are physically and mentally ready to learn more.

Teach them a few moves, maybe just one in a given session. However, do three or four of the moves previously learned. As in all technical instruction at the fundamental stage, it is best to start with a clear and brief demonstration. Then have each player work on the move with a still ball and no opposition. Every player should have a ball for this part of the sessions. Next, practice the move with a very slow moving ball and no defender. A guide line for introducing a move is 25 repetitions, which can be accomplished in less than two minutes. This is the proven number of repetitions necessary for basic retention for physical learning by learning research.

As success is achieved, progress to the game-related stage by working with a slightly faster moving ball, token pressure, and shielding whenever close to another player. Work up to the game condition (grid) stage by increasing the defensive pressure and speed, then make a game of it. Simple games such as hit another player's ball, hit the coach or super star under the knee, tag, etc. Add small goals or cone goals. Keep score, not necessarily by the number of goals, but perhaps by the number of times the move is executed. Another approach would be to reinforce dribbling moves in shortsided games: give points for usage of particular moves or correct shielding (side-on), or demand that before the ball is passed, a move must be used.

A highly successful method for combining many touches with developing specific moves is to dribble the ball back and forth between the insides of the feet three times (the ball goes back and forth, not forward) then immediately execute the move. Develop the move with each foot. From here, the activity progresses to more movement and increasing defensive pressure, then to shooting opportunities and smallsided games which focus on dribbling. Mandatory 3-5 touches per player scrimmages aid dribbling development enormously.

When players are in development, a good practice involves many touches of the ball. Coaches should consider at least ten minutes of dribbling practice per session, and of course, much more when dribbling is the focus of the practice. When your practice session focuses on dribbling, here is a good way to get nearly a thousand touches of the ball in the first thirty minutes of practice. A touch per second can be accomplished in this kind of activity, which offers far more variety than simply dribbling aimlessly throughout the field. Spend a few minutes at each of the following, and incorporate shielding wherever practical.

Turns are a critical part of dribbling effectively. Teach the scissor, instep chop, Cruyff and sole roll. The scissor move merely has the foot go around the ball, with the right foot it is generally done in a clockwise direction to maintain the best balance and control. The step over closely relates to the scissor but the foot goes over the ball instead of around it. The instep chop sends the ball from the inside of one foot straight across the body and in a quick motion is taken by the instep across the front of the body again and the player, having displaced his opponent, goes forward, passes or shoots. The Cruyff move is taking the ball with the inside of one foot and crossing it behind the standing leg to the other foot. The sole roll simply pulls the ball with the sole of the foot, often back toward and past the player and then forward to get past a defender or for a shot or pass. The rapid changes of direction and starts and stops are very effective in getting past opponents. Players who practice dribbling on their own will always distinguish themselves as competent. Ball control simply yields confidence, as indicated earlier.

- Each player with a ball, free arrangement in grid, center circle, or penalty box
- Each player with a ball, working around cones
- Relay races using pairs dribbling around cones is very motivating - even with high school age players
- Each player with a ball, moving in a random fashion around the demonstrator
- Each player with a ball, in pairs facing each other, pretending to take each other on, but when within two yards, using a move to dribble past each other
- Same format, but only one ball, each player taking a turn, and the other acting as semi-passive defender (in this activity go left and right)
- Two lines (no more than three players per line) facing each other ten yards apart, players in front dribbling towards each other, making a move, passing to player in line facing them, then going to end of opposite line
- Cones in a triangle, up to three players, each with a ball, making a move at each cone (stay at own cone, make move at left cone, then go to right cone)
- Entire team making moves in a grid, slowing down in traffic, speeding up in open space
- Three players in a monkey-in-the-middle configuration, each outside player with a ball dribbling to either side of a passive defender (players must have heads up to read move of other dribbler)
- Siamese Dribbling: one player leads and the other follows, copying every move. (After 1 min., switch leader and follower.)
- Accelerating through gate "goals" is an aid to vision while dribbling
- My favorite is a group with all players dribbling and pretending to take on any player they encounter

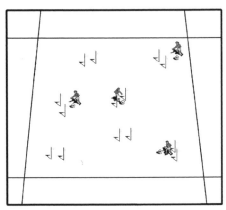

Diagram #4: Multiple gate goals for technical development. Do a move in front of each grid goal then accelerate through the gate goal.

Three players in a dribble/pass activity using 2 balls

1. X passes to Y who is in the middle
2. Y dribbles past passive defender X
3. X is now in middle and receives from Z
4. X dribbles past Z to the right side
5. Z receives from Y at middle area
6. Z dribbles past Y

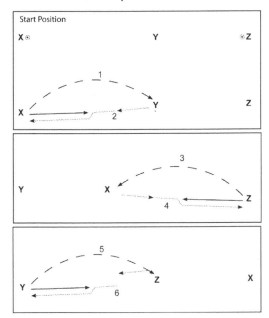

Diagram #5: Creative dribbling in groups of three. This was one of Weil Coerver's key activities

22

Dribbling the lines of the field can present another variation. Demand moves, backward movement, turns, changes in speed, some dribbling `sprints', dribbling lifts, and anything that creates variety and fun.

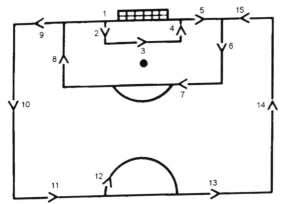

Diagram #6: Dribbling the lines. Follow the number pattern. This can also be done indoors following the lines of the basketball court.

A very simple basic exercise is a grid of 10 x 15 yds with 3 players behind each end line.

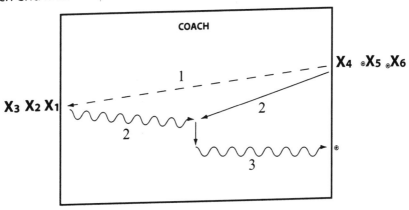

Diagram #7: 1v1 in restricted space

X1 tries to dribble over the opposite end line while X4 attempts to deny the end line: if X4 wins the ball he immediately passes to the coach. Progress to the defender, after winning the ball, dribbling to the opposite goal line.

Progress to 1v2, so two players come out to defend the dribbler. Proper steering is required by the first defender while the second defender must read proper angle and distance. Demand quality communication. Move to 2v2, still emphasizing communication and the proper exchange of the pressuring player. As soon as the first attacker completes a pass to his teammate, the second defender must immediately apply pressure, moving quickly as the ball moves and slowing down when approaching the new attacker. The first attacker must drop step immediately to provide cover. Do not permit the first defender to move a significant distance to provide pressure to the ball as this will often cause a defensive breakdown. If there are more than 12 players, consider two groups. If coaching alone, consider two groups, using players for service so you can observe both groups. This is also an excellent defensive exercise. Having two coaches definitely improves the quality of a session as long as the two complement each other.

"Spots" is a favorite; there are many ways to implement it but the simplest is a goal with a keeper and players taking on a defender from 28 yards away from goal. The defender serves a crisp ball to the attacker (dribbler) who immediately attacks the defender and takes a shot on goal. Each round players switch roles and move across the 18 yard line thereby attacking from many different angles. After every round (about 10 attempts, 5 each for each partner from the five locations) switch partners, generally winners against winners or capable dribblers against capable defenders. If players are having little success demand that the defender connect his hands behind his back. This not only facilitates dribbling success, but forces defenders to improve footwork & balance and not foul in the box which we all realize is very costly in games. Every coach looks to have a few players who can attack a goal, dribble and create a goal for a teammate or simply hold the ball long enough for teammates to get open or forward. As a result of instructing and permitting players to dribble, players with talent will develop creativity and flare which brings great excitement to spectators.

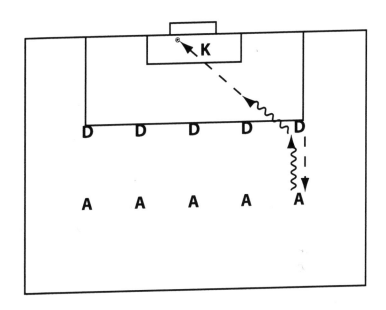

Diagram #8: Spots Shooting 1v1 - If you have 15 or more players consider 2 groups. If players hold the ball too long, which is unrealistic in a game environment, restrict the number of touches to about 7 touches.

Since dribbling is largely a question of personal style, the ball itself is the number one teacher of the player. You can accelerate learning by offering your players a great deal of 1v1 activities. Here is a basic one which has proven successful for all levels, from beginner to highest levels. Use a grid about 10 yards square, three balls, and four players (two per team). Two players go 1v1 in the grid, trying to score by shooting between the feet of the player standing still in the middle of the opposite goal line with feet spread wide apart. The goal-line players each keep a ball in their hands, so that when the field ball is played over the end line or scored, the goal-line player can immediately toss or roll the ball in to his teammate for a quick counter-attack. Goal-line players can not move except to retrieve the out-of-bounds ball. If the goal-line player is retrieving the ball, his opponent in the grid cannot shoot, but must shield and/or dribble till the 'goal' returns.

Diagram #9: 1v1 with rear support.

The coach should allow groups to play for a minute or two, then call for a quick switch; the "goals" become the field players for the next minute or two. Demand immediate transition; perhaps use extra players on the side lines to keep the ball in play; require specific moves. Your players will get a great workout as they develop dribbling and shielding skills. Many coaches use some form of this game in every practice, gradually adding players to develop a tactical progression from this 1v1 to 2v2, 3v1, 4v2, and 5v2 (see the next two chapters).

This is a basal activity that can be used often. Since it is totally game oriented, there is never a concern that the players will lose interest. This fosters maximum development.

The 1v1 exercise will reinforce the need for shielding. Players will find that when marked tightly and unable to go forward, they must place their bodies between the ball and the opponent, jockeying for position while maintaining possession and looking for an opening. (The concept can be demonstrated by a quick comparison: pick up the ball and dribble it like a basketball; as soon as a defender gets within range, notice how you keep your body between the ball and the opponent.)

26

Coaching points to emphasize are that the body intervenes from a side-on position (adding distance to the shield) while balance (strength) and vision are maintained. The player must keep cool under pressure, and shielding is working under pressure!

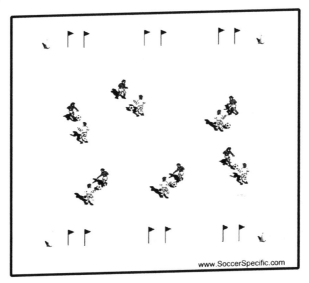

Diagram #10: Progression of 1v1 to Multiple Goals to Teams Attacking One Goal Two teams of six each with a direction. Each play 1v1 at first and a player can score on any one of his three goals. Then each pair is assigned a single pair of goals. Move to 2v2 or 3v3, again scoring on any one of their three goals and finally a full sided game employing all the players that can only score on the two central goals.

Shielding requires constant movement as you adjust to the defender's position. Playing 1 v 1 against a superior defender will reinforce this skill, as will 1v1 in a very confined area. To make a game of it, score by counting the seconds of successful shielding. Or add the option of dropping the ball back to your goal-line player after shielding for ten or more seconds. Another scoring method is the coach can randomly call "Stop!" every 5, 6, 7, 8, or 9 seconds and whoever has the ball gets a point. Play to a score of 5. The start can be both players facing each other with one foot on the ball.

As much as possible, 1v1 activities should involve finishing on goal, because scoring is a skill that requires continuous development and practice. You can progress from the human goal to the flat-faced goals which are very well-suited to many repetitions in a short time. This greatly facilitates economy of training (as well as space, since both sides of the goal can be used safely). Thus you can incorporate the 1v1 with shooting practice.

Need to get your goalies involved? Use portable goals in a 20x30 yard grid, with two field players going 1v1, and extra balls in each goal for quick restarts. Again, a minute to two at a time, then bring on two fresh field players. Resting players can retrieve balls. Several 1v1 pairs can work at the same time in the same area, providing an additional obstacle for both the attacker and defender.

1v1 with restricted number of touches for maximum realistic game situation. Can be done with one goal, in which case when the defender wins the ball he merely dribbles over the opposite goal line. With two goals with keepers, the defender shoots on the opposing goal.

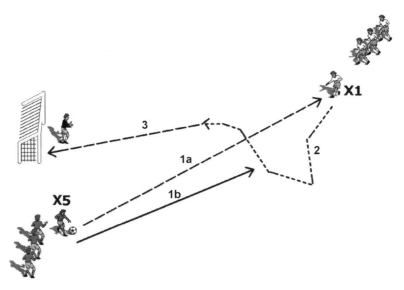

Diagram #11: X5 has served crisp ground ball to X1 who proceeds to attempt to score on the left side goal. X5 follows his serve and defends.

Coaching points:
Attacker:
- Attack the defender straight on toward the goal
- Attack with speed
- If necessary, slow down and gain control near the defender
- Shoot on first touch after beating defender
- Look for OPENING IN THE GOAL

Defender:
- Move at speed until near the attacker
- Then slow down, get low, keep eye on the ball
- Attack the ball right after the attacker touches the ball or anytime you think you can win the ball
- If ball is won, take a shot as soon as possible

Either use two groups with numbers greater than eight or even two groups going at the same time in the same area. This only increases the game relatedness with greater use of vision. Coach the activity but keep it moving at a rapid pace. Service should never be more than a second or two after the previous group's shot.

The 1v1 is vital because it is the foundation of the team game of passing and receiving. If no pass is immediately available, dribble. Once players can execute moves without pressure, it is time to put the moves into more challenging game-like situations. Small-sided games can be used to teach and develop dribbling skills in a more realistic environment. Your players then have the choice of taking on a man, taking a shot, shielding or passing, which is what the real game offers. To encourage dribbling, you can run a smallsided game with specific dribbling demands. For example, players must beat a man before they can pass, or they must touch the ball five times, etc.

The pivotal activity that really places dribbling in its full prominence and is game related, is to have a small sided game, anything from 2v2 to 6v6 in which the players must touch the ball at least 5 times before passing. I prefer 3v3 with one neutral who has no restriction so that he can help a team maintain possession in view of this difficult demand. This can be done as a possession game, to cone goals, to full size goals with keepers, but this insures that all players attempt dribbling. Another extremely useful game is to demand that every player take on a defender before passing or shooting, whatever the case may be. The demand here can be that you must beat someone or merely have taken him or her on. Taking them on means you can still use a layoff or square pass, beating someone means you dribbled behind the opponent. The day of the one-touch defenders and the dribbling strikers is long gone. All players in the modem game are required to be total players without regard for their position on the field. Recently, this even includes keepers.

All in all, young players even through high school must be given time to dribble at practice, and strongly encouraged to practice dribbling on their own. Players can benefit from dribbling instruction. In practice, give players dribbling experience in many 1v1 and shortsided games. Permit them to dribble in matches, even if they lose the ball! At least this way when they are 15, 18 or whatever they will be able to be constructive when no pass receiver is available. Better to lose the ball attempting to dribble than to kick the ball nowhere, or worse, to the opponent. As a developer of young players, encourage the art of dribbling!

First attackers who can dribble cause penetration, open passing lanes, create great difficulty to defenses and score goals. Equally important, frequently in the game in order to make a useful (penetrating) pass, one must create the space and time through dribbling to complete the pass.

For experienced players ages 14 or older, there still is a place for dribbling. This does not exclude one touch exercises or correction to players when there is a wide open player in a forward position who constantly decides to dribble and lose the opportunity for penetration. The notion that we continue dribbling ad infinitum is foolish. While we first attempt to develop a player who is confident with the ball, we still use passing/receiving activities for all ages. All players must learn to do what the game demands, that is why at the end of all sessions we play unrestricted football. Quality decision making will not occur if we only play unrestricted football during matches. There is no conflict between player development and playing good soccer in games as long as we are not overboard on either concept. Simply stated, there is great emphasis on development at younger ages, with tactics, fitness, functional training and winning receiving more emphasis as player get older. Even when coaching professionals, there are activities aimed at technical development as clearly exemplified by the great coaches universally requiring some fundamental technical training for their teams.

3

First and Second Attacker Passing and Receiving Combination Play

In a very concrete way, dribbling skill is essential to good passing and receiving. Dribbling is a series of micro-passes and collections; without this skill, the player is unable to hold the ball, and is forced to pass it at the wrong time or lose it. Furthermore, the feints used in dribbling can be used to disguise passing intentions. So by developing the individual art of dribbling, the coach is naturally preparing his players for the team art of passing. Since soccer is a team game, the single most important element in team success is probably the level of passing and receiving. Technically, successful passing requires skillful collection, disguise, proper pace, and short and long ball service accuracy; tactically, it depends on more deception, quality support, creation of space, communication, and variety. In coaching, our technical training should concentrate on the basic types of passes and receptions, while our tactical training should teach the concept of support and basic small group tactics.

Good training integrates both technique and tactics! The inside-of-the-foot, in passing and receiving, is basic to success in soccer, and is used more than any other technique. Train your players to master it with either foot. At the fundamental stage, stress the standing foot pointing to the target, the knee bent, the toes raised, the foot striking the ball just above the midpoint and the follow-through. The foot contacts the ball at three locations all on the inside of the foot; rear of big toe, just below the ankle bone and frontal heel area. The key to proper weight (pace or speed) of the pass lies in the follow-through, the result of a long stroke. Poor passes are often the result of short, choppy strokes, with no follow-through. The shorter the stroke, the smaller the `sweet spot'. The sharper timing that this requires is best left to highly skilled players operating at higher speeds. At earlier stages in their lives, players must use longer strokes. With youth, emphasize the follow-through.

Start with pairs facing each other passing back and forth from about 7 yards apart, striking a still ball. The toe up and opening of the hip often need frequent reminders with redoing the demonstration of the proper technique including the follow through. Once players are getting the ball right to their partners with a moderate pace it is time to attempt 2-touch. Left collections and right foot striking and the reverse is best for eventual speed of play. Encourage players to move to the ball to receive and after passing it to step back to make space. This is the very beginning of using space and making space which is fundamental to playing success. After this has been done in several sessions for brief periods of time, players might be ready to use both feet for one-touch passing back and forth. Be certain players are on the balls of their feet in order to have some success with the one-touch inside of the foot push pass. Offer encouragement for those who are doing well and sometimes it is best to have them re-demonstrate for the others. One might be surprised of the necessity of repeating this activity for brief periods of time, even with young teenage players. Since this technical instruction is often not the most motivating activity, it must be done for brief periods of time. However, it offers abundant repetition for technical improvement and will help as long as we move the players to more competitive game situations where they get the chance to use the skill in more motivating activities. Verbal encouragement and an upbeat tone from the coach in these technical exercises is often very helpful. This conveys the importance of what may appear mundane to players.

At the match-related stage, first add movement, then add token defensive pressure; perhaps a 3v1 in a large grid to aid success. Encourage the use of the weaker foot. Notice how the players use their eyes; they should look up before passing or receiving, and look at the ball while passing or receiving. This is important, as it leads to vision and communication. Players can then see the runs made by their teammates as well as their opponents. Hand signals, such as pointing where you want the ball, can also be very effective.

When players are ready for the match condition stage, increase speed and defensive pressure. If you want to keep the 3v1 format, make a game of it by scoring a point for every 8 (varies by age/ability from maybe 3 to 10) consecutive passes; whoever loses the ball defends.

This approach, used to emphasize technique, can be further developed into a 2v2 in a 10x20 yard grid; add small gate goals and score by passing with the inside-of-the foot through these gate goals. Building upon this format, you can add players and increase the grid until you have a small-sided game of 5v5 or 6v6. Impose specific demands, especially two touch, or weak foot only for scoring, to develop technique. If players cannot maintain possession, add one or two extra players to one team, or use neutral players who always help the attack.

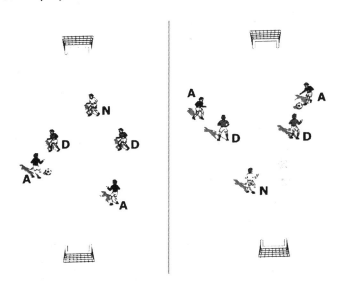

Diagram #12: Here we see 2v2, but it could be 3v3 or whatever number of players the coach has to accommodate in a shortsided game. For odd numbers, merely incorporate a neutral player. Here, two groups are shown working separately. Having one or two neutral players in this exercise insures that passing opportunities are constantly available, thus players will gain the experience we are seeking from this activity.

Since you should try to incorporate shooting into every practice, you may want to add goals, with or without keepers. This approach can be taken with any aspect of passing and receiving. Remember to impose specific demands only for a short time; then allow play without restriction. Encourage movement immediately after passing.

To encourage passing/receiving, consider the following:

- After every pass, require players to touch one or more cones on the perimeter of the field or elsewhere.
- Combination play (these always require movement)
- A simple sprint forward after every pass
- Player changes his position
- Divide field in half & no shot counts unless all attacking players are

in the attacking half
- Player must accelerate forward past his pass whenever he passes forward or square
- Divide field in half or into quadrants or tic tac toe and after each pass you must get to a new "box".

A tried-and-true method for combining technical and tactical work in passing and receiving involves the 1v1 exercise introduced in the previous chapter. After allowing players to take turns going one on one in a grid, give them the option of passing back to their keepers, who must return a one touch pass. This gives them a limited 2v1, as they can only pass backwards. But it will encourage communication and decision-making. The next step is to add a support player on each side; these players are restricted to their respective touch lines and to two touch passes. They support either attacker. Now the give-and-go is a real option. As before, they play all-out for a minute or two, then quickly switch positions. Better still, after using the outside player switch places with no stoppage.

Diagram #13: 1v1 with Wall Pass.

In this exercise, the second attackers learn where to support in relation to both the first attacker and the defender; they will soon learn that they cannot 'hide' in the path of the defender, but must move along the touch line to a receiving location. Since they must stay on the touch line, they only have to find the proper space along a single plane.

The next step of the tactical progression advances the second attacker's understanding of support. Use three players in a grid, one in each corner, with one corner open. Passes must follow the lines of the grid; they cannot be diagonal. With each pass, the player with the ball must have support from both sides. Walk them through the following demonstration: Whenever a player has the ball, she must have a supporting player at each near corner. This means that any player in the corner diagonal from the ball must move to the open near corner, just as a player on the field might move to support. See diagram 14.

Diagram #14: Basic support drill is used at all levels.

Once the players understand where and when to move, increase the speed and limit the number of touches. When they are able to perform this skill with some speed and control for a minute or two, add a defender in the middle of the grid. The first pass is free, then if the defender wins the ball or breaks up the play, he switches positions with the attacker who committed the technical or tactical error. At first the defender can play with hands behind back (this reduces his defensive pressure and also teaches the defender to use his legs and positioning more) and slowly increasing his effort to 100% by removing the restriction. Get to two-touch, and try for one touch with better players. Show how the outside of the foot pass can disguise the passers intention.

35

Keep score, such as a point for every string of 10 passes. Merely adjust the size of the grid for appropriate level for any group of players. Technical/tactical training such as this requires maximum effort for three or four minutes, then a short break. The 3v1 teaches players not only how to pass and receive under pressure, but also how to support the first attacker. The further development of this tactical progression culminates in the next chapter.

A simple excellent support contest activity is to have 7 or 8 cone goals about 5 feet wide spread over an area of 30 x 30 yards. Pairs pass to each other through all of the cone goals and whichever pair completes the task first wins. Progress to having 1 or 2 pairs be defenders (defenders must be at least 3 yards from any cone goal); they simply attempt to kick the ball 10 yards out of the grid. Another option is while trying to score, knock another player's ball out of the grid. This will force more dribbling. Consider no knocking other players' balls out until you have successfully passed to a teammate through one of the gates. You could progress to requiring a wall pass, takeover or overlap at each cone goal with or without defenders. This activity should foster communication (verbal, hand signals, runs, eye contact), heads up visual experience, pace, creating space and anticipation of teammate movements to facilitate winning the game. Play with two teams in the same area. The first team that passes ten times through gates to teammates wins. No passing through the same gate goal twice in succession. To bring support to game level simply have a shortsided game requiring 10 passes before going to goal. This will demand quality support in order to be successful! Only one touch shots also will require quality support.

This environment could also be used for dribbling activities for the first attackers. As a result of these activities and games, the role of the second attacker will come to many of your players quite naturally. They will discover how to support and make eye contact. Other players may need more instruction, but if you have taught them the roles of the first and second attackers (if not, now would be a good time), they will get the idea of where to move. It is not necessary that they learn the term second attacker, only that they know when and how to support. Support is the first step toward small group tactics, which have the purpose of creating possession and space for the attack.

Multiple cone goals have dozens of quality activities. Adjust the grid and goal size to your needs; two yards wide goals serve many purposes.

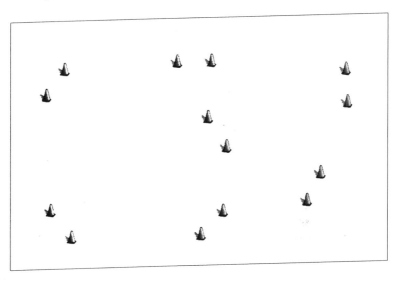

Individuals:
- Dribble through all goals: First through all goals wins
- Make a specific move at each goal: Cruyff, pull-a-V, step-over, pull back, sole roll (sideways, backward), Maradona spin etc.
- Go through the goal, TURN, go back through the goal
- Go forwards then backwards through each goal

Team Pairs:
- Pass the ball through all goals: First to finish wins. Last pair to finish does 10 toe taps.
- Option: Keep going until all are finished, but indicate your finish by the pair raising their hands when finished
- Option: Same as above but one pair defends against all the other pairs
- Option: All pairs try to score through every goal while defending against other pairs

Threes:
Threes begin the level of third man-on tactics; one player goes to a second goal while the two others complete a pass through another goal. Be patient and let players discover this idea and praise it when you see it! If it doesn't occur ask, "How can we go faster to win the game?".

Two Teams:

- Stage One: No defense. First team to complete passage through all goals wins.
- Stage Two: Defending other team's ball is permitted; kick it out of bounds no further than 20 yards. First team to pass through 5 different goals wins - best of 3 rounds.

The number of variations is unlimited. Truly games in which the ball and game competition does all the teaching necessary are extremely economical. If you choose to make a coaching point, be very brief.

Competitive games also allow individual creativity as opposed to boring line drills and drills that assign specific movement, space, time and other restrictions. These activities are by no means just for young children, surprisingly much older players get into the spirit of these games and will work hard (teach themselves). This format is especially great for warm-up as they can be adjusted to almost any topic.

Example: Today's topic is long ball aerial service. You must alternate going through the goals on one end with the goals on the other end. The team that completes scoring three goals first is the winner. Start without warning by simply tossing the ball across the centerline. This gate goal warm-up activity will foster accurate long ball service as well as fitness and firm strikes of the ball required for crossing. With more than 10 players consider 2 groups; neutrals are very much in order.

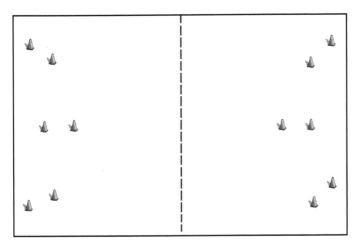

One can plainly see the great versatility of gate goal activities.

The next second attacker support activity shown below is also great for teaching cover for the second defender. Grid should be about 10x20 yards.

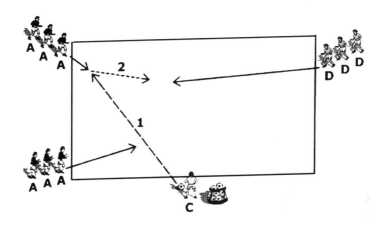

Coach serves a crisp ball to the attacking players (A), one from each line and a single defender comes out to defend the right side goal line. It will require a number of trials for the players to sort out how to support the first attacker with the ball, but in any case coaching points such as "stay wide and diagonally back a yard or two" can be made. At this stage loosely keep the offside rule in effect, which will preclude the second attacker from the run behind for the through pass. If the wall pass option is used successfully maintaining the offside rule, no problem. Encourage the first attacker to draw the defender in order to facilitate the second attacker's reception. Be certain not to lose focus on the supporting second attacker.

One outstanding coach I know only teaches one thing at a time, but frequently will compliment all excellent plays even if it disallows what he is coaching. He is impressive in the results he attains with all ages. He has done this for many years by his own intuition. Recently he was awarded a FIFA A license through the Scottish FA. I hesitate to recommend this procedure for all coaches only because it requires a great deal of experience and has an artistic element, which is not easy to duplicate if it does not come naturally. In any case, if this technique strikes your fancy by all means give it a try.

When doing cover, move to 2v2. So as not to duplicate this exercise in the second defender portion of the book, the coaching points for cover are made here: Sprint while the ball is moving, slow down and gain complete balance as you near the attacker, stay low with knees bent, feet shoulder width apart, SEE THE BALL, be goal side. Distance is critical: Never so close as to have the first attacker beat the first defender and you are unable to provide covering defense. Of course the absolute distance depends upon speed and guile of the various attackers and defenders and location on the field. As the coach you can manipulate the size of the grid and move to 3 attackers vs 2 defenders which will greatly complicate the situation. This is likely appropriate only for more accomplished groups as it now demands zonal concepts and abundant communication.

Train your players to anticipate becoming the second attacker in small-sided games: when a teammate is about to receive the ball, find a supporting position to safely receive that teammate's pass. Often this position is slightly diagonal behind the first attacker. The pass may be to the feet or to space. To emphasize the role of the second attacker, a 3v2 or 4v3 game can be used. Stipulate that first attackers can not penetrate by dribbling or passing until a second attacker offers support. At this stage, for training purposes only, the second attacker could yell "Support!" as he arrives at a good position. This way you can evaluate and correct the player's anticipation and understanding. (During the actual game of soccer, however, offensive communication is largely characterized by vision and runs, whereas defense has much more voice to it.) Once the concept of support is understood, some basic small group tactics can be taught. Introduce the tactic with demonstration and brief explanation, and have players perform it without pressure; try the activities suggested below, then add token pressure, and build up to a shortsided game which demands the proper use of the tactic. As a general rule, it is important to continue to play after executing a pass or movement. Following are the basic two-man tactics that develop the supporting role of the second attacker.

1-2 MOVEMENT (WALL OR GIVE-AND-GO)
As shown in the tactical progression, this very basic movement offers support from the side or front of the first attacker: one player passes to another and then accelerates to receive a return pass. One activity to gain abundant trials uses cones and is set up as shown.

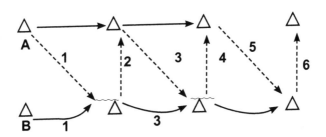

Diagram #18: Players return to the beginning of the line and reverse roles. The exercise commits the 1-2 move to muscle memory and develops timing.

Player A passes diagonally to B, who has accelerated to receive; B dribbles a short distance; players make eye contact and A accelerates to receive a square pass from B and the process continues. The wall pass can also be a one touch pass as players progress.

The diagonal pass could be backward instead of forward to emphasize support of the ball from behind the ball.

In the next variation, the through pass is emphasized.

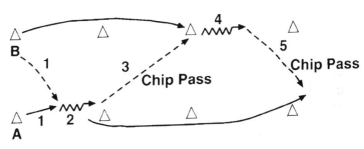

Diagram #19: Through pass emphasis and technical skill of chipping.

Player movement is increased and the chip pass is sometimes employed in this more penetrating 1-2 movement.

You can get more players involved in a single 1-2 activity with the following exercise, which highlights the dribbling passing connection.

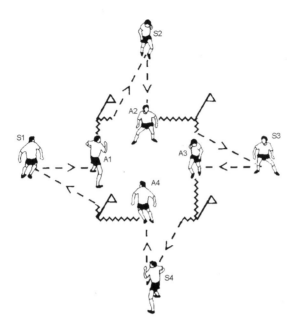

Diagram #20: Abundant 1-2 move repetition and definitely requires fitness. Grid should be 15-20 yds square.

Three to five players dribble around the square, passing to a server at each opportunity. Servers return a square pass to that player. Coach the servers; they are important to the success of this exercise. Servers should step toward the ball for receiving, and move back to create space after delivering the square pass. Start with two touch if necessary, but try to get to one touch for the wall player. Emphasize the first touch, as well as eye contact and acceleration, when coaching passing and receiving.

This activity offers many options. Dribblers should accelerate simultaneously with the pass so the receiver can see where the run is and then the receiver can focus on the ball in order to complete the play efficiently. They can pass square and servers can return a diagonal pass. Both passes can be diagonal, which increases the pace of the drill. Dribblers can add moves to disguise the pass. They can restrict passing to the weak foot or the outside of the foot. (It may help to go in the opposite direction). The square can be enlarged to facilitate accelerating to a drive (speed dribble). This abundant repetition will help immensely to develop the proper timing which is a critical for successful wall passing.

To develop the exercise even further, place the servers inside the square. Or have the dribblers pass to the server one station ahead of them. If your players can do these variations, they are ready for the final challenge: have the servers move along with the dribblers, first in the same direction, then the opposite! In any case, be sure to change roles after two or three minutes. You will easily achieve an abundance of 1-2 moves in a short time, while challenging your players to add appropriate related techniques. All of this develops timing and it is timing that makes the 1-2 movement so effective in beating a defender.

Since the ultimate aim of all passing movements is to finish on goal, you should work toward this in practice. Incorporate the 1-2 movement with shooting opportunities by adding goals. These next two separate activities can be done simultaneously using a single flat-faced goal. Use no more than six players in either activity, so that all players will be moving instead of wasting time in line.

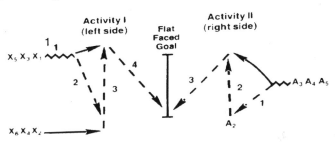

Diagram #21: Shooting using flat faced goals. On square balls shown, two touches are the most likely for success.

On the left side are pairs of players. X) dribbles a few times, then passes diagonally to X2, who returns a square pass for X1 to shoot. Insist on quality passes and changes in speed. Encourage low shots to the far post. Require players to retrieve their own shots in order to promote the good habit of following one's shot. For added interest require specific dribbling moves, specific passes, or specific shots.

On the right side the player passes to the wall player, who returns a square pass for a shot. The shooter retrieves his ball, then becomes the wall. In this and in many 1-2 drills, coaches often use a stationary player for the wall. While this is acceptable at the fundamental level, the coach should add movement of the wall player at the match-related level. So the wall moves to the ball, and after the touch moves back to create space (stretch the defense). At all costs, coaches must avoid performing the role of the wall themselves; this is something that the players need to learn. Progress to a defender on the attacker.

Continuous motion passing/receiving exercises are very efficient as they facilitate much repetition and simultaneously promote MOVEMENT which is so extremely valuable to player development as it is exceedingly game related. Shown is a wall pass continuous motion exercise with a minimum grid setup of 15 x 15 yards with six players, although more or less players will also work well.

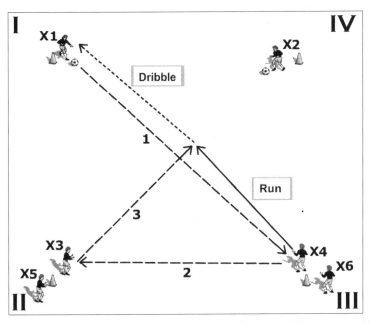

Diagram #22: X1 makes a diagonal pass and moves to location II; X4 passes to X3 and starts a diagonal run towards location I; X3 makes diagonal pass into the run of X4 and moves to location III. Once X4 has dribbled the ball to location I, X2 serves diagonally to X5 and the process is repeated on the opposite side.

Note X1 and X2 both have a ball. X1 prepares the ball before passing as required in all exercises. X1 passes diagonally to X4 who passes to X3 and makes a diagonal run to receive the return wall pass. X1 then moves to the "II" location. The next service starts with X2 and the same movement is repeated time and again. As always, demand stepping to the ball and eye contact communication. Focus on accurate passing, leading the wall pass receiver, a sprint run from the wall pass receiver and crisp one touch passing. While there is a necessity of instruction for receiving with the front foot, this exercise emphasizes cross-body collection for maximum control and accuracy. It simply is a matter that the correct progression for players is competency with the inside of the foot control before emphasizing front foot reception. For advanced players with inside the foot competency, I see no reason not to move to front outside of the foot reception. A common error with young players is not seeing the ball when they strike it. Top spin, with the ball hugging the ground, provides maximum control, which of course greatly aids speed of play, an important component of advanced level soccer.

With a larger group, consider moving to a large grid performing wall passes. Then move to a demand that the wall pass must be performed to an intervening player in the grid. About one ball for every four players should be about right.

Move to a game of two teams and every time a player performs a wall pass on an opposing player, score one point. Do this for about 15 minutes. Use a generous size grid and feel free to have one or two neutrals.

Then simply move to a full game with goals and keepers, but no shot can be taken until a wall pass is completed. For less experienced groups, any wall pass is acceptable, but for accomplished groups the requirement is to complete the wall pass with an intervening opponent.

Always end the session with unrestricted play. If a wall pass is completed in the unrestricted game without the coach having said anything about scoring, award 3 points for the wall pass. The points will clearly provide the praise you desire without any explanation. Clearly, wall passes (give and go, 1-2 movements) provide the mobility which has the effect of breaking down virtually all defenses, as evidenced by the success of the move even in professional matches.

DOUBLE PASS

Offering support from any direction, a double pass is merely a ball sent from one player to another, and returned with almost no change in position. This sometimes creates time and visibility for penetration. The player if behind with such time and visibility is called a window. From a position behind the ball with a view of the players in front of him, the window can see strikers who are being held at bay by the offsides law.

As the window initiates a double pass to a player in front of him, the defense is set in motion. A quick return to the window often opens space for a penetrating pass, such as a first time chip which upsets the defense or even permits a strike on goal.

As this brings a third attacker into play, it will be developed further in the next chapter. At this point, the coach can introduce the double pass as a small group tactic that can be used in combination with others, such as the double pass followed by the 1-2, shown in the following diagram.

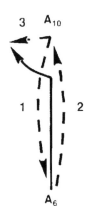

Diagram #23: Double pass can remove pressure to create time and visibility.

A10 passes the ball to A6, who immediately returns it to A10; then a 1-2 movement is executed. A6 then runs straight forward initially, so as not to telegraph where he will receive the ball.

Double passes can be used facing the touchlines in order to attain change of field; they are quite effective in throw-ins, and other times can even involve the keeper. At this point it does not make sense to drill extensively with the double pass alone, as it requires no movement, and if emphasized, might undermine the importance of movement in passing. Players with some experience should practice this tactic in combination with others. However, do point out in shortsided games where this would be very effective. Simple layoffs are more effective when done with diagonal angles as opposed to vertically as shown in the diagram above.

The emphasis on the principle of going to open space in youth soccer makes it important to remember that quality support from the second attacker sometimes requires going to the ball, and even running past the ball and the first attacker. In teaching this principle, the exchange is a very important technique which can raise the tactical mentality of second attackers.

The takeover is not actually a pass, not even a very short one; it is the exchange when a second attacker <u>takes</u> the ball directly from the foot of the first attacker. The takeover can also be faked, so that the ball carrier pretends to leave the ball for his teammate, but at the last instant takes it away himself. This is a great weapon in tight spaces. It exploits the moment when the first attacker has the choice of leaving the ball for a teammate or keeping it for himself, thus confusing the defense.

Some consider the takeover not an effective maneuver. This is false, but why is the notion existent? The notion results from takeovers that do not involve major acceleration on the first touch of the takeover, and the notion that the move is totally completed upon the takeover. Acceleration is critical as is the spin out move by the person who gave up the ball. The spin out creates an option for the person who took the ball causing problems for the defense. Frequently a square spin out causes an on-sides position for a shot in the goal area.

In takeovers, the first attacker is always in command. To keep the ball, he merely plucks it an instant before the teammate can take it. To give the ball to the teammate, he merely leaves it, while shielding the ball away from the defender. Takeovers are done from A1's right foot to A2's right foot, or left foot to left foot. Hand signals are sometimes used in this maneuver; but if the exchange is properly executed, such signals are unnecessary. Practicing this move using left foot to left foot allows for a easy right footed shot, when carried on in the vicinity of the goal. Key elements are initial eye contact, body language (45 degree angle to each other), both players moving, first touch by receiver must be long and quick to lose defender(s), taking the ball instead of a mini pass, and a spin out by initial player so possible support and penetration make the move even more powerful.

Takeover runs by teammates to the ball are frequently initiated when a teammate is in such an intense battle to maintain the ball that he cannot raise his head in order to complete a pass.

Option 1
Two lines face each other. The dribbling player and receiving player move toward one another and do a takeover.

Diagram #24: Takeover - Smooth takeover requires much repetition to become effective in match condition.

Option 2
Training for the takeover exchange can be facilitated with a circular drill which follows:

Diagram #25: Multiple Takeovers Center Circle can be the circle on a soccer field or for large numbers a much bigger circle can be created with cones.

Three to six players dribble clockwise inside the circle; a similar number move counterclockwise outside the circle. This creates a right foot to right foot takeover. Reverse directions for left to left takeover. Then ask players to move by crossing the circle line and now it can either be right to right or left to left foot takeover. Clear understandings of the movement are necessary to avoid collisions! When a player with a ball approaches a player without a ball, a takeover move is executed; that is, sometimes the ball is left, sometimes after a mini stop and an indecisive moment, the carrier keeps the ball himself. While the stop is extremely brief , it is just long enough to cause the defender to stop, then there is a rapid acceleration. If both players have a ball, they merely go by one another. Token defenders can be added, and pressure gradually increased. Culminate exchange activities with a shot on goal. Move to an active defender with full pressure and any takeover to get off a shot.

Stress shielding the ball and narrowing the spaces in order to `pick off' defenders. Do not let defenders slip in between the two attackers without committing a foul. Before the exchange, both players try to see as much as possible in front of them, so as to achieve maximum penetration immediately after the exchange. The spin-out move can greatly disrupt a defense.

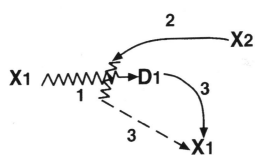

Diagram #26: Takeover Spin Out - After the take over the player without the ball should always consider a penetrating run (spin out) for a return pass. The first 2-4 steps are square (non-vertical) so that both are on-sides when confronting final defenders.

An advanced form of a takeover involves a player crisscrossing in front of a teammate. Here the defender and first attacker are moving slowly under control and a second attacker coming at great pace simply takes the ball, generally diagonally forward; frequently this action leaves the second attacker very open. This crisscross frontal takeover done at high pace can have the second attacker wide open for a shot or pass. Because this move is so infrequent it often offers great surprise.

Through the development of the second attacker, we have progressed from individual player techniques and tactics to two man techniques and tactics. A major goal of this training is to combine these tactics with rapidity, variety, and creativity. This so-called `combination play' advances the game to a higher level; therefore, it is a goal to strive for in the development of better players. The value of such combination play will be clarified in the next chapter, which illustrates the development of the third attacker.

Another simple exercise for combination play is sequence passing which merely has 4 players who are numbered 1 through 4. One always passes to two, two to three, three to four and four back to one. Now we merely have one do a 1-2 move with two, then with 3, then 4, and do a takeover with number 2 who also does a 1-2 with each player and a takeover with number three; play merely continues until the cycle has ended. For an added challenge add a defender to the exercise, but only after the exercise has been done at least three or four times.

Also, all combination play can be completed with groups of three.

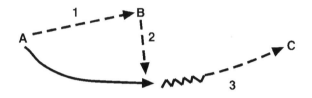

A passes to B and ran for 1-2, then dribbles and passes to C.
C dribbles in place until A checks away to make a space then checks to the ball and C completes a 1-2 move with A and passes to B.

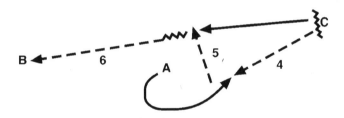

Diagram #27: 1-2 Move with Checking

The exercise is a continuous motion exercise that demands serious fitness. It also teaches how to make space for a 1-2 move and is great for timing. Excellent warm-up activity.

Since combination play is the very essence of the beauty of the free flowing game there can never be too much emphasis on it. Two combination plays done in immediate sequence can often destroy the best of defenses. The overlap is treated in Chapter 4.

The ideal culmination of any two man combination is a third man on. A third man on is nothing more than one more pass, usually one touch, which rapidly changes the location (direction) of play. When 'strings' (sequences) of combination play occur even the most lay spectators capture the beauty and excitement created! It's instinctive to see the skill and rapidity of thinking in these situations. Furthermore the most sophisticated of defenses is often broken down with such play!

4

Creating Space and Development of the Third Attacker

Another title for this chapter could be "Principles and Methods of Small Group Tactics." These concepts are for players who both understand and implement the roles of first and second attackers. The level of passing and receiving advances with the addition of third attackers, whose primary responsibility is to add mobility. They do this by offering width and depth, which are absolutely essential to the attack. This not only adds to A1's options, but also disturbs the defense.

While a certain amount of A3 development is functional, the basic principles hold true for any position or location on the field. Third attackers attempt to get behind and to spread the defense. When successful, they create the chance for a penetrating pass; when not, at least they draw the defender's attention away from A1 and/or A2, perhaps creating the chance for a penetrating dribble.

The technical aspect of A3 training is a refinement of the basic techniques of passing and receiving. These changes are mainly in terms of time, as A3 often must execute at speed in order to exploit momentary defensive confusion. The tactical aspects involve deciding where, when, and how to run, as well as cooperating and communicating with teammates. These tactical aspects take time, even with professionals! Not surprisingly, the addition of the third attacker(s) challenges the decision-making skills of all players. Thus the training for this role must incorporate a great deal of decision-making activities, rather than predictable drills.

The tactical progression (1v1, 2v1, 3v1) from the previous chapters can be developed into a very good introduction to the role of A3. The next step is 4v2, and takes place in a grid of about 10 yards. Less accomplished players may need more space. Each of the four attackers remains in his respective corner (but frequently move along the sides of the grid), while the two defenders attempt to win the ball. The object is for the attackers to split the defense with a diagonal through pass whenever possible; otherwise they must pass to one of the supporting players at the near corners.

Diagram #28: 4v2 - A1 was unable to complete the killer pass, but A2 had the opportunity and used it.

Tactically, this is similar to the real game of soccer in that A1 looks to A2 for support, and to A3 for the penetrating pass. Of course, this `killer' pass is not always on, when there is defensive pressure, so A1 must weigh the risk of the penetrating pass versus the safety of the support pass. Because the attackers are semi-stationary (only move to be in good location for the through pass), the possession player can more easily look for the penetrating pass.

At the fundamental stage, the coach can walk players through this exercise to introduce the concept of the penetrating pass to the third attacker; then increase the defensive pressure and make a game of it by scoring a point for every penetrating pass, or two points for every string of 5-10 passes.

Another option is every penetrating pass counts for two passes. The defender who was in the grid longer switches with the attacker who committed the technical or tactical error. Impose such specific demands as two touch only; award bonus points for the one touch killer pass or good deception. As in the previous stages of this tactical progression, players should go all out for three or four minutes, or until a turnover is made.

PEDAGOGY

When defenders are replaced by the player who lost the ball, I almost never permit stoppage time. While these amount to free passes as the defender picks up the vest, technical skills are still being developed. Play is continuous, without any stop. Also, do not allow the player to hand the vest to the next defender, make her pick it up, which eliminates the need for free passes and even adds a bit of flexibility. It is no wonder that so many teams are so poor on counter attack and not quickly transitioning to defense when the ball is lost. Teams get in trouble when opponents use quick throw-ins and direct kicks. All training activities must not allow stoppages which are nothing more than opportunities for losing focus and creating bad habits. Doing a counter attack or quick defensive recovery exercise will never compensate for the bad training habits of allowing constant stoppage transitions in training activities.

Along these lines, depending on the specific scrimmage exercise, I always place a vest about 15 to 30 yards from the goals. Whatever the restriction is for the exercise it is not to be followed if the ball is won in front of the vest. Usually a maximum of 7 (less for advanced teams) touches are permitted before a shot is taken. Passes are included in the number of touches. So in actuality we do quick counter attack every day while spending zero extra time on quick counter attack. That's economical training at its best! This of course simultaneously trains the defense for quick recovery.

The added benefit of this non-delay on transition situations in training increases focus, adds ball touches to the session and increases fitness. This eliminates the waste of time of running to nowhere without the benefit of ball touches.

Line drills automatically create these poor transition habits. The line drill must only be used for a minute or two to clarify the tactics with the appropriate techniques. Then immediately go to some sort of live action, continuous motion, defensive pressure, game activity and the like!

This very effective technical/tactical workout will help the coach diagnose the decision-making skills of his players: those who play safely versus those who play with risk. This information can become helpful later in deciding player positions; defenders generally need to play for safety, strikers more often need to take risks. But the emphasis here is on good decisions; encourage players to make the through pass whenever it is `on'.

TIP: When working with grids have players stand along the lines of the grid instead of the corners; instead of causing players to be stationary they should be encouraged to move along the grid line to provide proper support at all times. At an even higher level play 4 v 2 with no grid and whenever a ball goes out of control the entire group must move maintaining the 4 v 2. In this way there is no stoppage and the activity has more movement and is much more game like. Both ball support and pressure are immensely improved. This also improves transition a great deal. Demand firmly that players not cheat by using large unfair spacing. If a player insists on not maintaining a fair 4 v 2 distance merely make him or her into a defender.

To further teach the role of the third attacker, a 5v2 exercise is the next logical step in the tactical progression, as it offers more mobility, decision-making, and communication. In a circle of about 15 yards in diameter, five attackers keep the ball away from two defenders. The attackers are not limited to the circumference. As one player moves to receive the ball, the whole circle adjusts to the new situation.

Diagram #29: 5v2 with movement and the penetrating killer pass. For high level players 5v3 or 4+1v2 might be preferred. The +1 generally is in the central area changing the point of attack.

56

As A1 controls the ball, the closest support player moves close to offer support. This leaves the three remaining attackers to offer mobility: one should split the defenders while the others move wide. They need to move quickly and communicate, as the whole circle of players moves with each pass. As in the 4v2, the first pass is free, and the object is to split the defense, which is not always possible. Therefore a strategy develops, as the attackers use the short pass to A2 to draw the defense, then quickly follow with the penetrating pass to A5.

5v2 is often performed with the central midfield playmaker in the middle of the circle constantly changing the ball direction (constantly changing the point of attack). This can be 5+1 v 2.

Make a game of the 5v2 along the same lines as the 4v2. Since the 5v2 incorporates so much of the passing game, it demands coaching. Point out the reason for specific errors in technique or tactics. It is well worth the effort to offer regular reminders of feinting as it is difficult to over-emphasize its importance. Many coaches use the 5v2 in nearly every practice, emphasizing movement to support, moving wide or splitting the defense. It is also an excellent device for refining receiving skills: teach players to face the field when receiving a ball without pressure, to use two touch in playing a poorly passed ball, and to use one touch under pressure or when playing a perfectly received ball. Such quick decision-making is essential to the development of soccer players and to exciting soccer. This is a step toward combination play involving three or more players. A three man combination is not simply a string of passes from player 1 to player 2 to player 3; but it more resembles a two man exchange rapidly followed by a penetrating pass to a third player, or rapid change in point of attack, which surprises the defense. Another example would be a series of wall passes between two attackers, quickly followed by a through pass to a third attacker when the defense is expecting another wall pass. Thus the three man combination passes up the obvious for the more creative, more penetrating movement. A three man combination is characterized by sharp changes in direction, changes in speed, one touch passes, or a rapid series of two or more two man combinations.

Ultimately it must be encouraged by creating restrictions requiring it in a shortsided game. This is an absolute necessity because there is now defensive pressure, movement and goal direction. The carry over to the

11 aside is minimal, unless one goes from the exercise to shortsided to the full game.

Another instance would be the double pass followed by the 'window' pass, as introduced in the last chapter.

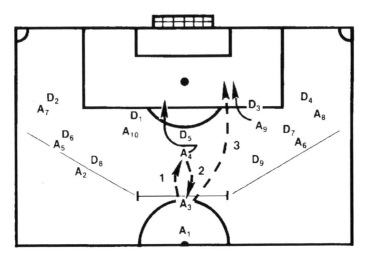

Diagram #30: Window Layoff - Window, through which player views the field in front of him and thus attains much useful information. A change in angle that allows the receiver to open his hips to the goal and teammates also helps a great deal.

A3 passes to A4, who is under pressure; A4 decides not to turn due to close marking and returns the ball to A3. A3, who has now surveyed the entire front line, chooses the best pass for a forward strike from among several alternatives (in this case a chip to A9).

Of course, shortsided games can be used to develop the third attacker. The objective here is to involve every player, even though only one player can have the ball at any one moment. Players should be taught not to be spectators when a teammate has the ball. The idea is simple: help the attack by running wide or deep. Spreading out is the first principle of attack, and it is best done by the attackers who do not have the ball. Once third attackers see how valuable they are to the attack, they may begin to realize how much fun this role can be.

A useful method in developing the tactical awareness of third attackers is to set up uneven sides, such as 6v4 or 5 v 3. The larger team exploits its advantage by spreading out, and can easily see the benefits of using third attackers to upset the defense or penetrate. Once the understanding has developed, the sides can be balanced. Now the attackers need to work harder to offer mobility, but their efforts pay off because this is highly match related.

At this stage, the coach can teach specific strategies for third attackers to use in freeing themselves of defenders and creating space. One basic method is the blind-side run, in which the third attacker gets diagonally behind the defender so that the defender cannot see both the ball and the third attacker. This creates a moment of confusion that can be exploited by a pass to space, allowing the third attacker to run on to it. In this play, eye contact and acceleration are still important, but this is a situation where hand signals can be very useful. Diagonal runs are particularly effective here. Also, square runs with a quick cut keep players on-side.

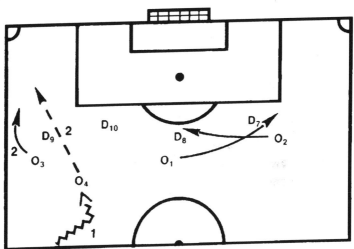

Diagram #31: Strikers Crisscross to Get Open - O1 and O2 are now really thinking because they are getting themselves open to receive ahead of time. The criss-cross can cause defensive confusion.

O4 (midfielder) delivers ball to O3 who has taken a through run on D9. O1 and O2 have both made diagonal runs and may be open to receive a cross from O3.

Checking also creates space and gets a player open to receive. Checks away and to the ball should be significant, both in distance and angle (not constant one step checks). Also, checking players, especially twin strikers, should check to two different locations so as to provide maximum problems for the defense. The jab step with a sharp change in direction is critical, as a player will not lose a marker unless the changes in direction are rapid and unpredictable. Sometimes when checking to a teammate a player will give a hand signal as to the exact location he wants the ball. Eye contact is always helpful. At the last moment, side-on reception is necessary to keep distance between the receiver and defender. While it is not always possible to keep eye contact with the ball carrier, it is absolutely necessary to take rapid intermittent peeks so as to get timing and best reception location to maximum advantage. Clearly, if technical instruction on checking and similar basic movements is not done at ages 8 through 13, the training of a 15 through 18 year old team to a high level becomes a monumental, if not impossible, task.

While checking to the ball is very important, there are times where the best check is TO THE BALL and then AWAY. With proper timing this is frequently done to receive a ball behind the defense. It is especially effective after many checks to the ball have been performed. When checking away, diagonal and square runs with a sharp change in direction will facilitate staying on-sides.

It is plain to see that checking is both a technical and tactical move. In fact, some of the items are hard to classify as either one or the other. Taking the change in direction as a simple example: A player has to have the physical strength for the change of direction, needs to do a jab step (technical element), and of course make the decision as to when to do the move (tactical understanding). One need have no concern about what is technical or tactical, or even if it is technical/tactical, but one must get players to be able to do it correctly and effectively. It becomes clear that merely being an athlete is not enough to be a quality player. One must acquire many basic fundamental skills and be able to apply them at the correct time and place in match conditions.

The modern game is so fast and played in such tight spaces that the bump check is necessary. This merely has the receiver check directly toward the defender (usually side-on) and then hope to receive the ball with the foot away from the defender.

Females often need some strengthening exercises in order to perform quality checking due to their differences in strength, wide base and other factors. Single leg jumps is one of the most common exercises to assist this development. Backwards running and bounding will also help to balance the strength between the quadriceps and hamstrings. All three exercises are also great for injury prevention, so time consumed on these exercises is well spent.

Another tactic for creating space by the third attacker is the overlap, which exploits the defensive tendency not to mark players behind the ball. This often allows an attacker to make a run from behind the first attacker to a penetrating position. Whether the overlapping player receives a pass or not, the defense must deal with this threat.

A pass is made to the outside midfielder, preferably from one of the center backs or inside midfielder since that will have concentrated the defense centrally. The outside midfielder, seeing or encouraging an overlap by dribbling to the center of the field, now has created space on the flank for the overlapping player to be open. The overlapping player may be open, or at minimum has drawn a defender away from the central area of the field. If he is open, he can receive and serve, lay the ball off or perform whatever appears to be his best move. Often the player drives to the endline and attempts a cross. The element that greatly assists success is the dribble inside and thus young players must be trained to create space for a teammate with this move. Naturally, there will be times when the inside dribble facilitates a change in the point of attack, a through ball perhaps, but it would seem reasonable that if the overlapping player is open, as is often the case, then this is a good penetrating choice.

Diagram #32: O5 to O7 while O3 overlaps. Then O7, having created flank space with this inside dribble, passes to O3. Dangerous opportunities are often created in this manner.

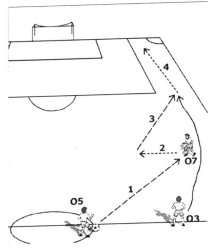

The overlap is generally performed in or near the attacking half of the field since most teams do not want to get defenders forward while they are in the defending third. Clearly, the intent of the overlap is to create a numbers up situation in a given area of the field to make it difficult to defend. Does the marking man to man defense convert to zonal coverage? Generally defenses do not like zones near and inside the 18 yard line. It seems to be that neither of these solutions is very good, thus it is clear to see that overlaps can cause confusion.

There are other types of overlaps such as an inside out overlap by a striker who in this case often becomes a server. Also there are far side overlaps that often allow two players against a single defender to have one of the two wide open for a change in point of attack pass. Probably the least attention is paid to east/west overlaps by central midfielders or twin strikers. The east/west overlap in the penalty area by players can really cause havoc. This is especially so because the ball is given very focused attention this close to goal so that the overlapping player can be open even in this crowded area. Dennis Bergkamp was the master of this move.

In shortsided training, encourage these space-creating tactics. Above all, teach third attackers to spread out the moment possession is gained or even anticipated, and first attackers to look for the penetrating pass. Score a point for each through pass. Instead of traditional end-line goals, place triangular goals on the field. This will encourage third attackers to exploit space and play the ball back to a dangerous area. In a real game, this goal will be replaced by a striker running into this area to receive a pass.

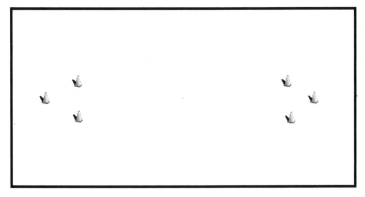

Diagram #33: Triangle Goal Encourages Gaining the Endline
The cones or obstacle course markers form goals with 3 sides.

Imposing such limitations as two touch or minimal dribbling will encourage players to look for third attackers. Award points for combination play or good decision making. Keepers can get a workout in this game, too; teach them to distribute to the open man running wide. Other suggestions include smallsided games with four goals -- one at each end, and one at each side. Or a gate on the perimeter that the ball must go through before going to goal.

Diagram #34: Four Goals for Establishing Width
Either team can score on the side goals. This creates an incentive for attackers to stay wide! Play continues without a stoppage when "goals" are scored.

A variation is to place these goals on the field and allow shots from any direction. At this point the players are involved in a match condition that can include shooting and goalkeeping. Reward third attackers for their anticipating, communicating, decision-making, and space-creating. Let them know that they are helping even when they do not receive a pass. Once players understand this, they can have fun in the role of the third attacker!

So far we have defined the basic responsibilities of the first, second, and third attacker, and suggested practical exercises and smallsided games that integrate these roles with technique and tactics. This approach to player development is most appropriate for young and experienced players.

Some countries that previously had abundant street soccer now find that they too must use these methods to develop players. While the Netherlands led the way in instruction for player development, many other countries are actively following suit.

All coaches must create a learning environment where attacking soccer is encouraged, and decision-making by each player is respected. Only then can we incorporate these attacking principles into the full game, refining them according to the location of players on the field. This so called `functional training' deals with the differences among positions, and should be taught only when the players have a foundation in the techniques, basic roles, and fundamental tactics elucidated in these early chapters. The next chapter clarifies the concepts of functional training by building on this foundation.

5

Principles of Defense

Yes, there is a defense, after offense! Defense may be half of the game, but should not comprise half of the instruction and practice time. Over-emphasis on defense at an early age can hinder player development. This is not to advocate only attacking instruction for an entire season. At youth levels, every player should spend some time as a defender and a goalkeeper, and learn to take pride in these roles. But the young player must first concentrate on the technical and tactical skills of attack, (ball control, dribbling, passing, receiving, etc.). Then she can learn ways to play intelligently when the other team has the ball. This is only possible when a team has well-coordinated goals and communication, which requires maturity. This may occur around age 9-13, though it varies with the quality of players and the coaches' beliefs.

Whenever there are attacking and defending counter parts, the attacking instruction comes first. For example, first attacker instruction precedes first defender instruction, dribbling precedes tackling, offensive restarts precede defensive ones, and so on. Good defense will not exist until opponents are comfortable with the ball and encouraged to play offense. In fact, the quality of a team's defense cannot be tested until it faces a good offense.

The decision of defensive style (high pressure vs. low pressure, man-to-man vs. zonal) depends upon the immediate situation, the personnel, the particular third of the field, and the score. For example, a team that is behind in the score may play high pressure defense in order to regain possession; a team that is ahead in the score may opt for low pressure defense in order to protect its final third. Higher level teams are able to switch intelligently from one style to another to adapt to these variables.

Virtually all high level play combines man-to-man coverage with zonal concepts. Therefore, the ability to play both man-to-man and zonal defense should be a primary defensive objective for the youth coach. This takes more than one season, but the benefits in terms of understanding and teamwork are well worth the effort. Defense is above all a mental disposition, where the mind drives the body.

Many young players intuitively mark tightly when they are close to the ball, and loosely when they are not. This is the first step toward zonal defense, and is easily developed in smallsided games. Encourage your players to loosely mark the attacker who is farthest from the ball. Then observe how these defenders cover the proper space. They should place themselves goal side, and be able to see their man and the ball.

Once again, the instruction integrates technique, principles of player roles, tactics, and finally, functional training. To progress immediately from technique to functional training hinders player development. This error leads to poor decision making and lack of teamwork. It only reinforces blind clearing kicks and over commitment by impatient defenders who are misled into thinking that their first objective is to win the ball. Such one-dimensional training creates one-dimensional players! It is much better to delay, then when you have cover you can be more aggressive in trying to win the ball.

In developing individual defensive skill, the many attacking activities previously described will expose players to most defensive situations. In these activities and smallsided games, coaches will be able to identify those players with the proper mental dispositions of good judgment, patience, and discipline. Such players can serve as models for the rest, since every player becomes a defender the moment possession is lost. What these players seem to do intuitively may be consciously taught to other players: Stay on your feet. If cover is offered by a second attacker, win the ball; if not, keep the attacker from turning with the ball; if the attacker does turn, force a back or square pass, or shepherd him across the field or along the touchline. Protect the space behind you. Be patient! Do not tackle when the attacker has full control. The moment to tackle is when the attacker is half turned, or has just dribbled the ball and no longer has contact with it.

Tackling when the attacker has contact on the ball requires the defender's all out effort and weight behind the ball. In this case, lifting the ball over the attacker's foot will usually help.

These individual skills are the foundation of small group tactics. Together they are the key to quality defense, which is team defense. Once again, the principles of player roles are the cornerstone. The principles of first, second and third defenders, discussed in Chapter 1, may need review before we apply them in training. Note that these defensive roles correspond directly to attacking roles; that is, while the first attacker seeks to penetrate, the first defender tries to deny that penetration; the second attacker offers support to help the first attacker, whereas the second defender offers cover to help the first defender. Similarly, third attackers try to lend width and depth, while third defenders attempt to restrict space.

A glance at diagram #1 in Chapter 1 reveals that the two triangles (attackers and defenders) do not exactly mirror each other. This is because intelligent defense is not simply a strict man-to-man proposition. True, the first defender, in applying pressure to the ball, can be said to play man-to-man. But the second and third defenders, in covering an area and a man, often use a partial zonal defense.

Even the best-intentioned parents and novice coaches are often unaware of this, and encourage all defenders to mark tightly at the wrong time and place. Indeed, the central issue of confusion in defending appears to focus on marking. Frequently, players on the field are making better defensive decisions than the instruction shouted from the touchlines. The second and third defenders often should not mark up tight! Strict man-to-man coverage permits the attack to determine the location of all players. Thus, the attack can take a strong defender away from vital space, exploit 1 v 1 situations, or crowd one area in order to open another. Against a smart attack, strict man-to-man marking can actually reduce defensive quality by eliminating cover and balance, thus preventing the defense from executing its major defensive objectives.

Even in a man-to-man defense, defenders should not mark tightly when they are outnumbered. As obvious as it sounds, two defenders cannot cover three attackers who are spread out. Tight marking in this case results in allowing one attacker space to penetrate, simply by reducing the 3v2 to a 2v1. Thus there is a need for players, coaches, and spectators to first and foremost understand the roles of first, second and third defenders. Only then will the concept of zonal coverage make full sense, and misdirection from the touchlines subside. Naturally, when a free back or central defender is free of man coverage, there is cover. In such a case, defenders can work more tightly.

Zonal coverage in soccer applies the concepts of first, second, and third defender roles to specific areas of the field and specific situations. It also relates to the attacking principle of four man width across the field, which calls for at least that many defenders. Three man width is never enough for a solid defense in the defending third; that number of players could not adequately defend the vital area in front of the goal. Two attackers would find it easy to get to the central area and beat the lone central defender with a 2 v 1. Even a single strong attacker becomes a great threat, especially as more young players develop the skill and confidence to take on defenders. Three man width diminishes the vital factors of pressure on the ball, cover, and concentration. It invariably reduces the defense to a man-to-man style, which is only as strong as its weakest link.

So, why are there successful 3-4-3 and 3-5-2 formations? The answer is simple. Almost invariably these systems have one or two holding midfielders whose main responsibility is defense, so in a sense there really are never only three defenders.

Again, 3 designated defenders does not mean the goal is defended by 3 players. It may be 4, but frequently it is 5,6 or even 10, especially on corner kicks and other dead ball situations.

Four man width, on the other hand, enables a team to maximize the defensive principles of delay, cover, and concentration. With four man width, two defenders can cover the central area no matter where the ball goes. This gives depth to the defense. If the ball changes fields rapidly, they can remain in the vital area while another defender puts pressure on the ball. Even if five attackers come forward, the defense still has a reasonable chance of denying a goal. Even if the free defender is forced to mark, there remains some form of cover from the keeper which allows for reasonable defensive safety.

If four man defensive width is good, is a five man defense better? Perhaps at higher levels, but not at the youth level. This would diminish the number of players committed to attack, and along with it the appropriate support and realization of success. It would distort the sense of offensive balance. In short, the quality and enjoyment of the game would suffer. Of course, encourage midfielders, even forwards, to chase back when needed.

In the final third, therefore, the defense must maintain four man width, with concentrated defense of the most vital areas, as in the diagram below, where the wingbacks have more area to cover than the center-backs.

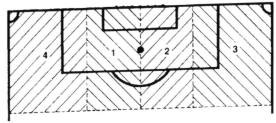

Diagram #35: Defensive Positioning
This is a lot of ground to protect, so even when we only designate 3 defenders, at least one midfielder knows his first responsibility is defense.

This coverage is generally considered the bare minimum, even for brief periods of time. When the attack involves more than four players, man-to-man marking may become impossible, and zonal coverage becomes mandatory. The first defensive principle of delay, with pressure on the ball, proves more vital than ever in this situation. Delay allows time for more teammates to recover and help. For reasonably sound defense, however, the team objective should always be to outnumber the attackers, especially in the defensive third.

Frequently, against only 2 strikers teams use only 3 DESIGNATED defenders, but in this case one midfielder is often a designated defending midfielder who generally stays behind the remaining midfielders. This player is often called a defensive screen. Of course, mobility among strikers, midfielders and defenders is high level soccer. In fact nowadays we not only emphasize a total soccer player, but we are more interested in a good SHAPE to defend and attack, instead of a player being in a rigid position. All combinations demand changes in player positions, and combo's always represent good soccer, but the team must still maintain a good SHAPE. This is as true for defense, as it is for offense.

But the real challenge to a defense occurs when the attack is numbers up. This situation forces decision-making and teamwork by the defense, and that takes time to develop. To accelerate this development, defensive techniques and tactics can be integrated in the next drill, adapted from the popular basketball drill where a 3v2 in one direction is immediately followed by a 2 v 1 counterattack. This drill is repeated quickly and intensely to force defensive decision-making in a numbers down situation. Keep some extra balls in each net. Here's how it works on half of a soccer field with full-size traditional goals or flat faced Coerver goals.

Three attackers face two defenders, as in the diagrams below. Player O1, in the middle, attacks goal A directly. One defender comes out to mark him, and the second must offer some cover. In a short time (two 30 minute sessions), the three attackers will score regularly, especially if they can reduce the 3v2 to a 2v1. The defenders may need to be alerted to this tactic, and try not to be drawn away from vital attacking space.

Once a shot is taken or possession is lost, D1 and D2 attack the opposite goal. Now O1 becomes the lone defender, as in the diagrams below. This is a simple 2v1, but emphasis can be placed on one of several areas: the training from attack to defense and vice versa, positioning, tackling, etc. This 2v1 will culminate in a shot or loss of possession.

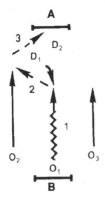

3 on 2 attack goal A. Two defenders are providing pressure and cover while the attackers attempt to occupy 3 lanes. Note excess players on goal line B.

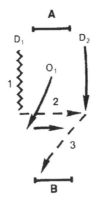

2 on 1 attack goal B. Here O1 defends against D1 and D2 who are attacking the B goal. O2 and O3 become defenders of Goal A.

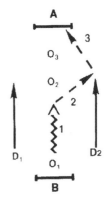

3 on 2 attack goal A. The cycle continues.

Now O2 and O3 become defenders against the next 3 attackers.

In this exercise, the rapid transitions from attack to defense challenges players to employ the principles of player roles in a constantly changing situation. Delay, pressure on the ball, and zonal play can be further refined if defenders learn to use the offside rule to their advantage, without becoming too flat. Good defensive coaching inculcates the importance of keeping the ball in front of the defenders. But once beaten, the defender can still help by immediate chase to get goal side. This may force the attacker to an early or hurried decision. Once some competency is established, keepers are added to goal A or both goals.

Coaching Points Consistently Needed:

In the 3 v 2 situation, instruct and remind players to maintain width, insuring the maintenance of three lanes so no single defender can cover two attackers.
Problem: Pressuring player tries to follow the pass in the 3 v 2 situation.
Correction: Since two defenders cannot mark three attackers, be certain the two defenders organize, implementing quality zonal coverage of pressure and cover. Also, the cover player must put pressure on the ball when a pass is made and the former pressing player drops to a covering position. Generally, players do not do this correctly on their own.
In the 2 v 1 situation, be certain that neither striking player is centrally located (aligned with the goal), as this places their teammate at a poor shooting angle. We want players to gain the habit of assuring that both players have a decent shot to present the defender with the most difficulties.

From this drill to shortsided games emphasizing defensive positioning and decision-making is a very short step. Encourage communication among defenders, especially from the second defender; the player in this role needs to let the first defender know that there is cover. This facilitates shepherding and tackling, and discourages the attacker from trying to take on two defenders.

The next stage of development is team defense, which hinges upon the particular third of the field. In defense, the safety/risk ratio in each third remains the same as on attack: Strikers can take risks to regain possession in the attacking third, midfielders balance safety and risk, while the final four plays mainly for safety to protect the space behind them. In general, there is tight marking in the final third by the final four defenders and some midfielders. Meanwhile, strikers and some midfielders lay a zone to cover midfield. Of course, defenders must work very hard (get to good positions) while the ball is moving.

At this point, it should be made clear that only two systems of play are recognized here. The 4-3-3 is advocated because it is a simple system that aids development and represents the most ideal balance of any team arrangement. The 4-4-2, with the extra midfielder, is a useful system later on for youth because it fosters direct attack, high pressure, creative striker movements and transition opportunities. Most other systems are only variations of these two basic systems.

There are many wonderful useful systems, but this book is about the neglected basic foundation material upon which systems are formulated. Once the basic principles are understood, formulating good systems is easy. What does not work is substituting systems in lieu of the basic player roles knowledge. When this happens, systems discussion are nothing more than a substitute (excuse) for learning the basic principles of the game of soccer.

As often as possible, we would like to stop the ball and regain possession before it reaches our final four. This requires players with the drive to get back very quickly when the ball is lost, and the anticipation to cut out passes. Back peddling and constant movement, even if it is only walking, are of great value, and need to be encouraged.

With these prerequisites, midfielders (or forwards) can then put high pressure on the opposing team and regain possession with some frequency. Even occasional success here would be a great help to a team's total effort. A quality defense requires strikers and support players who have learned how to play defense. They must especially realize the importance of chase, attempting to get behind the ball, as well as where and when their efforts will pay the greatest dividend.

No matter what system of defense or strategies for attack, successful teams always attack with all members working in unison. For defense, compactness and pressure on the ball is a must. For attack, the team must be more spaced out (depth and width) with players open to support possession and penetration.

Strikers must be more responsible for regaining possession in their striking third, even if this only provides occasional success. This is true if for no other reason than to force a keeper to kick a long 50/50 ball, which really turns out to be a ball that favors the defense. But as long as the ball is in the striking third, no matter which team possesses, strikers must play at full effort for high pressure defense to succeed. Loss of possession should not mean a rest for the strikers. In this third, forcing a flat square pass, especially close to the penalty area, is also a very helpful tactic; the interception of such a pass in the striking third could well provide a good shot on goal. Furthermore, strikers should enjoy the luxury of risk tackling. Defenders cannot afford to be on the ground, but a striker can risk a tackle, due to the number of players behind him and the distance from his own goal. Of course, when strikers are defending in the defending third, they must be more cautious, emphasizing delay as well as pressure on the ball.

Another high pressure tactic used by defensive strikers and midfielders involves setting a trap to regain possession and win a transition goal. The defending players allow the ball to go to a wingback, then close down on him with two players. Other defenders position themselves to deny a pass, as in the following diagram.

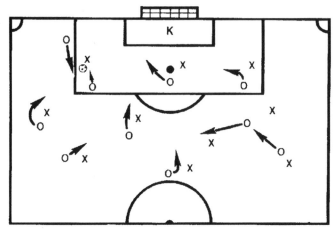

Diagram #37: High pressure trap. The offense (O's) are now attempting a trap to regain possession of the ball.

This is even more productive when the attacking wingback is close to the touchline, as the out-of-bounds is used to tighten the trap. Two defenders could get toe to toe, thus depriving the attacker from dribbling or passing. The extra defender for this trap is obtained by leaving the furthest attacker from the ball free. To succeed with such traps, strikers must feint a withdrawal; then after the keeper has released the ball to a defender, they must make an all-out effort. Unless they sell this fake withdrawal, the keeper will merely kick the ball long. These high pressure tactics require good conditioning, mental toughness, and awareness through coaching. To support these strikers when they're defending, the midfield `engine room' fosters quality tactics through using fitness for aggressive cover.

The major defensive task of midfielders is to prevent the opponent from moving the ball through midfield. Intelligent team defense will force the ball square or back. If pressure from a defensive midfielder forces a long forward pass, this may also work for the defense. Many long hurried passes are less than 50/50 balls. Even if these passes are directed toward a teammate, the defense is facing the play and gains an advantage. On the other hand, midfielders who remain in striking positions can easily cause a total team breakdown.

Of course, in a low pressure defense, these tactics would change radically. There would be less chance of regaining the ball in the striking third or in midfield because all or almost all players are withdrawing. In fact, low pressure calls for either no pressure or only token pressure in the striking third. To develop this style of defense, players can practice falling back to the midfield line or thereabouts on the full field instead of trying to win the ball. The coach merely directs the players to proper locations. The ball can be carried by the players or the coach. This type of activity must be brief, and only used with accomplished players.

A combination of high and low pressure is common nowadays. This involves a very strong effort to regain the ball as soon as it is lost. Good teams are capable of low, high or combinational pressure.
Low pressure really means very high pressure in the defending half, since a team doing low pressure may have its entire 11 in this area.

Coming to the final third, with four defenders against two or three strikers widely spread, one centerback may be marking the opposing central striker, and the two wingbacks marking the wings. One of the most obvious dangers is a centerback committing too early, which could allow another overlapping (or merely coming forward) player to go to goal unmarked. Therefore it is important that the centerback be an intelligent decision-maker and a strong communicator.

At present the sweeper concept hardly exists due to the fact that it can place two players onsides on both sides of the field which would make it impossible for the sweeper to be able to deal with both of them. This has been replaced with the flat back four which keeps players offsides much more easily, though the required communication and coordination in the back is considerably more difficult.

In the flat back four either of the 2 center backs closest to the first central runner will mark and the other is free to provide cover. Most often it might represent a rather flat curve shape as shown in the following diagram. Sometimes it more resembles a check mark.

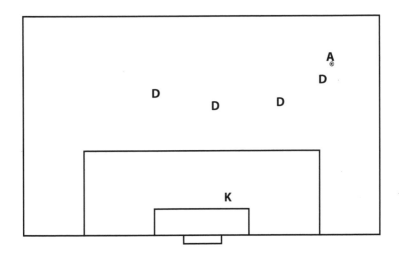

Diagram #38: Flat Back Four - must work together in great harmony.

The flat back four makes it more difficult to be able to play behind the defense without being offsides. The above examples show how to beat a sweeper defense rather easily, because it places attackers in on-sides position and unmarked. World Cup play which had only one SHALLOW sweeper among all teams clearly exemplifies that the sweeper concept is virtually non-existent because it is ineffective against teams that know how to attack it. Furthermore , the attack is simple, and the offsides trap is dangerous because it requires outstanding timing and depends upon nearly perfect officiating!

The sweeper system still used by some youth teams is effective because opposing teams do not have the sophistication to attack it. Frequently, strikers try to be open by being well in front of the defensive alignment, forcing them to have to beat a defender and then the sweeper and finally the keeper. This is difficult because the defense has exactly what it wants, that is, pressure and cover! In any case no matter the form of the defense, the desired goal of pressure, cover and balance prevail, and this always requires an abundance of quality communication. Individuals who are good individual defenders are not equal to players of the same caliber who in addition have good communication skills. Simply said, a quality defense requires a great deal of cooperation to be effective. To develop team cohesion in the defending third, shortsided games with specific limitations can be very useful. Full size portable goals on a field about the size of two penalty areas will allow for realistic problem-solving. Keepers can be added, and the field enlarged to include some midfielders. As always, reward good decision-making and teamwork on the part of the defense. One or two servers can be added to create a numbers up attack, but at first these servers may be limited to their defensive half. Other variations could include scoring a point for every good verbal direction from a centerback, for every successful collection, or for every time the ball is forced square or back. Thus, 6 vs 4 is a very common exercise to promote defensive organization.

Freeze activity is another useful approach during these games. One freeze of less than a minute of instruction for each five minutes of play is appropriate. More instruction than that destroys the natural flow of the game, and becomes boring. Players can learn from a lot of playing, and a little talking! The game itself is a great teacher.

These games will foster the development of a proud and cohesive final four with the proper mental disposition for defense: drive, communication, teamwork, and good decision making. While quality defense is a team effort, it is nevertheless built upon individual skills and the knowledge of defensive roles. This also pertains to the defending of the goal and to defending against free kicks, as we will see in the next chapters. Here are few of the most useful exercises for teaching zonal defense, recalling that virtually all teams revert to man marking in and near the penalty area.

While this first exercise is excellent for offense as well as defense, the purpose here is to develop pressure and cover.

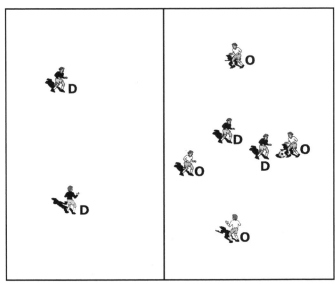

Diagram #39: 4 v 2 + 2
Generally adjoining passes are made until a through split pass can take place.

The 4 offensive players (0) play possession, 3 passes is a point. As soon as the defensive players win the ball they immediately pass the ball to their two teammates on the opposite half of the grid and they play possession and 2 players from the O team move to defend in the left side grid. Simple, but involves movement, which is preferred over static 4 vs 2 situations. This instills the movement on offense and rapid movement on defense when possession is lost. When doing this for defensive pressure and cover be certain to maintain focus only on the defense! Be sure that all players assume a turn at defending. There is no point in doing this for defensive purposes with players who have not developed the necessary possession skills.

Here we move into the very functional positioning of the back four.

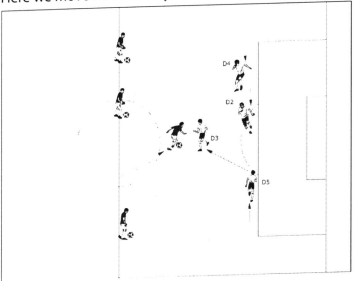

Diagram #40: Learning and rehearsing the very specific team defensive roles is very important. This sliding movement is fundamental to team defense.

The coach simply calls out a number and that attacker dribbles forward and the nearest defender applies pressure, while the next nearest goal side defender provides cover and the remaining defenders slide toward the ball. The furthest defender should not cross the nearest goal post. The two nearest players to the defender providing pressure in the case of D2 or D3 being attacked requires double cover due to the danger of the attack in a central area (diagram 41).

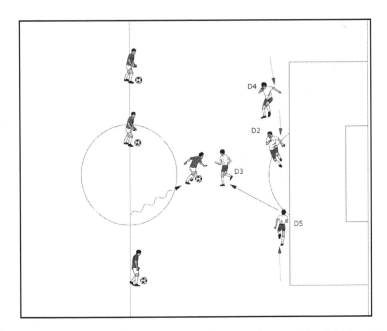

Diagram #41: Note that with penetration in the central part of the field, TWO defenders must provide cover while the other defender attempts to provide balance.

In Stage II the attacker goes at an angle so the decision of who will provide pressure is more confusing and demands more communication. Next the coach serves the ball to one of the 4 attackers. Continuing to focus on pressure and cover, though advanced teams might consider balance in the later stages of the progression.

Next the four players pass the ball to one another, using skip passes occasionally. After 5 or 6 passes they begin to attack. The defense is adjusting to every pass.

The next activity has many possibilities of 6 vs 4+K or even 5 vs 4+K. 7 vs 5+K (or 6 vs 5+K) is very useful since it also includes the defensive screen midfielder in the *scrimmage*. Once the defense has some success, encourage the six to attack by going to goal.

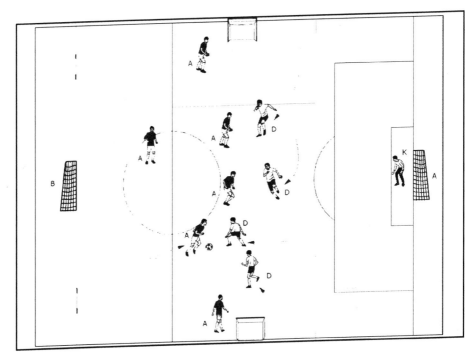

Diagram #42: Shape and marking: 6 v 4
Two strikers, 4 middies vs the back four plus keeper. Note the pressure, cover and balance displayed by the defense in this diagram.

In this exercise again we are trying to preserve defensive shape and still mark the ball when it reaches the vital shooting area. Four lanes are set up. Each defender is placed in a lane. Outside defenders can occupy their lane and the adjoining lane, while interior defenders can occupy their lane and each lane on either side.

When defenders win the ball they can send the ball in either the large goal (B) or either of the two small goals. Keep score, any goal counts one point, any defenders getting the ball through any one of the three goals is a point. The offsides law is in full effect. This makes this a great exercise for both offense and defense!

Move to using all available players such as: 8 v 6+K or even have 2 keepers, one in each goal.

Defenders can also dribble the goal line. Encourage a great deal of mobility and combination play for the attackers while the defense maintains shape, pressure and cover. This will force learning how to pass attackers on to a fellow defender. Balance is automatic due to the restriction placed on the activity. Off sides is in affect and can be kept by non-participating players, assistant coaches, or even players in the activity with the coach as the final judge.

Progress to full play using all players in this environment and then just play unrestricted.

DEFEND OR EVEN WIN THE BALL FOR A QUICK COUNTER ATTACK!
The strikers will have to learn in this environment how to work together and provide quality defense. Of course, the middies will generally provide verbal communication to their attackers to work hard because players don't want to lose.

This activity is good for pressure, cover or balance and it is equally good for penetration, support and mobility. In fact, no matter what your emphasis is, the other five responsibilities will be developing. Generally you find that in order to use it for cover you will have to give some instruction to attack in changing the point of attack. If this is not done the demand for quality cover may not be needed and thereby render this activity less useful.

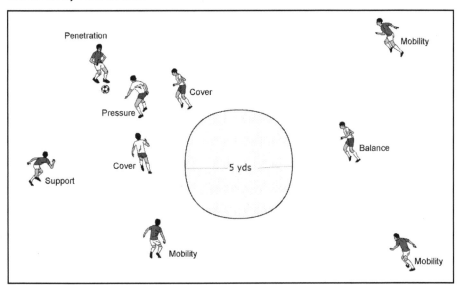

Diagram #43: Excellent for defensive and offensive roles: 6O v 4D
Generally this is a very motivating activity for players. Note that attackers (dark shirts) are spread through entire area while defenders (white shirts) are more compact.

Each gets a point for the following: Attackers dribble into the circle. Defenders dribble off of any touchline and leave the ball. After calling out "One Thousand One, One Thousand Two, One Thousand Three", they can take the ball again and score by doing the same by going off any other touchline. The attacking team must get the ball before the count is completed. Attackers only have to go out of the circle and can immediately go back in. Therefore this is a great quick transition activity. It also involves serious fitness! Substitute regularly. Often the players do all the substituting on their own so the coach can truly coach this activity. Again we have an activity that is excellent for all roles, but the focus here is defense!

This is a very rigorous activity so play 6 attackers against 4 defenders and sub players in and out so all get to play. Players not engaged can get drinks. Attackers attempt to dribble into the circle and defenders provide pressure and cover to deny the attack. Stay focused on cover, although as previously mentioned this is a wonderful activity for any of the responsibilities of offense or defense. Younger teams have little patience off the ball, so quality changes in point of attack will not be in evidence, therefore this is a great time to get the offense to spread out.

Finally we do not want to forget the necessity of strikers playing serious defense (see diagram 44). Three quarters of the field is set as follows: 8 vs 8 (3-3-2 formation) plus keepers is ideal but numbers of one or two more or less can be accommodated.

Teams play standard rules except defenders score one point when they hit the 4' x 4' goals in their defending area. Regular goals scored count 3 points. The demand is for strikers in the attacking third to play square in an attempt to force square and backward passes.

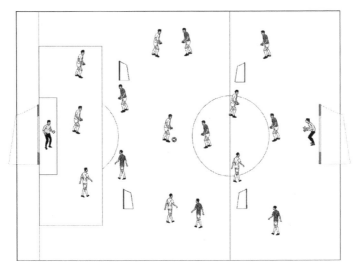

Diagram #44: Strikers Defending - strikers defend the mini goals in their attacking third Strikers working together to develop serious defensive pressure. This denies a possession rhythm of your opponent.

Another fundamental activity which is steering players so that teammates know where to be to assist in cover is four players per group in a grid framework as shown on the following diagram.

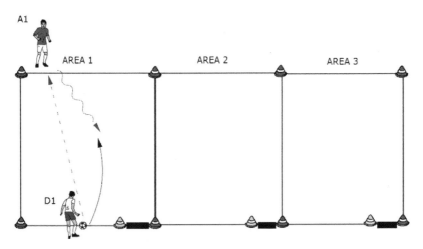

Diagram #45: Defensive Steering - Areas are 6 yds x 6 yds
Steering is a very important skill so that the cover players know on which side they should be. Usually goal side and steer players to outside, but not in defenses that steer players to the middle.

Defender (D1) passes a crisp ball to attacker A1 and immediately follows his pass to force the attacker into the small area to his right (the bold black area). If the attacker crosses the line outside of the bold area the defender has failed. If attacker is forced into bold area line or won the ball he has succeeded in steering the player for his teammate.

In less than 5 minutes move to a single attacker against two defenders still demanding clear steering to the covering player; the cone is removed so the two defenders are defending the entire end line of their grid. Four grids can accommodate any number of players up to 24 players.

Technique: Defenders should move at full speed when the ball is moving, but when they get close to the attacker they should take small steps and lower their body profile by bending at the knees. They should be in balance on the balls of their feet with back somewhat erect. Eyes should see the ball and with peripheral vision see the player's hips. The moment the ball is out of control right after a touch is the best time to win the ball. If you do not have cover be patient and keep the player in front of you, but close enough to deny through passes. If block tackling do so with commitment.

Plainly there are many enjoyable active player environments for teaching defense. The beauty of these activities is that the ball and the game is still the gold standard of instruction.

Finally any activity with many goals will place great pressure on defenders and their keeper. These difficult environments demand much communication and quality pressure, cover and balance which can only help your team when the actual game takes place. This set up can exist at both ends of the field with adequate numbers or it can be used with the offense simply attacking the defense. Counter goals for the defense can be placed on the far end.

Diagram #46: Developing Defensive Tactics
There are innumerable multi goal activities that place a great deal of pressure on defenders in order to improve defense.

Another excellent game is a single goal constructed from 3 flags which both teams attack and single keeper defends all three faces of the triangle goal. Approximately 6 yards is about right, but again many adjustments are possible. This is a great workout for your keeper, especially if you demand proper footwork. Shuffling, drop step, half turn running, quick movement toward the ball may be some of the footwork movements you might want to observe. A garbage barrel can be substituted for the 3 flags, but this is done without a keeper. This can be done in a grid 40 x 40 or simply use half of the field.

We try to get defenders in the habit of passing to the keeper any time they have someone on them and they are facing their own goal. Naturally if the lane to the keeper is unsafe then we must try to put the ball out of bounds on a touch line, though there are some occasions when a corner kick must be conceded. In any case train to avoid corner kicks. The keeper is encouraged to point where he/she wants the ball, but always out of line with the goal.

Because second defender cover can be awfully poor in terms of player development in strict man-to-man systems, I do advocate some zonal instruction, if for no other reason to fully develop the second defender responsibilities of cover.

6

Functional Training in the Defensive Third

Understanding the principles of attack can help players create intelligent exciting soccer. These principles can be refined, according to the particular area of the field. For this purpose, the field is often viewed in terms of thirds; that is, the attacking third, the middle third, and the defending third.

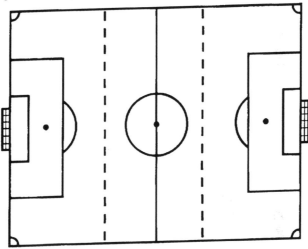

Diagram #47: Thirds of Field to Assist Functional Training
The dotted lines show the three 'thirds' of the field.

On attack, the relationship between maintaining safe possession and taking chances on penetration varies through each third of the field. In the defending third, safety is the greatest concern; players cannot afford to lose the ball here. This is no place to take chances. This is not to say that defenders should blindly clear the ball at every opportunity. Dribbling is also permitted, but only if the situation is safe. In the middle third, safety is balanced by a small amount of risk; players may risk more dribbling or penetrating passes when there is a good chance of success. If the ball is lost at midfield, it is not as critical as a ball lost in the defending third, where shots can be taken. In the attacking third, chances must be taken if goals are to be scored! Playing it safe (that is, merely maintaining possession) will not create scoring opportunities. Scoring requires taking risks, with the understanding that possession may be lost. To summarize: in the defending third, play safely; in midfield, balance safety and risk; in the attacking third, take risks.

The principles of attack correspond to the roles of the first, second, and third attackers: penetrate, support, and mobilize. Simply spreading out across the width and depth of the field will help achieve these principles; therefore, players should be trained to spread out as soon as possession is gained or even anticipated. Once the roles of first, second, and third attackers are understood, players will do this automatically, and the coach can then refine their decision-making as to where and how to use the field. Such understanding will ensure that players run intelligently; that is, not everyone will run away from the ball nor toward the ball every time.

This can be accomplished in shortsided training, adding players gradually to reach 11 aside. At this stage, functional training can begin. Functional training involves adapting the principles of play to a particular third of the field, particular player roles, and considering the safety/risk ratio.

Attack is often begun by a team gaining possession in the defending third of the field. A keeper or defender who mindlessly kicks the ball as far as possible creates a mindless mental set. If the defense develops strategies for mindful possession and forward movement of the ball, a higher level of the game is achieved. The long ball may be used, but there should be an intended receiver.

As can be imagined, methods of attack depend to a large extent upon the opponent's style of defense. Therefore, a word about defense is in order here. There are two basic approaches to defense: High pressure and low pressure. High pressure describes a defense that tries to dispossess the offense anywhere on the field. Low pressure refers to a defense that falls back to its own half before applying defensive pressure. Both approaches have their place in the game, and will be discussed in later chapters; what is important at this point is that low pressure defenses drop back to cover some portion of the field in front of their goal. This leaves the attacking team's backs unmarked or with token pressure. Therefore, it is safe to use the backs to begin the attack.

A long punt may be unwise for several reasons. Non-professional players are often not very accomplished with air balls. Also, if the opponents only have 1 or 2 players forward in a 4 back system we are sending a ball to 6 vs 9 with the additional problem that the defense is facing the play and merely has to hit the ball forward for instant success, while the team in possession is moving away from the ball and often need to complete a drop pass for any modicum of success. Furthermore, it is better to play at moderate pace and chose an opportune moment to rapidly change the pace and begin an attack. The element of surprise always puts additional pressures on opposing defenses!

In the Defensive Third - Using Wingbacks on the Attack

Against a low pressure defense, there is no point in a rapid, risky long ball attack from the defensive third (unless the defense has been caught in transition). Under the normal pace of the game, facing low pressure calls for a full spread of offensive players across the width and depth of the field (full depth means use of approximately 1/2 the length of a field by the field players), and of course a low risk of dispossession. If the goalkeeper has the ball, the wingbacks become the support players. They make bent runs with no thought of stopping until they near the touch line, or the keeper has released the ball to one of them or to a teammate. Wingbacks must not lose eye contact with their keeper; the bent run ensures vision of the keeper and upfield areas.

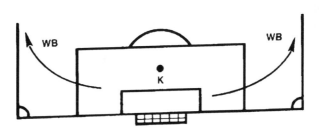

Diagram #48: Defenders Wide to Spread Opposing Defense
Wingbacks need to take very wide fast runs in order to be open. They frequently need to anticipate this action.

In training, it is often necessary to work with both wingbacks at once, so they get accustomed to making a proper run even when they do not receive the ball. This allows the keeper to deliver the ball to the better run, while also encouraging the keeper to look to both wingbacks. Normally, if the ball comes to the keeper from the right, the left will be open and force the defense to run considerably.

When the ball is delivered to them, wingbacks always check back to the ball in such a way as to maintain a view up the field. Whenever possible, having hips open to teammates (allowing maximum vision) is a good habit. The wingback should receive the ball with the foot furthest from the keeper (the foot nearest the touch line). The ball should be closely watched onto the inside of the foot, then directed immediately forward with a single touch. The wingback can then again survey the entire field.

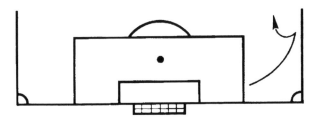

Diagram #49: Wingback checking back to the ball.

Target vision is a primary point of instructional emphasis. A player should look at the field before the release of the ball from his teammate, during flight, and immediately after the first touch. Since good keepers feint some throws, the receiver should also be taught to alternately survey the defense and the keeper until the keeper has fully released the ball.

If danger arises, the wingback must be prepared to run back to the ball and return it to the keeper; if the keeper is unavailable, the ball can be cleared upfield or sent out-of-bounds. But frequent blind clearance kicks should be discouraged. Stress good decision-making.

Most systems want diagonal balls forward, as this yields some penetration and relative safety of completed passes. Thus, inside players will frequently use the outside, and flank players should look inside as well as upfield.

If the wingback can move forward, she should do so immediately. If there is time, the long skip pass to the striker is considered. This receiver requires support by a midfielder.

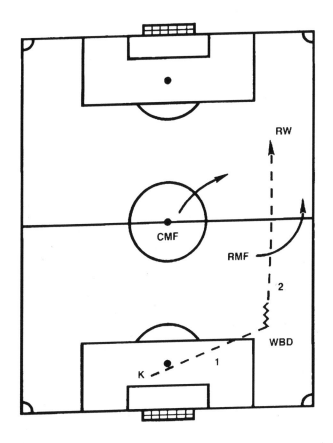

Diagram #50: Skip Pass Requires Support
The long skip pass demands support from teammates. Note CMF and RMF have moved behind RW to support the long ball service.

This long ball may yield an early strike on goal.

Midfielders must be alerted to the necessity of 'checking out and in', taking runs away from the ball to lure a defender, and then quickly checking back toward the ball to receive a pass. Distant players must go even farther away from the ball so as to deny defenders cover and concentration. Spreading out facilitates much of this, allowing for 1-2 movements, outside and inside overlaps, useful diagonal runs and wingback support of the ball. The following diagram illustrates a 1-2 movement between a wingback and a midfielder.

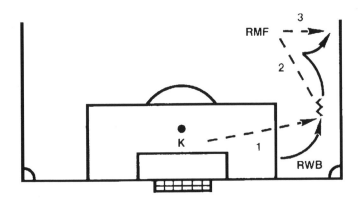

Diagram #51: Combining with midfielder to move ball upfield.

Following is a suggested progression for attacking out of the defensive third against low pressure defense. The first step involves two wing-backs, a keeper, and a server. The server takes 20-30 yard shots on goal. The keeper makes the save, then delivers to the wingback. Repeat until bent runs with good eye contact, quality collection, and upfield vision are well established. When players reach proficiency, add one defender who covers one wingback as soon as the shot is taken. The keeper, of course, delivers to the other wingback. Demand quick, accurate execution.

The next step adds the two central defenders to the team being trained to build out of the back and at the same time add a second defender against them. One defender marks a wingback tightly; the other defender is about 15 yards from her wingback. Upon the keeper's release of the pass, the defender challenges for the ball. Ensure the success of the activity by varying the distances, but allow little or no time for the wingback to waste before she delivers a ball back to the *keeper* or other open player. Work at a rapid pace, even to the point of becoming a conditioning activity, but maintain quality as the first consideration.

Adding midfielders to the activity will give the wing backs a target. Then forwards can be included to receive a penetrating 'skip' pass (one which skips the closer player to reach a more distant player). A smallsided game can be the final step: score a point for each good decision by the wingbacks. This can end up being 11 vs 5. The 5 could be two defenders against the defense, 2 defenders against midfielders and 1 defender against the two strikers. Eventually work toward more realistic numbers such as 11 vs 8.

This type of activity should last less than 30 minutes of a practice. It may require two to four practice sessions to complete. The rest of each session must involve many touches of the ball, shortsided work, and game-like decision-making (possession) activities which provide more fun, realism, and conditioning.

Sometimes it is more efficient to have the 4 or 5 players that you want for specific instruction to either start early or have them stay afterward for this type of specialized functional training. While assistants might be doing possession or other specific training, not everyone has the luxury of one or more capable assistants. If you are on your own, small group training before or after practice creates a more efficient coaching and learning environment. High level coaches have learned how to use assistant coaches effectively.

In the Defensive Third - Using Centerbacks on the Attack

In a game, the wingbacks and most other players may be marked, which is characteristic of high pressure defense. Since some teams use three strikers, these three players are more likely to pressure the `final four'; that is, the two wingbacks and two centerbacks. By contrast, the 4+Kv2 situation can also be exploited by using the centerbacks to move the ball through the defensive third. With three pressuring players, the long punt is used more often.

In a subsequent workout, the above progression can involve two centerbacks instead of (or in addition to) the wingbacks. As before, a server shoots on goal from a distance. Immediately after the server's shot, one centerback moves to one side of the goal outside the penalty area, while the other moves to the opposite side of the goal just outside the penalty area. This lends width and depth to the attack building.

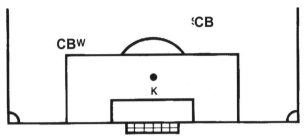

Diagram #52: Midfield Checking
This spread generally yields an available receiver.

A server shoots on goal and immediately covers one of the two centerbacks; the keeper delivers the ball to the unmarked centerback. If players can face upfield, they should certainly do so. Side-on reception is constantly encouraged. But frequently the centerbacks must face the goal or touchline; therefore, voice communication is critical. As soon as the keeper sends the ball to one player, the other back supports and is looking upfield and providing eyes for the ball carrier. Players with such vision should use commands such as "Turn!"; "Man on!"; "Take it outside!"; "You have support!"; and "Back to the keeper!" Subsequent passes (2a, 2b, 2c) are suggested in the following diagram. Back to the keeper is less common with the rule requiring foot passes to keeper be dealt with by feet instead of hands, but it is still used.

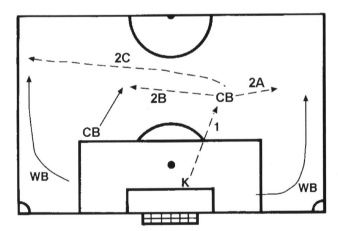

Diagram #53: Building out of the Back
The final four make space for each other in this way. Often 5-8 passes are required before returning the ball to the server. This builds technical/tactical skills and confidence in passing/receiving for the back four players.

The essential element is to make it impossible for two or three opposing strikers to cover four defenders (remembering the keeper makes five) in a full field game. This is accomplished by spreading out across the width and depth of the defending third of the field. Improper positioning allows one opponent to cover two players.

To add realism to the situation, the keeper may choose to kick a long ball to an added target player who simulates a 1 v 1 attack at midfield. This reminds players of the advantages of a 1 v 1 at midfield or in the offensive third.

Another option is distribution to a midfield player, particularly an outside one. In fact, this could be the preferred choice because it permits some penetration and the player has his defenders as support players.

Diagram #54: Possessive Keeper Distribution
Good hard runs with checking back to the ball gives quick reacting keepers many choices. Note #1 where the player makes space by running forward then checking back to the ball.

1. Check away and back to ball midfield run
2. A drop kick line drive distribution to midfielder
3. Either a turn, or as shown a layoff to a teammate
4. The teammate attempts to pass diagonally forward.

Like the previous progression involving the wingbacks, this activity can be gradually enlarged to include more players, maintaining the emphasis on safety in moving the ball out of the defensive third. Spending time practicing the entire system against some defense will develop proper runs and communication.

Preparing the final four for attack takes some individualized sessions such as the suggested progressions above. Once the system is learned, a half hour every two or three weeks will help maintain it. Technical weaknesses, such as inaccurate long passes, sloppy collections, and poor dribbling, must be corrected and practiced. Furthermore, all players must be trained to always look forward for open teammates upfield. This is always the first option, but it may not exist.

Tactical considerations can begin with the keeper. Sometimes a single failure in moving the ball out safely causes the keeper to kick every ball long, or to overlook one side of the field. In training the final four, look for these common tactical errors: poor runs (not bent) which limit visibility upfield; lazy runs which are too late or slow to help the attack; fear of using centerbacks even when they are wide open; and a tendency to possess even when the other team does not withdraw. This is the time to send the long ball up field. Tactical problems at midfield often include `choking' the attack by not moving forward as soon as the keeper has the ball, or not checking back to support when the final four have the ball.

On the team level, the reliance on the blind long ball out of the defending third is a liability. The "If in doubt, kick it out" syndrome should give way to a more positive approach: "I have a good pass that I will execute well." There are times, under extreme pressure, when kicking the ball out of bounds or long is necessary. The guideline for these clearances places the priorities in the following order: "high, long, wide." The blind header or long kick, however, usually reaches the opponent. Often times, if there is enough time and space for a long delivery, there is probably enough time and space to do something constructive with the ball. High level soccer is characterized by quality passes, and even the long clearances have an intended receiver. In any case, there are great rewards for teams that learn patience and possession in moving the ball out of their final third. Such play sets a tone of teamwork, confidence, and patient development of offense by allowing every player to dribble, possess, and combine. Furthermore, it allows defenders to strike and score. Above all, it encourages all players to think. And it is only with thinking that high level soccer can be attained!

At a high level players could be instructed to an extended building out of the back that involves a significant change in point of attack. This allows ball movement to do most of the work while the opponents have to do a great deal of running to slow down the attack. In this case, the ball initially goes to the wingbacks and a diagonal ball to the central midfielders is delivered, which in turn is sent to the opposite side to an outside midfielder or even a far side overlapping wingback.

96

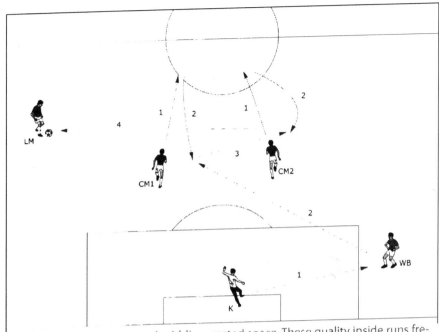

Diagram #55: Note how central middies created space. These quality inside runs frequently open up possibilities on the flanks.

Note that the wingback should have the option of both central midfielders if both make good angle checking runs. Note option 2a, the skip pass is given preference since that player is likely to have the least amount of pressure. In some cases the two central midfielders may use each other, especially if the ball goes to CM1 and under pressure he may lay the ball off to CM2, who in turn could serve the ball to the left outside midfielder or the overlapping wingback. The key is the overlapping wingback going at full pace so as not to be hidden behind his own outside midfielder for any length of time. This option is very often open since the defense was concentrated on the attacking team's right side. It causes a great deal of work in terms of reorganization (marking) for the defense. This higher level tactic will take time to develop so that it moves quickly (successfully). While all of the basic fundamental movements need rehearsal, these more sophisticated movements can add excitement and enjoyment to your team. Obviously this is for more advanced teams, likely age 13 or older.

No amount of tactical or technical training will make up for the lack of energy, hard work and a tough minded disposition on defense. Good defense demands determined tackling and rapid transition. These qualities probably supersede all other aspects of defense. The coach can aid these portions of defense by clarifying their importance and offering positive reinforcement of these attributes. Goal scorers and highly skilled players get the attention of the press and spectators, but the coach needs to balance that unbalanced notoriety by teaching the importance of winning and sustaining possession, denying goals, determined tackling, quick transition, etc. By the same token, no amount of individual quality defending will make up for poor team defense, which requires quality communication, cover and balance.

Defense requires all eleven players with serious effort. Four quality defenders cannot make up for poor defending by strikers and midfielders. Pressure on the ball will deny numerous quality services. If there are innumerable quality services into the defending penalty area, no amount of defense will be effective for 90 minutes. While the best defense is to have possession of the ball, it is unrealistic to expect to have the ball for an entire match, therefore properly prepared defending is a necessity.

Nothing is more beautiful than the total soccer player, playing on a team that uses both short and long passes and balances possession with penetration. Varied rhythms causes lack of easy prediction by the defense and greatly enhances scoring. Not surprisingly, no one does it better than Brazil. This can be overly dramatized because there is seldom mention that Brazil has won the ball more in their offensive half, in fact they are number one in this regard in 3 of the last 5 World Cups. This is obviously outstanding defense more than offense which is constantly touted. I guess this merely suggests that Brazil is very balanced in all aspects of football.

7

Functional Training in Midfield

The mere mention of midfield launches many soccer coaches into heated argument. But it is important to remember that the great midfield debate takes place off the field, and concerns professional teams. Youth coaches need not be unduly influenced by such theoretical discussion as the merits of the Dutch system versus the Italian. This chapter focuses on the development of intelligent midfield play in accordance to what the defense does. While the approach is a systematic one, it encourages decision-making, and actually fosters creativity.

As in the final third, the principle of spreading out still holds true at midfield. Remember that we are dealing with an area on the field, not a position per se. Just as play in the defensive third is not restricted to the defenders, midfield play is not restricted to midfielders; all field players often find themselves as linkmen for strikers and defenders and must play the game accordingly. In other words, they must balance safety and risk, get support, try to penetrate. With numbers up or even, attack quickly and directly; with numbers down, build up slowly and work for an opening. Some back passes may be necessary in order to balance risk and safety.

At midfield, the roles of first, second, and third attacker still come into play; but now there is the addition of rear support for safety. As in the final third, the midfield attack usually takes what a defense gives. Thus the choices of getting the ball through midfield vary according to the defense's tactics. On occasion, it is good to impose your own style to test and surprise the defense. Johann Cruyff instituted the ball controls the game system at Barcelona many years ago and it has kept them in good stead since then.

Here the instructional emphasis covers the various choices at midfield, but in even plainer terms: Pass to the open man!

In any third of the field, the attack generally needs at least four players in that area. It is nearly impossible to have proper ball support and some mobility without four or more players in the third of the field where the ball is. With a three man midfield line, four man width across the midfield is generally created by one of the final four moving into the middle third. Of course, the four man width at midfield can be provided by any of the four defenders and the midfielders.

Whether the ball is delivered to midfield by the keeper or a defender, front runners move up to create forward depth and some defenders stay behind the ball to give depth from the rear. Now the midfield offers width and intelligent choices to the first attacker (player with the ball). Let us look at those choices, beginning with a midfield attack against a high pressure defense.

Since high pressure defenses cover players all over the field, attacking forwards often have only one defender between them and the goal. Therefore, the first option would be a long ball to the wing or even the center forward who is in a central location or drifting out toward the touchline. This tactic requires multiple rear support from midfielders. The advantage of this direct attack lies in getting behind several defenders with one pass, and in the tendency of the defenders to allow open lanes on the wing. It is very effective when it connects with a player who is strong in collecting (esp. air balls) and distributing or shooting in traffic.

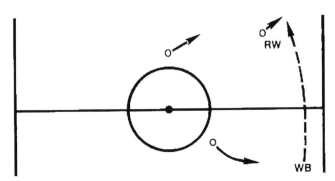

Diagram #56: Long Ball Wing Strike
The long ball direct attack might be best exemplified by the Celtic and Rangers teams from the British Isles.

This can be an 'over-the-top' ball forward, or more commonly the striker checks back to the ball, in which case it might be a ground ball. This form of attack requires sprinting support of the strikers to be effective.

A second option against high pressure would be a 1-2 movement with a midfielder who is checking back. This would beat a single defender who is pressuring the ball, and does not require the long distance accuracy of the first option. Other two-man tactics (double pass, take over exchange, and overlap) can also work here, as high pressure defense may be susceptible to a 2v1 attack. Here the 1-2 involves a wingback and the center midfielder. Angular balls in both directions greatly facilitate players having many options with their teammates.

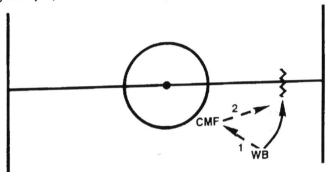

Diagram #57: Wing Back's 1-2 Movement
This play sometimes utilizes up to 30 yards - - in any case the distance varies considerably from one occasion to another.

The third option is a long diagonal pass. This change of field often catches a defense moving the wrong way, thus opening a channel of attack. Like the first option, a long penetrating pass takes several defenders out of the play. Strikers may then be able to get free for a shot on goal.

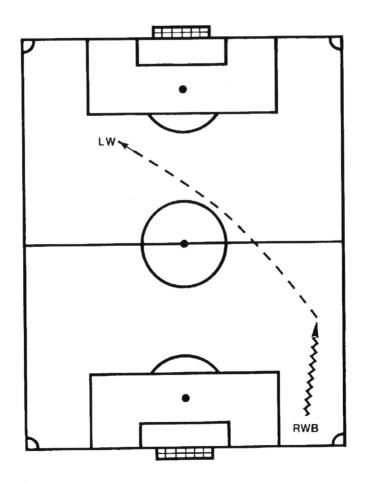

Diagram #58: Diagonal Long Ball Service
The finish can be direct, or a layoff, cross or combination play can precede the shot.
Obviously, this option is seldom available.

Against low pressure defenses, the use of wingbacks as explained in the previous examples can advance the ball through midfield. Combinations involving the centerbacks and-or marking backs are also effective. This option shows a slower and more patient movement of the ball. The keeper distributes to the wingback, who combines with a centerback or midfielder. The diagram shows a 1-2 movement, but a takeover exchange or an overlap could also be used in the event of sudden defensive pressure.

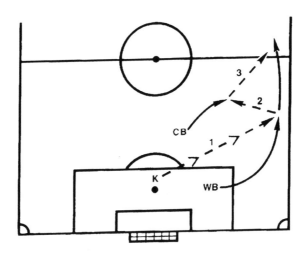

Diagram #59: Keeper Building Attack
Building attack from defending third and through the midfield. All of these movements could also be performed by midfielders or any combination of players.

Another option is a long dribble (usually called driving) through the midfield by one of the final four. This can surprise a low pressure defense which retreats too slowly, or a high pressure defense which leaves a back unmarked.

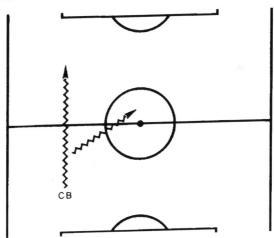

Diagram #60: Dribbling Centerback Attack
A Dribbling attack. With more total soccer players available than ever, high level play has become more characterized by defenders who dribble when safety permits. This is frequently done by midfielders.

Angular runs with the ball can even be more effective as there is always the possibility of occupying either two defenders or no defenders at all, both of which favor the offense.

In developing good decision-making and skill at midfield, the following progression is suggested. As always, the coach can adapt these activities depending on the players' needs. The first step uses short passes in developing possession and exploitation of the midfield area. Four players use the entire width of the field while passing the ball from touchline to touchline, then back again. After every pass the two outside players must touch the touchline. Emphasize upfield vision, crisp passes, movement toward the ball, and efficient collection throughout the circuit. Involve the entire team in this progression as width is a necessary concept for all players.

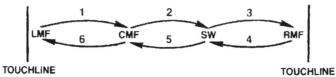

Diagram #61: Midfield Change in Point of Attack
Midfield width permitting changes in point of attack. Always be certain that players are close enough to support each other and far enough apart to disallow any defender from covering two players. Naturally, the players would be in a much more Zig Zag alignment.

After each pass, the player must move away and be prepared for a return pass. Emphasize the importance of each player moving toward the ball to receive it. Naturally, this is a very crooked shape.

The next step uses the same format to introduce the skip pass. On the first circuit, the first pass is to the closest player, and the second pass is a 'skip pass'. Every other pass is a skip pass until the ball returns to the first player. This time the first player begins with a skip pass and the other players alternate accordingly.

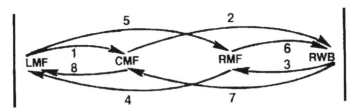

Diagram #62: Skip Pass
Rapid change in point of attack as result of long ball usage.

When players grasp the concept, add forward movement through the length of the field. Players can go in both directions simultaneously, creating a passive defense for the various groups. For all ages, emphasize accuracy. Better players should use air balls for the skip pass, and can try proper bending of the ball and even takeover exchanges.

Wall passes and overlaps going east and west are also effective in breaking down a defense. Be certain that the full field width is maintained through the entire exercise.

Finally, do any and all of the above actions while moving up and down the field, adding keepers and one or two defenders and have players shoot on goal.

One of the most likely tactics of midfield play is for the central midfielders to play off of each other. This concentrates the defense to the middle of the field which opens up the flanks. Among the most common ways for central midfielders to work together is to use each other for a double pass, heel pass, 1-2, a takeover or even a mini east-west overlap. Central midfielders are usually able to work in tight spaces and though all the possibilities are not easy to perform, they generally have the skills to perform such interplay successfully.

When central midfielders do any of the above in the "Staging Area", an area about 40 yards wide and 20 yards deep starting from a couple yards from the 18 yard box, defenses are placed under extreme pressure due to the proximity to the goal. From there, through balls, possible open flanks, shots, and chips to strikers all present dangers to the defense. In addition, the defenders paying attention to the central midfielders allows strikers better chances to get open.

A very game related exercise is to merely play, designating this area and only allowing one player to defend against the two central midfielders, demanding an exchange between the two followed by any of the above mentioned exchanges. Numbers of approximately 8 vs 5 will allow players to have some success in this tactic. Once a modicum of success in training in this manner occurs, it is time to remind players to consider this tactic in a real match. Obviously, this experimentation should take place initially in unimportant matches or matches against lesser opponents. This will facilitate gaining confidence to try it in higher pressure contests. The only down side of this extremely useful and somewhat sophisticated training is seeing some results in training may require 40 minutes of play before players gain some confidence. Still, it will require several such sessions. However, it will be worth it as the team can eventually experience great success as a result of this training. This often opens up the flanks in the final third.

While a great deal has been made of offensive play in central midfield, flank play and crossing by outside midfielders also requires training time and clarification of technical and tactical details. One point will be made here that appears to be a problem regarding the outside midfielders. That is, the expectations often placed on them are sometimes not only unrealistic but unnecessary, especially with 4 man defenses. Expecting your outside midfielders to defend the first or second attackers in your defensive third while at the same time expecting them to be major attacking players serving crosses in the box is asking a lot, probably too much. With four man defenses, outside midfielders can be more attack minded while with a three man defense, obviously a more defensive posture is required.

Little has been mentioned about central midfielders defending. Suffice to say an able, high energy, good tackling player with good anticipation in transition is always a valuable asset. It seems that virtually all the memorable teams in the last couple of decades have had such a player. The ability to win the ball simply gives an attacking midfielder many more chances to create goal scoring opportunities.

I guess the point made in the opening of the chapter, that is that midfield raises controversy and excitement, has been well made. In any case, possibly some of the most important elements of midfield play have been touched upon. The final point is that without a degree of sustained possession in the midfield it is very difficult to gain a rhythm and scoring opportunities. Purposeful possession, possession that seeks penetration at all times with degree of safety, creates the final piece of the midfield puzzle.

Fortunately or unfortunately, depending on your own view of midfield play, it must always be adjusted to the personnel available. Actually, that might be the key element of successful coaching. We must all learn to enjoy the players in addition to enjoying the game to be recognized as a quality coach.

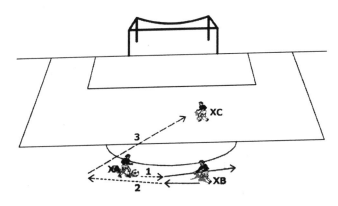

Diagram #63: The diagram shows the two central midfielders assisting one another through use of the takeover. The same movement could also involve XA dribbling past XB and performing a heel pass. Maybe the most important point is that we must provide adequate training (time and activities) of the central midfielders with one another.

Advance to a match-related activity, set up a scrimmage of 11 attackers versus 6 defenders and a keeper on a full field. The team of eleven should possess the ball and change fields in each third, finishing with a shot on goal. (They may need a dry run without any opposition.) Obviously, no team should ever be so stretched out, but this will allow good practice in changing fields and developing width. The team of six defenders is divided into three pairs. Each pair must remain in a particular third of the field while defending against the attacking team. In a subsequent stage have no restrictions on the defending six. This could also be done with three such areas on half the field or half the field plus 15 yards.

Diagram #64: Change in Point of Attack - LINKING
team must remain spread out, but still go toward every pass. This is a great activity -- try it and after one or two occasions incorporate your own wrinkles!

At some point the team must move up an down the field as a unit, just as they would in a game. This connecting, often called linking, is critical to quality team play.

In this situation, insist upon four man width wherever the ball is. One of the final four must join the midfield, two of the midfielders must join the forwards when the ball is in the final third. The final strike is made by a cross with all three slots (near post, far post, and penalty spot area) filled. This progression can work up to the match condition by building up to 11v11. If you do not have 22 players this is a good time for a scrimmage against a weaker opponent in order to build confidence in your team. Reward every change of field, and use low pressure defense. When the attacking team is repeatedly successful, change the defending team to high pressure. Now the attack must be more direct. Look for a change in attacking tactics; the offensive change in behavior must come from the players. Once it does, the coach can secretly signal to the defense to change back and forth from low to high pressure. The offense must learn to react properly on its own, using both direct play and deliberate build-up. At this stage, midfield play will approach a higher level of soccer. Players will observe a defensive change and learn to adapt to it. They will seek to exploit change and learn to respond appropriately. They will seek to exploit space wherever the defense allows; at a more advanced level, some players may even create chances where none appear to exist.

This adaptation to the defense and exploitation of space are the objectives in teaching systematic forward movement. Despite some claims to the contrary, a systematic attack actually encourages greater creativity. The mere elimination of confusion fosters the imagination, and the four man or more width allows choice. Teaching systematic tactics demands a special effort on the part of the coach; but all this planning, choosing, and practicing will allow the attack to take place without all concern being focused on merely maintaining possession.

Once players do not just knock the ball into the final third, nor forget where the goal is, the proper mental framework is partially understood. Once they realize that the midfield is an area in which we PROBE to put the ball into the box with reasonable control, midfield play is fully understood. These exercises not only teach the proper techniques and tactics, but they also inculcate the proper psychology of midfield probing. The initial premise that players must clearly understand the basic roles of first, second, and third attackers now holds true more than ever. These basics must be achieved before teams can succeed in the tactics and functions that make versatile midfield play a major part of exciting soccer.

8

Shooting and Functional Training in the Attacking Third

All too frequently, players and teams are criticized for weaknesses in attacking, yet more often than not, these youngsters receive little or ineffective instruction about attack. The mere mention of attack is a long way from developing the skills for attractive attacking soccer. Of course, spending a great deal of time on the tactics clarified in this chapter, without accompanying technical instruction and practice, is not enough. But when combined with psychological, technical and tactical instruction, this chapter offers proven methods for increasing the frequency and quality of the greatest moments in soccer - - the scoring of goals!

In the attacking third of the field, the safety/risk ratio emphasizes risk; that is, taking chances in order to put the ball into the net. This requires an understanding that possession is often lost in the attacking third. Against a good defense, merely maintaining possession is not enough to create scoring opportunities. A team must be willing to risk losing the ball, though not to the point of recklessness.

It is almost impossible to find enough time to train adequately for finishing. Developing finishers still demands shooting exercises which provide the repetitions necessary to perfect the technical aspects of quality power ball striking, accuracy and heading. It is just a matter of understanding that a quality technical shooter still needs training beyond shooting, so there is a need for finishing which involves real game situations.

Again, shortsided games using full-size goals and goalkeepers in a small area afford numerous finishing opportunities. If players have learned the correct shooting technique, and followed the progressions in finishing, they can then begin to develop the mental toughness that goal-scoring requires.

Goal-scoring is an attitude. Shooting is merely kicking the ball toward the goal, while finishing is putting the ball into the net that has a keeper tending it. Therefore, players should be taught to think in terms of finishing, not just shooting. This is not simply a matter of semantics; instead, it deals with the development of a positive attitude and the proper mental framework. The biggest mistake in the attacking third is a mental one -- failure to shoot! Players must be taught to look for the opening in the goal.

Another critical mental factor is timing. In today's game, there is no longer the luxury to stop, look, and play. Nor can players run to space only to stand and wait for the ball; they must arrive as the ball arrives. All players must be alert to the timing of a run. With a full speed run there is a chance to get open at an ideal location. Since there is always the pos-sibility of a quality defense or slight technical difficulty by the striking team, attackers must also be instilled with the habit of second effort and follow-up on each striking attempt.

Of equal importance is the realization of when to shoot. Many play-ers think that they have to get fully behind the defender before they can shoot. In fact, all they need is a `window', the width of the ball, just enough space to get a shot past the defender and on target. Thus they can benefit from the encouragement to shoot early, as soon as a win-dow or reasonable chance to score presents itself. Keeper errors, visual screening, rebounds, deflections, and just plain luck all increase the chances of scoring, but only when shots are taken, and mostly when they are taken early, but in accordance with what is available. The men-tal preparation and decision-making in the attacking third are based on the principles of player roles and of attack. But these principles are slightly adapted because of the space limitations in this part of the field: deep in the attacking third, teams must often penetrate across the field, and the classic triangular formation of first, second, and third attackers often become compressed. Forward penetration gives way to getting the ball to a scoring location.

The previous chapter points out that there is nothing automatic or stifling about systematized midfield play, and this fact holds true in the attacking third as well. It is vital that players know what to do in the attacking third; that is, to make good decisions from knowledge which avoids panic. Therefore, we will examine the choices available to the first attacker in the finishing third of the field.

The first option will begin near the touch line entering the final third. The wing (or player in the wing's role) will drive toward goal, and if he beats the defense and has a reasonable shooting angle, will take a direct shot on goal. The first option for any attacker in or near the penalty area with half a chance should be to finish! This may seem obvious, but players often neglect this option. Only realistic practice will perfect the techniques and set the proper mental framework.

It is well researched that most goals are scored from close, inside 12 yards. Nonetheless, the mental set of taking available opportunity is a must. Obviously, if a player is marked and a teammate is wide open the pass must be given. What must not happen is a player in 1v1 situation passing to another player who is in a 1v1 situation.

The use of 1v1 contests which culminate in a strike are excellent preparation, as are 1v2+K and 1v3+K in the penalty area, illustrated below. If necessary, have defenders connect their hands behind their backs, heads or a similar restriction. This will afford enough advantage to the attackers for success. Furthermore this is good for developing defensive footwork skills. Also players can be placed along the sides for 1-2 movements to ensure success of the activity. The attacker (A) beats D1 with a dribble, then tries to beat D2 and finish on goal. Defenders are confined to their individual grids, and the keeper may not leave the goal area until the last defender is beaten. Set up several stations, each with groups of four to eight players. Move to full pressure and keep score to encourage maximum effort. Rotate defenders. Since this activity focuses on the attack, avoid coaching the defenders. Good instruction often avoids confusion by working with one element at a time, and teaching that element well.

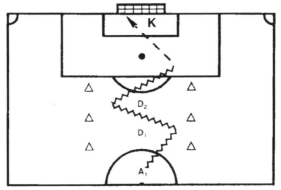

Diagram #65: 1 v 1 v 1 v K Developing attacking confidence. It also puts a player in an exercise in which he continuously moves TOWARD the goal.

Since attackers often find themselves marked by two or more defenders, they must learn to deal with this situation in practice. A 1v2 + K activity offers such a challenge, and also helps an attacker to feel relatively `free' in a match when he/she has a 1 v 1 opportunity.

In diagram #66 allow the attacker to receive the ball from the servers before the defenders become active. Gifted players will find ways for defenders to interfere with each other.

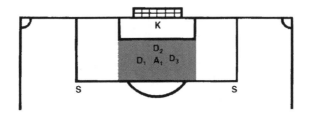

Diagram #66: Shooting: Every Man for Himself
1 v 3 + K Attacking confidence; move servers to create many varied situations. Ground, driven, bouncing, slow rollers are all wonderful possibilities. Each of the four players can alternate being the attacker.

On any trial, each server has a ball, and either may serve. At early stages, defenders have hands behind their backs or weak defenders may be used, but work up to attacking success against full pressure. The rewards of this activity are great and well worth the effort. In some cases, the two servers may receive a pass when A1 is under pressure, but they must return the ball one or two touch to A1; servers cannot shoot.

Another option is merely 4 players with every player taking on the others. In this situation a coach serves the ball, attempting to give opportunities for all four players. Serve ground, driven, air and even bouncing balls throughout the entire shaded area. This is an exhausting activity: therefore change personnel or provide rest regularly. Players love this game of every 'man' for himself.

In these activities, as in a real game, the attacker is generally advised to shoot 'worm burners' to the far post. The goalkeeper usually concentrates on the near post more than the far post. At first you might want to restrict the keeper to the near post. Also in actual games there is a better chance for other attackers to be on-side at the far post, especially for a rebound or keeper deflection finish. Later, chips or near post shots should be taken when they are the best choice. Again, players must be allowed to make decisions in the workout if they are to develop decision-making ability during games.

Another suggested activity that encourages finishing and decision-making involves a pair of regular or flat-faced goals. A neutral server delivers the ball to one player, who attempts to beat the other with a shot on goal. The server can begin by alternating serves, then repeating serves to the player who scored last, and finally offering neutral serves for which the players must compete. More players can be added, or the server can become a second defender. Another variation is to serve air balls, and limit scoring to head balls. The versatility of these goals allows for other 1 v 1 activities on the outer faces of the goals.

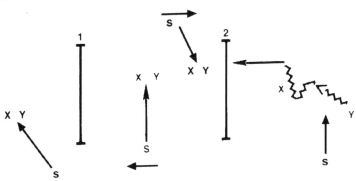

Diagram #07: Shooting Galore: Here both sides of two flat faced goals are being used. Each Shooting on first opportunity. These 2 goals are accommodating 8 players – 16 players when alternating pairs - 4 keepers could also be added. Alternate servers.

Of course, reasonable shooting chances do not occur every time a strik-er enters the attacking third. The second option, therefore, is to cross the ball. The player usually tries to gain as much ground toward the goal as possible before crossing, since this creates the most dangerous angles on goal. Receivers can then face the goal for a powerful first-time shot. The problem of off-sides is also eliminated when the server nears the goal line.

The preferred dribble or drive aims for the end line, attempting to stay within 15 to 25 yards from the goal, as shown in diagram #68. A drive to the goal line as shown by A, as opposed to B, is greatly preferred.

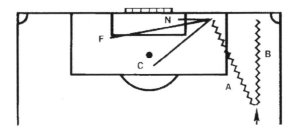

Diagram #68: Filling Goal Area Slots
Giving the receiver good shooting angles.

There are three target areas for the cross: far post (F), near post (N), and center (C). Ideally, all three areas would become occupied by attackers just as the ball is about to arrive. The central goal area should be exploit-able by any number of players.

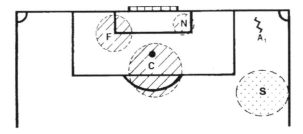

Diagram #69: Service Target Areas
F, N, and C lined areas are the target areas for serves. Send driven balls to area N, loft balls over the keeper's head for area F and pass ground balls to area C in a crease to an oncoming teammate making a late run.

If the defender forces a blind cross, in other words plays well enough to keep the winger's head down, the cross should be a lofted ball to the far post, over the keeper's head and out from the goal line. The receiver can then face the ball and the goal without an awaiting keeper. For this cross, emphasize the non-kicking foot pointed toward the target. If the wing can make eye contact with a teammate at the near post, the cross is generally a low driven instep kick that the receiver can deflect toward the goal with the head or foot, or flick on to a third attacker. This requires timing and heading skill, which are the result of much practice. Higher level soccer is characterized by such technical and tactical capabilities as the flick-on.

Another choice is a ground ball to the central area. In any case, a 'friendly' one touch shot is preferred. This play depends upon the keeper's position, defenders' and attackers' location, as well as skill and field conditions. This is an excellent option for young players as it creates mindful football.

Frequently the best a server can do is to serve the ball between the defense. If the entire team is trained in this regard, all runners attempt to fill lanes between defenders. This provides a far greater connection between server & receiver, and can result in goals.

The words wing, striker, attacker etc., are used somewhat interchangeably. This attack can be used with any formation, system of play and with teams composed of very differing attacking talents.

Crosses are frequently only as effective as the receiver's heading skill. Players need to master two types, the attacking header (for passes and shots) and the clearing header. Both types are useful to all players because strikers must clear balls, as in defending against corners, and defenders must pass air balls to the feet of their teammates and occasionally also shoot. The emphasis of the attacking header is on getting the ball down. The ball should bounce perpendicular to the keeper's feet, usually close to the goal line. Contact is made with the frontal area of the forehead (the flat part). For the clearing header, contact is made higher on the forehead (more on the hairline). Stress distance and height.

Attackers must specifically practice the scoring header, since it requires both concentration and confidence. Without practice, all techniques deteriorate, but those that demand courage need additional work. In lieu of a cross, the wing may pass a perfectly weighted ground ball to a supporting attacker (S, in dotted area Diagram 69) for a one touch shot or cross. In this case S usually serves a long diagonal ball to the back post area; at the corner of the 6 yd box.

Often young players cannot loft a ball to the far post or drive a ball accurately to the near post; therefore, the emphasis should fall on the pass to the near central area. At higher levels all four options should be fully developed, though individual skill, team style, and opponents ability may determine the emphasis.

Since a great number of goals are scored from the area between F, N, and C, why not put attackers there? The answer is that this area must remain vacated so that it can be exploited by any one of three people coming into areas F, N, and C at speed. What is not wanted is a player parked in the central goalmouth as that will allow the central defenders and the keeper easy positioning.

Functional training for the cross can teach your players their individual responsibilities. Let's focus on who might try to strike at each area. A coach must be open minded to variations best suited to his unique personnel. While the basic system is sound, the coach can adapt variations, depending on the players' skill and attitude. Sensible adjustment and emphasis of a basic system might be wiser than trying to invent a whole new system. Minor changes allow for many options, which the coach needs to adjust due to variance in team skill, individual player strengths and personnel available from game to game.

Anyone can fill anyone of the suggested areas, but in a typical 4-4-2 one would think that the first runner, the target striker would most often be at the near post, with the far post being-other striker and the area just inside the "D" of penalty area would be a central midfielder if the ball were coming from the flank.

In any case without creativity, blind side runs, eye contact, inside overlaps, combination play (especially third man runs), heel passes, flank overlaps, midfield support runs into the penalty area, and split second decisions all manner of organization is still not likely to succeed. With the addition of these elements and a bit of organization one can see a significant increase in scoring.

Another alternative, especially when service is delayed, is depicted in diagram 70.

Generally, the center forward would go to the far post area in order to blindside the central defenders. Since the center forward is usually marked by a good defender, it is advantageous to remove this defender from the vital near post area. The far post area presents opportunities to score with the head, and center forwards are most often willing and able to head the ball from this vital location. Other players could occupy the far post location; the left wingback or left midfielder are logical candidates, especially if they can head the ball well.

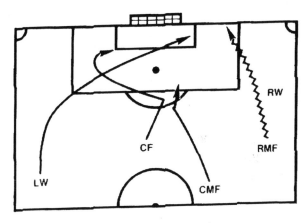

Diagram #70: Paths to Goal - Filling the 'spots' in attack.

The near post location is frequently attacked by the left wing attacker (diagram #71). This requires a lengthy run across the field, which can upset the defense. Forcing the defender to change sides of the goal, or to pass his marking responsibility to someone else can cause confusion. The attacker may also be able to outrun the defender to arrive at the near post unmarked.

If the crosser is deep in diagram 71, path 1 is the first option; if the crosser is not deep, path 2 can be taken to maintain an on-sides position. A disguised and quick movement along path 3 can then exploit the near post area. Maintaining on-sides is fairly simple for the left wing because she can see the ball and the deep defenders throughout the approach. With a two man front one would go near post and the other far post, often after having crisscrossed each other.

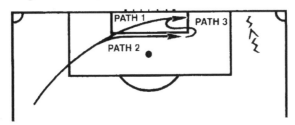

Diagram #71: Wing Crossing the Goal
Wing run with full visibility for maintaining an on-sides position.

Of course, the wing attacker can receive anytime after entering the box, and then take a shot. On the other hand, if the wing does not receive the ball early, he should continue toward the first attacker to offer support. The point is not to remain stationary. Successful strikes at goal are characterized by timely movement.

Central area C is often assumed by the center midfielder, who is often chosen because of the ability to offer quality support to teammates. In this case, however, an attempt at early support may well deny a shot on goal. Because this is an easy area to get to early, the major problem with this location is early occupancy. Patience must be emphasized, so that the midfielder will learn to arrive at the last possible moment, running at speed. Teach the basic movements first, and only then coach timing.

Along with the timing of this run, all involved players must be taught what to do if the ball arrival is delayed: all three players merely rotate clockwise with right wing attacks, counterclockwise with left wing attacks. This allows visual contact with the ball and movement, while forcing decisions among defenders. Any breakdown may result in a goal. After players have practiced this attack, it merely becomes a general pattern in which creativity is encouraged. But, during the training period, maintain discipline. Variations are permitted only after the general pattern is established. Once the artist knows the media, he can become fully creative.

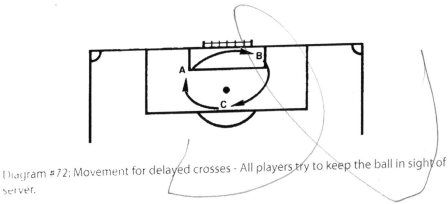

Diagram #72: Movement for delayed crosses - All players try to keep the ball in sight of server.

The run to area S (diagram #73) is generally made by the right midfielder, although it could be the right wingback. In any case, this player is the second attacker, and as such must concentrate on the role of supporting the first attacker. Any player who goes directly to area S is likely to be marked. Therefore, he must be in the general area, but still able to sprint to a desirable location to receive the ball. Changes of direction and speed facilitate the support function.

This could be accomplished in many ways, but the key is to provide support through bent run movements while the wing attacker works for a quality pass. A run as shown in the diagram below may blind side the defender; then a cut can be made in front for a one touch shot, or a bent run back to receive. In any case we want this player to attempt to get free for a shot on goal or pass to a teammate.

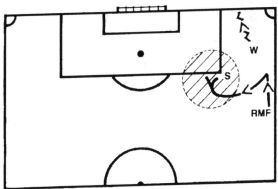

Diagram #73: Service Support
All players near ball should be working hard to attain a shot on goal or service.

Once a team has mastered the basics of filling the critical attacking areas, the particular locations N, F, C and S can be filled by anyone. When such a free lance occupation takes place, the general order is as follows: the first player who can get to the near post does so, the second player takes the far post, the third player fills the middle. This order permits all players to use their vision effectively; no one needs to look backwards, which may cause one not to see a ball delivered to them.

Here is an effective activity for teaching your players to fill the attacking slots. Groups of four players stand about 18 yards from the 18 yard line.

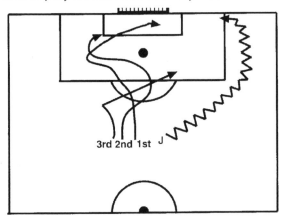

Diagram #74: Filling Slots
Using 4 players; Filling three attacking slots plus a server, while integrating fast thinking. Later on it will be a habit; it will merely be a reaction which is faster, therefore more efficient.

Ground balls to behind the penalty spot are emphasized. One player is given the ball and dribbles to the goal line just inside the penalty area. Service is to all 3 locations, but the area just behind the penalty spot is emphasized. Then the first runner to the near post goes wide outside the near post six yard box timing his run at the near post for when the dribbler delivers service. The coach either holding shirt (or verbally) releases the second runner to far post who is also wide. Then the third runner for the penalty area is released. THE MAJOR FOCUS IS PROPER LOCATION RUNS AND TIMING. All this is done with no warning to the players of who is to do what; the guy given the ball is the server, first released player goes near post, next released player goes far post and the last player released moves into the"D" of the penalty area.

Then add a single defender and keeper. The single defender marks one runner; changing who she marks on each occasion. The server MUST serve to one of the two open runners. I found this exercise remarkably valuable in creating scoring opportunities and actual goals. In time 2 or 3 groups can do the activity at the same time, either with assistant coaches, or captains. Again a flat faced goal could accommodate two groups. Generally the whole team is trained, but obviously strikers are engaged in this activity more often and for greater periods of time. Simply move from this stage to a shortsided game (anything from 5 v 5 to 8 v 8 is appropriate), still using full sized goals. Goals scored from a goal line cross count 3 points while direct dribbling goals count 1 point. Be certain players fill the slots, approach the goal from angles taught and that players do not arrive too early.

Though this training does not exhaust the possibilities of wing attack, it does teach players the major options, thus mitigating confusion. It will also encourage players to attack on the wing, making better use of the entire field. This approach is highly recommended before attempting to develop direct attacks up the center of the field. These more direct attacks are characteristic of higher level teams that are already capable of wing attack. On the youth level, direct attack often deteriorates to kick-and-run, poor decision-making, lack of patience and improvisation, as well as, impoverished technical development. Nevertheless, direct strikes are a part of the game, requiring intelligent training that should minimize its negative aspects at younger levels. But this training should occur only after the fundamentals of wing attack have been mastered. Since reasonably developed defenses seldom allow a through ball directly at the goal, direct attacks require someone to run behind the defense while staying on-sides, turn the ball at the goal or quality combinations creating a shot. Players need to practice this difficult skill so that they can prepare the ball with one touch, turn quickly, then shoot accurately and powerfully with the second touch. Ability to turn both left and right in a variety of ways is a great asset.

Using this drill, train players to receive ground balls to either foot, and air balls to the foot, thigh, chest, and head. Then add disguise: on a turn call, feint a touch, let ball through legs and then pass it. Another feint involves the inside of one foot to one touch the ball behind the other foot, setting up a pass or shot. The players' creativity comes into play here. As might be expected, this activity should culminate with finishing on goal.

Direct attacks require strikers to learn running east/west to stay onsides and then cut when the ball is delivered. It frequently requires the server to chip the ball over the top so the ball does not drift to the keeper. This is also avoided by the strikers not running in line with ball and the keeper; always trying create an angle so their hips are facing the ball and the goal. The server should try to serve to the striker that is in this advantageous position. The crisscross by the strikers attempts to cause defensive confusion; also one can check to the ball while the other supports or goes through. Strikers creating space for each other requires much work with just the strikers against defenders in the near (about 36 yards from goal) penalty area. If the midfielder can serve to the far striker this puts the other striker in the immediate vision of his other striker. This facilitates an early successful strike on goal.

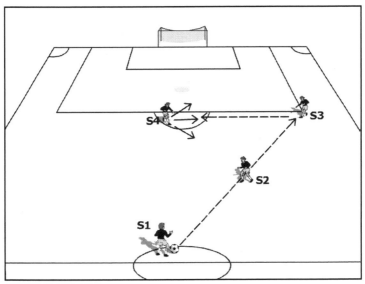

Diagram #75: Skip Pass
Service to striker involving a skip pass -- this often requires layoff support

To develop this skill arrange three players in a line. Player X1 passes to player X3; player X2 becomes a defender. The passing player must make the proper call: "Man on!" if the defender marks closely, "Turn!" if the defender gives space. After turning player X3 can pass to player X2 and the drill continues. Player X3 remains in the middle. Rotate players every 2 minutes. If player X3 cannot turn, he must shield, then move toward player X 1 to create space to turn, dribble, or simply pass the ball back to X1.

124

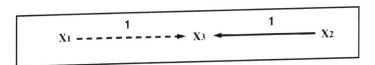

Diagram #76: Communication
X1 would tell X3 "Man On." Man on would indicate a return pass to X1. The other command is "turn", in which case X3 would pass to X2.

Shortsided work for the day should score a point for every successful call of "Turn!" or "Man On!" For every mistaken call, deduct a point. Let teams keep their own score and call it out. The thinking while playing is a feature of the real game. Soccer requires a great deal of thinking about several things at once. Sometimes we're measuring our opponents speed, style, etc., yet we are playing to score (soccer is almost never played the same way when we are winning as opposed to losing). In addition, we may be trying to conserve energy but not give up too much. All this is done while still playing, reacting to support, warding off a tackle, penetrating, etc. Much of this is reaction, but some of it is conscious thought.

Accomplishing all that is outlined here is likely to be a long range plan of at least two seasons for a team which meets twice a week during the season. However, this is no reason to avoid training for a quality attack. Once players have learned one systematic attack, they will have an easier time learning others. Certain formations lend themselves better to certain types of attack. Systems using traditional wings obviously suit themselves to the wing attack system advocated here, whereas a double striker formation offers target players for direct attack. Naturally it is only a matter of emphasis, since we must do what the game demands and there are occasions that lend themselves to one or the other type of attack! Of course the choice of formations depends most directly on the individual players' abilities and weaknesses. Nonetheless, in either attack players should understand how to fill the slots.

Some motions that are part of a more direct attack are often characterized by a 4-4-2 formation. First and foremost, having two strikers does not mean the team strikes with only two players. It means that there are two DESIGNATED strikers. We still need 2 or 3 others to join in the attack in order to score goals with some consistency.

The two designated strikers must work together - - often in tandem, one in front of the other, but not usually flat across the field, except once they reach the line of offsides, usually near the penalty area. In this way they can work TOGETHER because obviously two lone strikers working alone are not going to score many goals. However, on defense the two strikers might be flat. Furthermore, one striker is usually on the strong (ball) side of the field while the other attempts to stay somewhat centrally.

If one can hold the ball to allow midfielder or wingbacks to get forward, this will help enormously.

What follows is a number of options to goal, but generally any given team would probably emphasize 2 or 3 options best suited to the talents of that particular team.

Obviously anytime we have a capable dribbler and he finds himself 1v1 this simple option of taking the opponent on is still VERY POTENT. In any case the layoff, 1-2 move, takeover and the overlap are potent weapons for attaining strikes on goal. Since these basic combinations are potent all over the field for possession and penetration, train the entire team in these basic attacks on goal. In this way you accomplish finishing, penetration and possession - - this is economical training at its' best. Besides, players enjoy shooting exercises; this will keep team motivation at a peak.

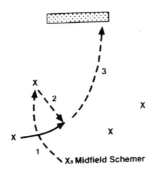

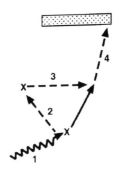

Diagram 77: Layoff
This is a simple delivery to a target player, then a layoff for the other striker for a shot on goal.

Diagram 78: 1-2 move
Another simple option is a 1-2 move by the 2 strikers or ANY two players, though frequently at least one of the two strikers is involved.

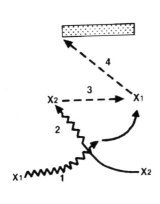

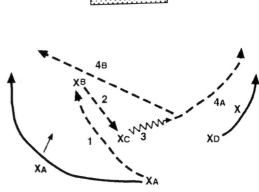

Diagram 79: Takeover
Here a simple takeover is performed; the original dribbler spins off and receives a pass and takes a shot on goal.

Diagram 80: Third Man On
Layoff to third man on. Pass to target player with layoff to other striker who dribbles while an overlap takes place. Shown is one on each side but either one or the other is sufficient. Now player dribbles, generally across field because he doesn't need penetration, he just needs time in order to serve a pass to 4A or 4B the overlapping players. This frequently is the essence of an entire team attack.

9

Strictly Shooting

A) Shooting Activities
B) Shots on Goal: A Novel Idea
C) Causes of Poor Shooting
D) Twin Strikers Training

Many coaches are frustrated when they observe their players missing easy shots. Interestingly few teams do enough shooting to perfect the technique; and equally important have inadequate practice in order to have composure when shooting. First of all shooting requires a great deal of practice, and secondly a major part of shooting must be in game like conditions with a keeper in goal and defenders forcing the shooter to do so quickly. Quickly does not mean rushed, it means composed but taking as little time as necessary. It means taking a one touch shot when possible and if necessary taking a two touch shot. In other words one must also make good decisions quickly as to what is the best option. In summary players must be competent technically, make good decisions and do so with composure. Easier said than done. In any case adequate shooting and finishing training is necessary. Usually the word finishing brings into play being able to get the ball in the net past the keeper in game conditions.

One area of concern and a common fault among players is the desire to spend a good deal of time striking dead balls which is not very game related except for direct kicks. Another problem is many players who are unable to drive a ball with any degree of competence spend much wasted time on bending balls. The third area of inefficiency is players aim for the upper 90 before they can competently strike a ball low with authority. Some of this is a result of when players are young it is a challenge to lift the ball to any significant degree. The second reason is permissiveness of the above behaviors.

Those instructing players must become more convincing on driving low balls to the open areas of the goal.

Another area of concern is choosing the correct surface for a particular shot. Specifically a shot with the keeper in goal from 18 to 30 yards has little chance of scoring without using the surface of the power instep kick. By the same token using the power instep kick inside of 10 yards rarely makes sense. From one to ten yards invariably requires the accuracy of the inside of the foot push pass surface in order to obtain maximum accuracy which is the main requirement from such a close distance. Also refusing to head the ball when the header allows the earliest possible shot causes shots to never even be taken. Probably the most difficult area to coach is having players look for the opening in the goal instead of deciding where the keeper is. Some research indicates that built into the human instinct is to seek a target as that was our evolutionary process to the rabbit, fish or whatever game early man was hunting. It may sound like a word game to say look for the opening in goal instead of where the keeper is. It is not a word game. Very experienced coaches who have used this teaching strategy have seen positive results.

Another fallacy even witnessed with experienced coaches and players is shooting for the near post when the far post offers so much more opportunity. Any deflection from the keeper could easily allow a teammate to be onsides and finish the original shot. At the near post no teammate could be there soon enough and be onsides to finish the original shot. Another shooting fallacy is taking shots from goal line areas. While goals are sometimes (rarely) scored from this location it is invariably on a poor keeper. Almost never are goals scored from that location in real games of parity with competent keepers. Furthermore, service from this location provides excellent chances for a teammate finishing on goal. This is often seen in professional matches and is something that should be trained for so that players know proper shooting location versus serving locations.

On corner kicks shooting success often depends upon being back from the desired (best) location so that one is moving forward which allow a far higher jump and allows one to legally overpower an opponent. The location should also place one with a 45 degree angle from the ball to the goal. This means starting a bit away from the goal so one is moving forward and toward the goal. Needless running around before the ball is to be served is wasted energy. A defender close to you and facing away from the corner is ideal as she cannot see the ball. You can see the ball and your forward running is difficult for an opponent who is back pedaling to stop you.

Blind side runs on defenders, especially in crossing situations including the early cross and long diagonal services gives an attacker a huge advantage. Timing a run for any and all situations is learned through experience, however questions to players regarding there choices in regard to the final sprint to shoot may help them gain insights they may not have thought of on their own.

Finally following shots is an important attribute of the good finisher. Actually this is easy to train for. Simply require following ones own and other players' shots all the time. Naturally doing sessions specifically aimed at following shots will also help.

Not quite as obvious is the infantile behavior for potential through balls is for the receiver to stand in a straight line with the goal. It is best for the receiver, generally a striker to create an angle with the ball and the goal in order to have hips open, thus ready to receive and shoot. Open hips reception will allow a striker to see the ball, the goal, teammates and opponents. Furthermore players delivering the ball to strikers should look for a player that is properly positioned in the triangle configuration of sever, receiver and goal. The linear situation is often merely a pass to the opposing keeper. It would be a good idea to instill this behavior for serving teammates to reiterate frequently where the receiver might better be placed to receive the ball.

Almost without saying wall passes, mini east/west overlaps and take-overs followed by a spinout are extremely useful in the penalty area. Any movements which will either pick off defenders or cause them to exchange their man to man responsibilities creates defensive problems. What follows is several simple fun shooting activities. Most are competitive and also many are actual games that increase interest in shooting effectively. Some authorities discourage having players chase balls sent over the top of the goal. By now it is clear that I favor positive player focused behavior, but I do not think that having players retrieve their own ball when they sent it over the top of the goal will hurt them.

A) SHOOTING ACTIVITIES

Some of the following activities are technical, some for young players while other for mature players and many involve tactical strategies and some are totally game related and useful for many age levels.

1) Circle shooting: Two goals anywhere from 30 to 50 yards apart. It is done with or without keepers, but certainly after 2 or 3 occasions use a keeper.

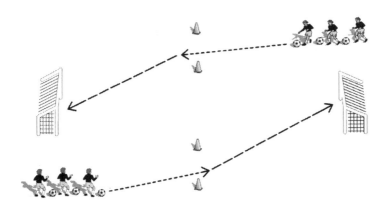

Diagram 81: Circle shooting accomplishes many repetitions in a short period of time. The next shooter goes when the previous shooter goes through the gate.

Every player has a ball and merely dribbles through the gate goal (cones or obstacle course markers) and on the first touch through the gate takes a shot. Be certain players head directly toward the goal and prepare the shot with a slight angle. However the player goes straight to the ball. The last touch should be far enough out in front to facilitate a power instep shot. Demand low driven balls to the far post. If the keeper gets scored on at the near post he must run around the goal; this insures the keeper covers the near post as he should in a real game, and does not 'play the drill', behavior which will destroy any activity the coach designs. Players merely go in a circle and shoot and follow their own shot and retrieve their own ball. Do not have the keeper retrieve the balls because he must protect the player retrieving the ball. Keep it moving quickly and be certain to change to counter clockwise for some period of time.

Variations:
1) Is a wider cone area with a line defender or even a box area of about 5 x 5 yards
2) Place a mannequin about 12 yards from the goal and require chips
3) Have a player act as a wall passer for the shots
4) Require service from the opposite goal line and then the shooter receives and then shoots
5) Require beating the keeper before the shot (obviously developing dribbling skill)
6) Add a defender who starts out about 6 yards behind the shooter; if she wins the ball she shoots. Always demand game speed going to the cone area and then convert to control preparation touch for the shot. While this is extremely simple, it can even be done with U-6's, the enormous amount of repetitions it facilitates makes it a useful technical exercise. For added fun have players keep score and after 15 minutes check on the number of goals various individuals scored or even have two teams and watch your defenders and defensive middies out score your strikers and attacking middies. Go figure!

2) Yeagley Shooting: This exercise merely has every player with a ball at midfield and dribble and shoot a power instep drive from about 22 yards (less for younger players), then take an inside of the foot accuracy push pass shot from a ground ball served about 12 yards out, and finishing with a header hand served by the coach or an able server near the goal line. First play 5 rounds where everyone gets the full three shots. Then after that if you miss two shots you are eliminated and finally those that are left whoever scores all three shots wins. Yes, multiple winners. Remember eliminated players are always required to do something such as juggling. In some cases so the others are not standing around too long whoever makes 2 shots first wins. Use your own wrinkles. What's nice about this exercise is that it gets players constantly shooting and moving **to** the goal. Also it teaches them from far away to use power, when close to place the ball, and they get some heading shooting experience as well. Emphasize getting the heading shots to go down to the goal line by using the frontal forehead instead of the hair line, which is used for clearing. With large numbers have two separate groups.

3) Baranello Shooting Fitness: Have two teams on both sides of the coach about 30 yards from the goal. Both players run around the goal in opposite directions and when they reach about 6 yards out from goal the coach serves a neutral ball about 5 yards which the two players compete for; whoever wins the ball attempts a shot and the other player defends. If the defender wins the ball they shoot. When the previous pair touch the ball the next pair go so this is a quick moving exercise. With numbers use two groups. After x number of rounds, generally about 10, one team wins, the others pick up equipment, donkey jumps, or whatever. Adjust the distance to your purpose, but usually about 30 yards is about right for mature groups.

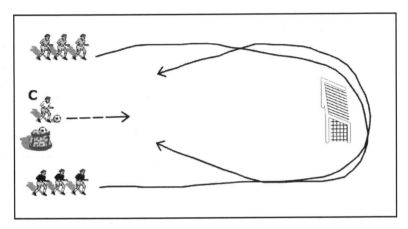

Diagram 82: Fitness shooting will invariably elicit full effort from all players.

4) Goal Line Numbers: Two teams one on each side of the goal on the goal line. Every player has a number. The coach is also on the goal line with all the balls. There being two of every number, one from each team, the coach merely call out "Three's" and the two three's run out to win the ball served by the coach about 16 to 25 yards away. Have equal pairs to make it competitive. Variations: Call out two or more numbers at the same time. At the very end send a ball out about 35 yards and call out "Everyone". With more than 12 players use two different groups. Avoid games of elimination such as "World Cup", instead play games of inclusion.

5) Anson Dorrance's Carolina Lightning: Two teams, one team in a line about 25 yards taking one touch shots from a square ball served in rapid succession straight across the 18 yard line and the other team defending the goal. If possible each team has her own goalkeeper, or one permanent goalkeeper. The defending team has one player inside each post of the goal on the goal line and every time a goal is scored a player from outside the post takes their place. The player leaving goes to the end of line outside the goal. If a ball is served and no one gets to it for a shot the shooting team loses a point. After 10 non-goals, saves, over the top or whatever the two teams exchange places on the fly and the server serves a ball that must be shot before it stops. The shooting team by the same token should be setup and ready to defend the shot. Be sure non-goals are called out loudly by the defending team and goals scored by the shooting team are also called out. After 5 rounds the team with most goals wins. Everyone is responsible to be certain the server has many balls at her feet at all times. Shots over the top are retrieved by the shooter. Demand everyone works to have balls at the serving location! This is a good time to make sure there are no prima donnas, as those individuals destroy any team building efforts you make. Have an assistant to the server for organizing balls for the server. This is a shooting, defending and rapid transition competitive game.

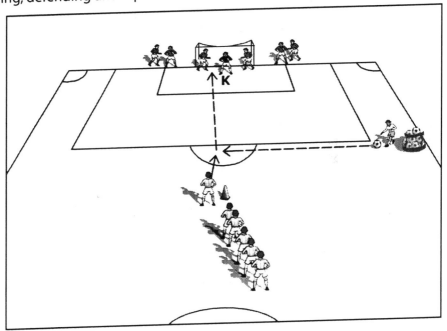

Diagram 83: Carolina Lightning engenders a good effort even after a rigorous practice. After a couple of rounds have balls served from the left side.

6) Kings Game: About 30 yards between goals nearly full width of the field.

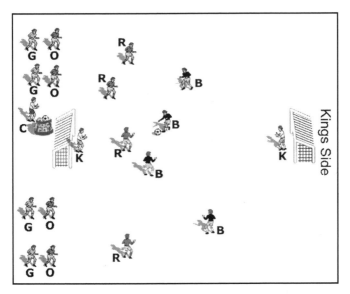

Diagram 84: Guaranteed your players will request this game!
B= Blue Team   O=Orange Team   R=Red Team   G=Yellow Team   K= Keeper

- Kings are always on the right side attacking the left side goal.
- If Blue scores they remain Kings.
- If they fail, shoot off target or out-of-bounds, Red is issued a ball from the coach.
- If Red fail to score, shoot off target or out-of-bounds, Blue is issued a ball and game continues.
- If Red scores they become Kings attacking the left side goal, Blue leaves and Orange come on to defend.
- Put more simply, if you score you become or remain Kings.
- Every time someone scores, a new defending team comes on.
- If a shot is off target or out of bounds, the other team gets the ball and play continues.
- So whenever there is a score a new team comes on. Since this is a rapid transition game there is no stoppage, and if a team can score while the other team did not come on soon enough, it counts; in fact the object of the game is defending and scoring rapidly in transition.
- At times 2 or 3 teams come on in a single minute, so even when you just left the field you have to move quickly to get ready to go on again.

- A fringe benefit is that this is great training for keepers as well as the field players.
- Option: Every time the ball is lost a new team comes on. This is a very rapid game.

All players love the Kings Game!

6) Varied Goal Scoring According to Area of the Goal Struck: Everyone is playing to a goal which is in the center of the field. Often played with younger players with groups of 5 or 6 players and a small 4' x 6' goal. Can be fun for any age group. A score on the front of the goal, the regular area, counts 3 points. A score on either side area of the goal counts 2 points and a score at the rear of the goal counts 1 point. This can be varied so only the front and sides count or whatever. Play to a score of 10 for a winner. It can be played as two teams or every man for himself. With several goals there could be games of 2v2 or 3v3.

6) 1 v 1 Spots: Equal pairs play 1v1 to a full size goal with a keeper.

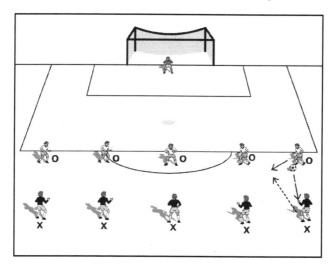

Diagram 85: Spots gets many 1v1 chances in a short time to a full size goal.

When using a keeper only one player goes at a time, but in rapid succession. Flat disc's are really best. The distance of about 10 yards between the server/defender (D) at the cone and the attacker (A). The server serves a crisp ground ball and the attacker attempts to score by dribbling past the server/defender. Both players attack from the same cone before moving to the next cone. If you play without a keeper, pairs go without regard for the other pairs as generally there are only two pairs working at the same time because of retuning to the spots and retrieving balls takes time. The other pairs only help to create further token defense. After eight minutes new pairs of competing are created with winners challenging winners and losers against losers. Sometimes there are ties and they also play against each other.

Coaching Points: Defenders try to steer the attacker away from the goal and the attacker tries to get central for a shot. The attacker always wants to make the goal as big as possible by having a central location. If you notice players shielding and consuming long periods of time, restrict the attackers to 8 touches. Also demand that once there is enough room for a shot or the defender is beaten you must <u>not</u> take another touch! You could have two teams and keep score that way, but generally scoring is on an individual basis.

9) Bull Pen Shooting: Two teams with goals about 25 yards apart and all extra balls in the two goals occupied by a keeper. Simply play, there should be a shot at the least every 10 to 15 seconds. Regular game rules. If the coach desires, when an available shot is not taken, call it a turnover and award the ball to the opposing team.

Variations:
1) Hit the target player who can shoot or layoff the ball; she must also follow every shot.
2) Have a midline and all shots come from behind the line
3) All shots must come from in front of the line
4) All shots must cross the line and the shot can then be taken from any location
5) One neutral server on each flank and all balls go to a flank server before a shot is taken
6) A server from each team on both sides or the field who are undefended and serve before a shot can be taken. Variation: every time they serve they return to interior play and another player goes outside to serve
7) End line neutrals that must serve to the team that gave them the ball; with this option chipped by balls away from the keeper can be served.

The options in Bull Pen Shooting are limitless and players from 7 years old to professionals enjoy this simple outstanding shooting game.

10) Volley Shooting: Flat Faced Goal: Player A on one side of the net serves over the net, either by hand or with a chip to player B who aims a full volley shot low at the net. Then the ball is simply served to the other side for a low volley shot.

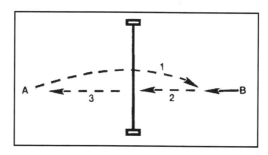

Diagram 86: The ability to shoot volley shots helps goal scoring a great deal.

Options include half volley; receiving the ball with the body on full run then shooting on second touch; heading shots; two receivers, one setting up the other for a shot; addition of keeper; two players competing for the shot. For more realistic finishing , add a defender.

11) Circle Shooting on Flat Faced Goal: A circle of cones is placed around the goal about 15 yards away. Players are all outside the coned area. Players can only go into the cone area to retrieve balls, which must be sent outside the circle area instantly with 1 or 2 touches. Whoever gets the ball first has possession. In this activity there are two teams; both teams can score on either side of the flat faced goal. However, prior to any score the team must change the ball from the side they won the ball on to the other side. For even more fun have the teams change the ball from one side to the other two times. No shots can be taken in the circle area. After a score the team can score again, but must do so on the opposite side from the initial score.

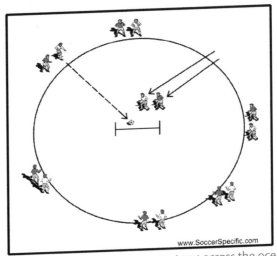

Diagram 87: Peter Duckworth's scoring game came to us across the ocean from the youth division of the Premier League.

Combination play can be incorporated. Touch restriction can be imposed to facilitate speed of play. The game has many wrinkles to it, but clearly involves many skills including technique, vision, shooting, change in point of attack and much more. One unique option is to have a single keeper defending both sides of the goal.

12) Gate Keeper: Can be any dimensions the coach chooses. Here the area is 30 yards wide and 18 yards deep with the goal centered on the gate. Gate should be about 3 yards wide.

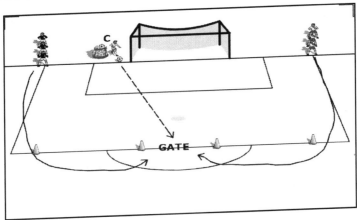

Diagram 88

One player from each team sprints from the goal line around the corner cone and must run through the gate. When players go around the corner the coach serves a slow ground ball about 15 yards out. Whoever gets there first attacks the goal, the other defends. Generally played with a keeper. As soon as the previous pair goes through the gate the next 2 players go avoiding the necessity of the needless calling out by the coach, "Next". This keeps it moving and makes players attend to the activity, allowing the coach to give pointers instead of wasting his energy on keeping the activity moving. Players also keep team scores. Besides the team winner at the end, ask which individual scored the most goals. This is predominantly a youth shooting activity, although on occasions done through age 15.

13) Bill Buren's Cone Ball Game: This game merely has an area about 30 x 40 yards with 4 yard wide cone goals with a ball on the top of the large style cones. Any cones will do, but the large cones with the hole on top make it a bit easier. Players simply play a shortsided game anywhere from 3v3 to 6v6. No keeper nor can anyone stay in the goal area, which has dimensions of 6 yards square. Whenever a shooter knocks a ball off the of a cone he must replace it with his ball wherever it went, but the game continues immediately with the ball that was knocked off the cone in quick counter attack fashion by the opposing team. The numbers down allows the offense to have an open player that fits this game perfectly as it really is a game for perfecting passing/receiving and shooting. It also involves very purposeful dribbling and 1v1 possibilities. Surprisingly this is a good game for all ages.

14) Learning Proper Weak Side Runs: This is a line drill that should be done for a very limited time, but due to drifting outside middies to the center of the field, frequently too early thus choking the strikers and reducing chances it is meant to have them understand the proper run from a wing position. Best to have two groups working on two different goals, but with 10 or less one group is fine.

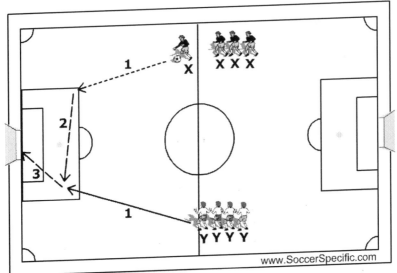

Diagram 89: X speed dribbles to the corner of the 18 and then serves a cross to Y who shoots. Both X and Y follow the shot to goal. X's and Y's change lines on each round.

Often a coach or field player is put in goal that simply knocks the ball down for a follow up shot. A coach or field player is used so as not to give the keeper a bad habit. After 5 minutes reverse the direction of service. Move to a scrimmage requiring service to the weak side and demanding the run that was rehearsed in this exercise. To be effective the scrimmage likely needs 7 v 7 with 2 neutrals. Weak side one touch shots count 5 points instead of one point. It just seems so counter productive to bring the ball all the way down the field and have good service and the ball drifts past everyone without anyone even having any chance at all to shoot the ball. That combined with the fact that too many players going right in front of the goal allows the defense to be compact with little fear of anyone scoring. Understandably expecting players to assume a team position, instead of a personal position or run is requiring a reasonably high degree of tactical understanding. But sometimes something very simple with a brief explanation just might get the concept across.

142

Phase Play

Phase play has players assigned a specific area with a given assignment.

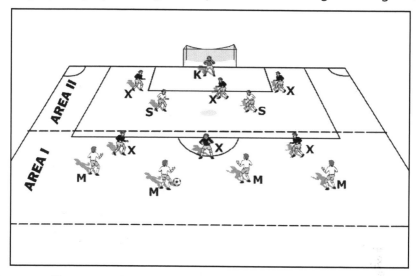

Diagram 90: There are probably hundreds of different situations that the coach may use to teach through phase play. One example is given here for understanding the concept. The 6 X players are defenders, 3 in each area. The M's are midfielders on the same team as their two strikers (S). Thus 6v6: Each group is confined to their own area of the field. Use the full width of the field and a bit less than half of a field, thus each area is 20 to 25 yards deep.

Here there is an attempt to provide many chances for middies to find the strikers, sometimes referred to as linking. Clearly the strikers will have to check to and away from the ball to get open. Also crisscrossing could be encouraged or even required. Midfielders have 4v3, allowing them possession while the strikers attempt to get free. While this environment has a very worthwhile purpose, it is strongly recommended that after a brief time one or two midfielders be allowed to move into Area II to join in the attacking of the goal. This is in keeping with the emphasis throughout this text on mobility. Of course any variation would be acceptable such as two midfielders joining the attack and allowing one of the defenders from Area I to also go into Area II. Phase play is only limited to the coach's imagination. However, no matter what phase play was employed, spend a good deal of time with the unrestricted play because in the end that is what the team must do in actual matches.

THE FOLLOWING EXERCISES ARE FOR SMALL GROUPS WITH ONE COACH WITH THE BULK OF THE TEAM AND ANOTHER ENGAGED IN THE FOLLOWING FUNCTIONAL SHOOTING ACTIVITIES. Some of these could be special session. There is great power in these small group and individualized activities. Either as small group special sessions or as a separate session the focus and quality of retention in either format is extremely powerful.

The first is as simple as having the keeper in goal and strikers simulating breakaway situations by attacking the goal by dribbling from 50 yards out with a defender who starts about 6 yards behind the striker. Be certain that until the striker gets close to the keeper he is dribbling at full speed. This sort of dribbling is usually referred to as driving. It is sad when the coach displays frustration (often anger) when players miss easy breakaway opportunities, and yet they have never been trained for it. In those cases who is really at fault?

Serving strikers and having them turn and shoot is a necessary part of technical shooting instruction. I have seen Rudi Voller, the great German striker, do this for 45 minutes. The receiving and turning using both the inside and outside of the foot, Cruyff (ball moved behind the standing leg), the dummy move and whatever other favorites the striker has displayed should all be done with abundant repetition.

Move to working with twin strikers on shooting, involving service to them from many different angles and distances. Key items to do are takeovers with a spinout return pass in east/west direction, wall passes with each other or the attacking midfielder and east/west overlaps. Once a defender or even two is added the object becomes scoring a goal using any manner of getting it done!

Diagonal chips to each other are often a very effective way to get your teammate open for a good shot. Certainly one would hope that the offensive midfielder is proficient and uses this tactic when the game situation demands it. When incorporating the offensive midfielder, proper layoffs positioning is in order. Proper means that the midfielder does not stand straight in line with strikers, but instead creates an angle for reception. The midfielder must keep a distance great enough to have space to move to the ball and time for the shot. The layoff must be on the ground and paced so the shot can be taken with a single touch.

Throughout the instruction encourage bent runs. In the shortsided and full scrimmages, emphasize blind side runs; this is nearly impossible to clarify when only working with strikers. Encourage use of the weak foot for close shots when it is the correct thing to do.

Certain inside overlaps can be taught by merely serving a ball to the outside for the one striker to cross to the other, and/or another attacking player.

Is it remotely realistic to do all of this in a single session? Maybe not even a short season. Hopefully there might be enough time, especially with two or more coaches that at least 20 minutes a week could be devoted to strikers movements and tactics. This is another reason why the one man show , the coach not getting assistants leaves a program deficient.

The composure of finishing is unrealistic unless we spend serious training of shooting and finishing. In addition players total motivation is raised by the shooting activities enumerated in this chapter. That alone is reason enough to be certain to allocate adequate time to these activities.

B) SHOTS ON GOAL, A NOVEL IDEA
Good things can happen when the shot is on goal, while shots not on goal are free goal kicks to the opponents.
1) You can score a goal
2) Keeper can mishandle and you or a teammate can finish it for a goal
3) A teammate can redirect the ball to an open area of the goal
4) Opponents can have a hand ball resulting in a penalty kick
5) A poor clearance can give your team another shot for a goal
6) Keeper or field player puts it over the endline resulting in a corner kick
7) Opponents hit ball resulting in an own goal
8) You have not yielded a goal kick to your opponent
9) Opponents get ball out of penalty area, but your team regains control and have a quick counter attack
10) You are reinforcing your habit of getting shots on goal, instead of reinforcing a bad habit

Other nebulous occurrences such as a better chance the official will call a foul also come into play, if the official thinks the contact denied a goal. Any defensive or keeper lapse in focus or error can cause a goal. Certainly wet ground and unusual bounces are a definite reality.

The bottom line is that serious training to keep shots low and on frame is likely to pay huge dividends. It really isn't that hard to keep shots down if properly trained for. Even volleys can be kept down and volley shots often have great pace so they always represent difficulty to the keeper.

One old sage said, "I have never seen a shot go under the goal line". While there may be a bit of sarcasm there, or wit, however you choose to view it, no one can dispute the fact. Any and all attempts to have your team get shots on goal will pay dividends.
It is no exaggeration to say that many games are decided by poor shots, which if on goal may have been goals resulting in a victory.

C) CAUSES OF POOR SHOOTING

There are numerous reasons for poor shooting in games, but the most prominent reasons may be the lack of practice, incessant hitting of dead balls and the desire in early ages to lift the ball.

Lack of adequate practice includes lack of proper training. Not only is there not enough time spent on shooting and then not progressing to more finishing types of experiences, but the technical aspects of shooting a moving prepared ball are often lacking. Knee over the ball might be the most important of the neglected details of the power instep kick. There are many other pointers, but the approach angle is often the reason for this. If the knee is lifted only a slight angle of approach is required. But without the knee lift players having stubbed their foot into the ground begin to approach the ball at severe angles, which often causes a circular motion as opposed to power forward follow through. This is a difficult habit to alter if a youngster has been doing this for a number of years. There are many other technical details that can be noted, but that is left to more complete sources that strictly focus on very beginning players.

Shooting a prepared ball requires a proper angle and distance that must be practiced. Hitting a moving ball means the non-kicking foot be placed on the side and in front of the ball so that by the time the kicking foot reaches the ball it is not way out in front, which of course causes the ball to rise, often over the goal. Weil Coerver, the famous Dutch youth coach, maintained that shooting for the upper ninety was only to begin at age sixteen and mostly for professionals. All in all this means adequate technical shooting and tactical finishing requires much repetition, but also requires the scrutiny of an observing coach who encourages and demands numerous quality repetitions in training activities. The dead ball problem is partially a result of the all the youngsters thinking they are Ronaldo or one of the other great dead ball finishers. This is not a bad thing, except they have not gone through the amount of training of such professionals. Before practice and games we can observe all of the players shooting dead balls and yet only one or two will do it in the game. But the real problem is they CANNOT DRIVE A BALL and shoot worm burners like the accomplished professional. Driving the ball with power and accuracy is greatly neglected while much time is spent on bending balls. Furthermore, many can only hit a banana ball, spinning counter clockwise for a right footed kick, losing a great deal of power. Thus thousands of players bend the ball not intentionally, but do so because they cannot drive a ball. Striking the center of the ball horizontally and vertically is not that difficult if one is taught to do so, and of course practices the skill. It demands seeing the ball when it is struck, and maybe this simple idea is among the most common problems.

Regarding the lifting of the ball when it is not the most appropriate technique is also common. Putting top spin on the ball especially with the push pass is very easy and with the advent of so many low ball goals being scored professionally nowadays, more attention must be given to this area of ball striking. Messi could be used for dozens of skills that he performs well, but keeping the ball down for shots is certainly one of his more prominent techniques.

While there are many reasons why more goals are not scored, it is not because of the rules as so often sighted, but it does have much to do with the lack of quality technical, tactical, fitness and mental training, particularly at early ages. This chapter touches on many of those details. Only visualization of finishing is not covered in detail because that is in the domain of sports psychology that better covers the details of focus, visualization and similar psychological aspects of finishing. One source that is concise is "Sports Psychology Basics" by this author.

D) TRAINING TWIN STRIKERS

This supplement was added due to the fact that the 4-4-2 is very common and yet seldom do you see any significant coordination between the two strikers. Usually both appear to playing completely on their own as though there were not another striking partner. While a minor portion can be attributed to the creative or improvisational nature of strikers, more likely it is a lack of training. Thus the basic concepts of successful twin strikers are enumerated here. While one may have some difficulty in thoroughly training all that follows, certainly everyone can train those items that they think are most valuable to their particular tactics and the personal attributes of their strikers.

Simply have the twin strikers and their substitutes do the following: In time add the schemer or any offensive middies. Once the strikers have a modicum of performance of the items indicated it is time to have a keeper in goal and some defense.

Start by clarifying the **tandem concept**: Until strikers reach the line of the offside trap on offense tandem is preferred. Tandem strikers should not be in line with one another and/or with the ball and be at a distance that will facilitate connecting between each other. For mature players 15-25 yards apart, naturally varying considerably depending upon ball location, teammates and opponents. On defense generally twin strikers are square and steering play to the flanks, though there are other options.

Quality **checking** is critical. Start with the technical aspects of jab step and significant distance of the check. Also demand an angle going away and a different angle while checking to the teammate with the ball. A very important detail is to have twin strikers be cognizant of each others checking so the they check to different creases so as to enlarge the chances for successful reception. If both check in the same line with the ball the chances of receiving are much less as the defense's job is greatly reduced.

Crisscrossing is a major movement, which causes problems to defenders as to whether they will track their mark or switch marks. Tracking their marks puts the defense out of shape and passing on a mark invariably causes the striker to have a bit more space. In some cases if one defender switches and the other does not, the striker is actually completely free. Tactically the main fault with crisscrossing is the tendency of players to go too far forward and thus go offsides. Tight crisscrossing in a nearly square east/west fashion will also pick off a defender from close marking.

Running the line will keep striker onsides because they can clearly see the line of defense. The big advantage comes when the trap is moving forward and the striker is already moving and merely cuts behind the defense to receive in an onsides movement. By time the defender stops and turns the striker can possible be safely on their way to goal. Running the line is also very useful by being first to contact the ball on penalty kicks and is also helpful on direct and indirect kicks.

Almost without saying the **combinations** of wall passes, mini east/west overlap and spinout takeovers must be rehearsed. These are so valuable that you should have the whole team do them. In any case the twin strikers need to become comfortable with these movements especially in and around the penalty area, thus this training is done in relation to goal.

The **heel pass** can really disrupt a defense. This movement really becomes easy to perform once it is trained for. This is extremely useful movement for the central middies. Actually it is very useful for all middies since the movement can be used productively for an outside midfielder with an inside midfielder. Use of the sole roll is acceptable for short distances, but the actual use of the heel allows for greater distances. Some would consider the crossover of the legs heel pass a bit of a hot dog move, but is absolutely is not. The crossover heel pass allows accuracy over significant distances. It certainly is worth exploring with your players to see if they see value in it.

The **dummy play** becomes truly the dummy play when a player lets a ball go by them and they are not certain that there is an open teammate behind them. My advice to players is to be certain that whenever they let the ball run for a teammate, that they have checked to ascertain that someone was there to receive it. Otherwise take control of the ball yourself! By the same token letting the ball run for oneself also demands that no defender is there to intercept.

Chipping through balls should be coached so that even when the keeper is some distance away the chip is not in line with the keeper. Actually all chips have much greater success when they are chipped diagonally. This often increases the visibility of the receiver and takes the keeper out of the equation. While this is not an easy skill, or at least even at the professional level we see balls that are not chipped even though it was required, maybe we can train younger players and eliminate this problem. Occasionally one finds a player who is capable of quality chips and even uses this skill in game situations. Such a player may even bend the chipped service. This is rare, but once in awhile is spotted in players as young as 15. This is a great time to point out to other players how effective this skill can be. This is "Catching them being good" at its best!

Layoffs have become even more prominent in recent years due to packed in defenses. This is especially valuable when the players behind the strikers are able ball handlers. Once the striker has determined that the layoff is going to result in a shot it is best to train them to go to goal seeking rebounds. Layoffs provide the best chance for clear shot at goal if they are sent at an angle. Naturally the defense is already in line with the ball, otherwise the striker would have shot the ball himself.

Open hips, which are so often heard of are a result of being out off line with the ball and the goal. This simple concept seems to be seldom clarified to the strikers. The triangular shape of receiving player, goal and ball increases vision so the player can see the ball, goal, teammates and defense. That should certainly facilitate the player taking one of the better options available.

Flicks to teammates is also a valuable skill. This can be trained for by having the whole team with one ball for every four players simply dribbling, passing/receiving and flicking balls to teammates. The flicker needs to call out the name of the player she is flicking the ball to.

Distance (spacing) is important. The main thing is that there are numerous players working very hard to be open for support and for shots when we get to the final third.

This next activity was inspired by Laura Kerrigan: Improving twin strikers is a wonderful session for improving technical, tactical, fitness and mental outlook in an economical environment.

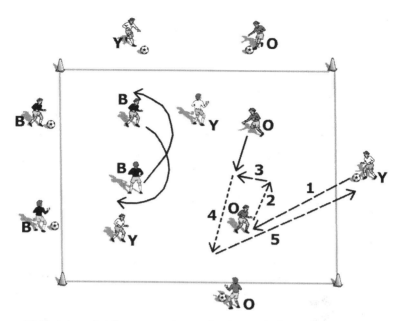

Diagram 91: Training of strikers to work together instead of in isolation. For mature players the grid should approximate 40 x 40 yards. Outside players should be 3 or 4 yards away from the grid to reinforce the movement to the ball and make space to get open after passing the ball.

Simply put the whole team in pairs using several colors of pinnies; one pair inside of orange, one outside and the same for yellow, red and blue. All players on the outside have a ball. Interior players are given a desired movement such as crisscrossing. The pair visually, hand signals and/or verbally communicate to a given player on the outside, do the crisscross, receive the ball and exchange it between them and return the ball to the outside player who gave them the ball. All pairs are working simultaneously fostering a great deal of communication and visual development. After each desired skill the inside pairs exchange with the outside pairs. Maintaining a 15 to 25 yard distance between the two strikers is critical. That way they are close enough to use each other and far enough apart that one defender cannot cover both of them. This is done with the whole team because it is valuable to all. Central middies, a central midfielder and an outside midfielder, centerbacks, a centerback with an outside back, and the many vertical working relationships all need this working together development. This fosters quality movement of the ball among players using many technical/tactical skills.

Other possible desired movements:

- Double pass between members of the pair and return ball to outside player who gave them the ball
- Checking: Demand angle away and angle to, while partners never end up in the same place
- Wall pass between the pair: Demand eye contact and acceleration to receive; also a quality one touch pass
- Takeover or takeover with spin-out return: demand acceleration upon the takeover
- Overlap: Demand a hard run, ball pushed well to one side (away from run) and lead the receiver
- Split as if a midfielder were coming through, and strikers want to create space for the midfielder, get open to create options for the midfielder and at the same time stay on-sides - best done going to goal
- Collect and speed dribble; pass to partner who does the same and return to deliverer
- Heel pass; receiver, dribble past teammate, then heel pass the ball
- Dummy pass to teammate; be certain teammate is there before performing a dummy pass
- ADVANCED - Short high chip to teammate
- ADVANCED - Flick from one teammate to the other; start with hand service
- ADVANCED - Head the ball to the partner's feet

By exchanging inside and outside players after each skill we can demand quality as players are in a one active to a one rest-recovery cycle. This is excellent interval fitness with the ball. It might be a good idea to have the schemer deliver the pass while strikers go to goal while the rest of the team does their functional skills. Doing three or four of the many options listed is about right for a single training session. Works equally well for 3 strikers, obviously using groups of three.

None of this precludes options such as an inside/out overlap for the striker to become a server and other creative movements. One would assume that nearly every team has some awareness of filling the slots. An awareness of the near post, far post and pull back areas clarified earlier should be trained for. Lead up activities and game options were clarified in detail earlier in the text. One touch shots must also be trained for as every coach has seen loss of possession and no shot taken because a player took extra touches. Flicks might not be the highest priority, but some teams may want to use this option.

While this is an excellent way to get many repetitions of several valuable options, the grid activity is no substitute for repeating these tactics in going to goal, and eventually going to goal with a keeper and defense in a game situation.

10

Possession

Teams at all levels almost always have a portion of the training session devoted to possession. Possession allows a team to get forward with some degree of control. Without possession teams are merely kicking the ball into the final third, having little chance of success due to the fact that there are frequently four defenders besides a keeper, against normally one, two or three strikers. Furthermore the ball is going toward the defenders and they usually have good size and are chosen for the position because they are skillful and strong in the air. Often, the most the offense can hope for is to head the ball back toward one of their teammates. All in all, without a degree of possession, long balls launched into the opponent's deep territory are wishful balls. This is not to say that this should never be done, especially if the defense was lax in getting back, in which case we might get an opportunity to get behind the defense. Again, this is rarely successful with modern day keepers who can defend many yards away from their goal.

Possession also provides abundant opportunities for passing/receiving, combination play and is extremely game related so that technical/tactical development transfers to the actual game.

Without some degree of possession, it is difficult for a team with the lead, to maintain the lead. Giving the opponents possession provides many opportunities to create scoring chances. This is not in a team's favor, especially when there is a great deal of time left in the game.

Quick counter attacks have always been a method of scoring, but they are becoming increasingly more important with the modern day zone organizations that are fortified by timely marking near the penalty area. If you do not have possession in the attacking part of the field, there is little chance to re-win the ball close to the goal you are trying to attack. It is not frequent that a team that is attacking and in their attacking part of the field will return the ball back to their defending third. Even when they do, this is done when there is plenty of time and space, so that gaining possession from a quick counter attack in that situation is extremely unlikely. This leaves the best opportunities for quick counter attack when one has had possession in the opponent's final third, or at least in their half, and a team regains possession after having lost it briefly.

All of the above leads to modern day football in which high pressure is played. The era of allowing teams enormous easy possession is essentially gone. Allowing such possession permitted too many quality services into ones defending area, and thus the stringing of ten and twenty free passes that was common until about 1986 has virtually disappeared. Therefore we must train for possession.

Obviously there is no need to mention that when the score is 5-0 in the first half of a game we might want to keep possession solely for the purpose of good sportsmanship. Since this occurs in less than 1% of high level games or situations where there is parity it requires no further elaboration.

This leaves us with possession as important, but not in isolation to a given purpose. First and foremost possession should have an eye on controlled penetration, especially if the service has a chance of ending up in a goal. Aside from this there are many types of possession for many different purposes. We might want possession on the flank because we are either very good there and score from crosses or the opponent is weak on the perimeter. This is only a couple of reasons, however there are dozens of other reasons for the same tactic. We might have a great target player that we want to play off of; still we want to get him/her the ball with some decent percentage of completion. In short, there are many types of possession for many different purposes.

Possibly the beginning level is having two teams in the same area, each with their own ball simply passing to one another. The coach should constantly encourage spreading out to use the entire space. The token defense here is that the other group is in the same area causing a bit of visual confusion and the necessity to not pass a ball to a teammate when there is an intervening player. An option in this activity is to require sequence passing which would cause the necessity of more dribbling since it would be a bit more difficult to find an open teammate.

Demanding combinations in possession activities is also extremely useful and common with all teams that have already been instructed in the fundamentals of combination play. Having two groups doing the desired behavior of the session in the same area is an important basic coaching pedagogy. It should be used often to avoid wasting time. If players cannot perform the tactic with token or no defense, what is the purpose of trying to do it with defensive pressure? Thus, this is a useful pedagogy to use often for the fundamental stage of training sessions.

A group of the whole with a ball for about every 3-5 players could lead into the possession activity. About 4 balls for 16 players is about right, depending on the coach's training goal. This is a common lead up to hundreds of different sessions. This is not a ball for a particular group of four, but 4 balls for the whole group with everyone working with everyone. Fringe benefits are team building, communication, visual skill development, movement, collection and dozens of basic skills.

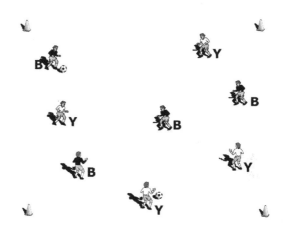

Diagram #92: The coach keeps demanding use of all the space and combinations.

At the second stage one could have a dividing line in the grid and place two members of each team on opposite sides of the dividing line. In this case of 4v0 for the two teams, there is a demand that every pass must go to the opposite side of the grid.

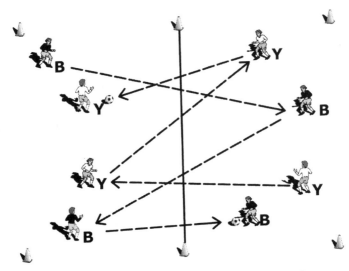

Diagram #93: Two and one touch will aide anticipation and visual development.

Besides encouraging spreading out a long pass is required (demanded) and long range vision is encouraged. Clearly players are gaining confidence in maintaining vision in preparation for when there is a real pressuring defender. This technique can be used for difficult topics even at the higher levels. It allows success of whatever is being taught and saves time. Also, it avoids failure of what is being taught, which can instill a bad habit and make learning more difficult for no good reason.
Let's begin with some simple formats that do have a true opponent but allow possession even with teams that are not very accomplished. In this case we might have any number from nine to eighteen or more players. We simply create 3 teams. In this example we have 5v5 + 5N, with all 3 teams somewhat balanced. Five blue are opposed by five yellow with five red players outside the grid.

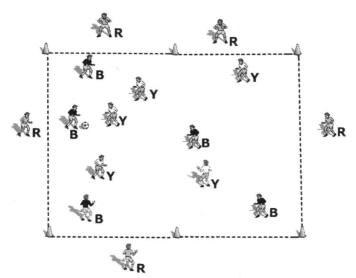

Diagram #94: The neutrals outside the grid greatly enhance success.

Note that the neutral players are away from the grid. This is virtually always done because we want players in any exercise to move to the ball when it is passed to them. This will become even more critical as we get to the advanced exercises in which the receiving player dribbles into the grid and another player takes his place on the outside. This mobility is much more like the real game, but players must be ready for such movements.

The size of the area would vary according to the skill level AND THE PURPOSE OF THE COACH. Scoring is by completing six passes or whatever. It could be the most completed passes in a given amount of time. Often the only passes counted are the ones that are within the grid (not the ones to neutrals outside the grid), although if the coach were trying to emphasize 'play what you see', she might count all passes. Frequently no double-double passes with a given inside player and an outside player are permitted: that would be from inside player B to outside player R, back to B and then back to R. Again one must decide how does this possession relate to today's topic? From B to R to B more than likely would be permitted. For third-man-on development, require B passing to R, then R must pass to a different B player with one touch. Only mature, accomplished teams would likely engage in this level of activity. This would require less balls per the number of players. For the 5v5+5 neutrals, 2 balls would likely be the maximum. Players on the outside would

159

generally be restricted to two touches, but it could be one or even three. Personally every time a ball stops with undefended players I call for a turnover. A still ball allows teammates to be marked and creases to be closed. This is generally not constructive for game success.

Possession, which incorporates service with an angle, is shown here. Again very different numbers of players could use this exercise; here it is shown with 4 v 4 inside with each team having 2 outside players.

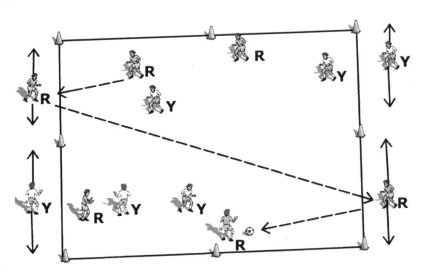

Diagram #95: This is very effective for developing long ball penetration service. Note that players outside the grid are expected to move laterally.

Here the players are even further away from the grid because after three passes in the grid the ball is served to a teammate outside the grid, who receives and with the second touch SERVES THE BALL to a teammate on the opposite side of the grid. The players cannot cross the central cone of the grid. This of course is providing experience for long ball service penetration in the actual game. The size of the grid largely depends upon the length of service that is realistic for the players involved.

Option: This could be done with the receiver/server going into the grid to be part of the possession activity. Of course, then players in the grid will fill their spots, or it could simply be played with outside players remaining there permanently. In which case after every 3 or 4 minutes the coach switches the outside neutrals. At higher levels where we are attempting to develop leadership and having players take more responsibility for coaching each other this can be done by the captain or simply as the whole team learning to make these moves on their own. Pia Sundhage, our former National Team women's coach, is huge on encouraging players to coach each other. Our local high school coach of boys, two time state champions, encourages an enormous amount of latitude to his players---naturally this is a very talented group that is ready to take a great deal of responsibility for everything they do.

Another possession activity that focuses on delivery to a target player has a player on each end of the grid.

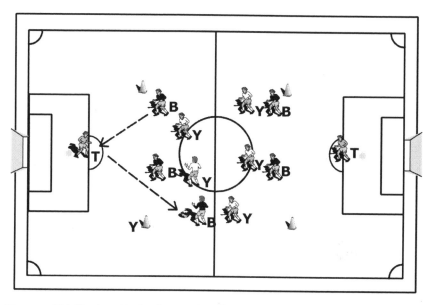

Diagram #96: Depicted is the first option (Stage D in which the target player lays the ball off to a teammate in the grid. Here each team is playing in a specific direction.

If necessary use a neutral in the grid in order for there to be a good chance to completing 3 passes regularly. In this exercise after the 3 passes, as quickly as possible, a team serves a long ball to their target player who can in Stage I return it to the grid, but later on can shoot. Option: The service can be required to come from a layoff in the grid. Option: A player must leave the grid to support the target player and the two of them go against a defender and keeper. Usually the grid is about 40 wide x 30 long with the target player about 15 yards from the grid and 20 yards from the goal. Therefore the goals are about 100 yards apart. Of course there are many options to this basic format, which the coach will tweak to his specific purpose(s). For instance, if the coach wanted to further develop the playing between his two strikers he could put another striker out of the grid. If he still wanted one to act as a target player he would place the second striker closer to the grid and well behind the target player to receive layoffs and then possibly they would attempt to score against a keeper and one or two defenders. This is a great format that has limitless options! It is best when the format of going to goal is being used that the coach have many balls just outside the grid and she serves another ball into the possession activity when service out of the grid is made. This keeps up the fun, ball touches and fitness of the activity.

An excellent format that incorporates an enormous amount of game related playing is when we have two grids side by side. Numbers can vary considerably, but here it is shown 4 v 4 on each side.

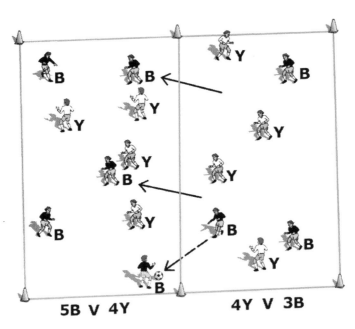

5B V 4Y   **4Y V 3B**

Diagram #97: Twin grid movement. This activity can be adjusted to various numbers of players with a maximum of eight.

After three successful passes by the B team in the right grid, a free pass is made to the left grid and one B moves from the right to the left grid, making a 5B v 4Y. However, if Y had intercepted the ball and sent it to the left side grid, one Y would have moved to the left side, creating 5Y v 4B.

It really sounds complicated, but all the players need to know is that it is always 5 offensive players against 4 defenders and that players have to move from one side to the other to always create the 5 v 4. Obviously a coach would not choose this format unless he planned on using it regularly because the first time it is presented requires a few minutes before players even get any rhythm (success). This clearly is only for rather accomplished teams from about age thirteen and above.

Having one neutral, especially if you had an odd number at practice could also facilitate the possession. One of the many benefits of this exercise is an enormous amount of visual development, mobility and need for serious hard work on defense. The grids could be as large as 20 x 20 yards with the total therefore being 20 x 40. However adjust to your purpose, player's ability and the numbers you are using. It would seem reasonable that if the exercise started with 3 v 3 that the space would be reduced.

Options: Allow players to dribble across the dividing line between the grids, restricting touches, demanding layoffs for service, involving a overlap or wall pass in changing grids, changing the number of required passes before changing from one side to the other. For developing quick transition, quick counter attack and speed of play allow the ball to go from one side to the other with a single pass. At very advanced levels one could require an air ball that is headed to a teammate when the ball crosses the center grid line!

Another possibility is gate goals in all four corners of the grid. Each cone goal is two yards wide and has a player next to it. The coach merely points to the player in the corner near the gate goal and if the player is in the goal and is pointed at, he **gets out** of the goal. When pointed at if he was not in the gate goal he **goes in** the goal.

The coach can have zero, one, two, three or even all four goals open. Clearly with all closed it is a possession activity, with one open there certainly is a high demand on vision, especially if the coach is constantly changing the environment. The coach can keep the activity competitive (have score constantly be close) to insure motivation. This game is often played to a score of 5 goals. The grid can be any size; with 5 v 5 one would think a grid in the neighborhood of 20 x 25 yards might be appropriate. If players begin to act like goalkeepers simply demand man marking or provide a no defending area near each gate goal. Options: Dribble through gate or goals can be scored by passing the ball through the gate AND received by a teammate.

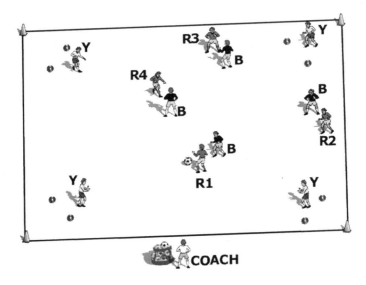

Diagram 98: 4v4 with the 4 Y's tending the goals. The R's appear to be attacking the top right side goal. B's are marking tightly. If R4 could get free, she could attack the top left side goal. Clearly these situations demand hard work on the part of the defense!

Color games of possession can also be fun and constructive in order to get a team to value the ball and not kick the ball to nowhere or play overly vertical. If we have each of three players in four different colors we can have the team that lost possession be defending against the other 3 colors. Or we could designate a taboo color for each team; that is, a color they cannot pass to. So with the rainbow team defending, yellow, blue and red are in possession. But, yellow is not allowed to pass to blue; so blue is yellow's taboo color.

- Yellow taboo to blue
- Blue taboo to red
- Red taboo to green
- Green taboo to yellow

164

This becomes a very visually demanding exercise and probably forces a fair amount of dribbling, shielding, thinking and support from the appropriate possible receivers. You might end this activity with two equal teams Y+B vs R+G.

Another possession activity that discourages too much short passing at the expense of penetration and quality service is something I developed years ago. It's called **tic-tac-toe** because the grid is exactly that!

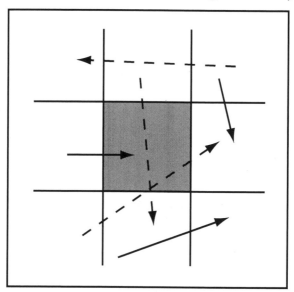

Diagram #99: All dotted broken line passes are legal; all bold solid line passes are illegal, meaning they are turnovers.

We have two teams. No one can be in the central shaded area. Every pass must go through anyone of the 9 areas before it can be received by a teammate. Any pass to an adjoining area or in the central shaded area is a turnover. Three completed passes is a point, play to a score of 5. Generally one or even two neutrals are required in order for teams to develop any degree of success. Option: One pass can be made to an adjoining area, but then the next pass must skip an adjoining area. Again vision, thinking, quality ball control, long ball service accuracy is demanded. **Creating space and then checking to the ball is an absolute requirement for success in this activity.**

I think the point that possession has an inexhaustible number of options is clear. The point is that it is a critical skill and almost every session has a possession activity in it. There are hundreds of possible activities with dozens of wrinkles for every kind of possession activity. For maximum benefit the coach must tie the possession activity to his training goals for that day. As seen with the above examples with a little careful planning that is always possible. The carryover, transfer of learning to the actual game is enormous because possession activities simulate the game except there generally isn't any shooting. They are competitive, require thinking, and involve all skills. If one chooses to say it does not involve shooting, this is only partially true since all shooting is merely an accurate pass or service. This is not to denigrate shooting activities. Personally we do scrimmaging AND shooting activities in nearly every single practice that we have.

Some of the simple formats of possession are more difficult because they may involve only two teams, equal numbers on each team and movement. An example is 4v2 in a tight grid of 10 x 10 yards and when defenders win the ball they instantly deliver a pass to their teammates on the other side. This recreates 4Y vs 2B defenders on the right side. This is a very rigorous exercise, but very useful. Be certain all take a turn at defending. See diagram.

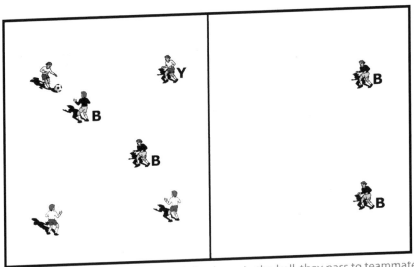

Diagram #100: As soon as blue (B) defenders win the ball, they pass to teammates on the right and join them in possession. Any two yellow (Y) players go to defend.

Frequently the whole topic of possession is handled in a totally differ-ent manner. Channels on the outside of the field that have no defense permitted in the channel in a scrimmage situation can facilitate crosses, overlaps, even both at the same time, or whatever the coach desires.

The cone/vest game is merely played with two teams anywhere from 2v2 to 7v7 with the most appropriate about 4v4 with four players each having a cone and vest in their hands. One team is the cone team the other the vest team. Whenever the cone team passes and uses a player with a cone, the cone is dropped. Whenever the vest team passes to a player with the vest, the vest is dropped. Which ever team manages to use all the cone/vest holder first wins. In other words when all cones/vest holders have no cones in their hand, that team wins. The total area might be about 30 yards by 30 yards with cone/vest holders spaced throughout the perimeter of the whole area. Option: Every time the cone people use a cone/vest player that person drops the cone and picks up the vest. In this case a team must be the last to use all four cone/vest players consecutively in order to win.

Another common possession activity is 4+K vs 0 to start. Here players simply pass the ball around the back and then the coach adds one or more attackers who are defending. This could build up to anything but frequently one would move to adding a defensive midfielder and hav-ing four attacking defenders. This creates K+5 vs 4 attacking defenders. This obviously is trying to build possession for defenders, especially in team tactics for teams such as Barcelona that like to build attacks very safely.

Maybe the most common possession exercise is six attackers against four defenders and a keeper. Here we are trying to give the attackers a better chance to succeed and possibly build certain patterns that suits our personnel and style of play. Consider 7 vs 5 + K. While this is a bit more game related it is an excellent exercise that in many cases allows the whole team to play. In a manner of speaking, this is not strictly a possession activity.

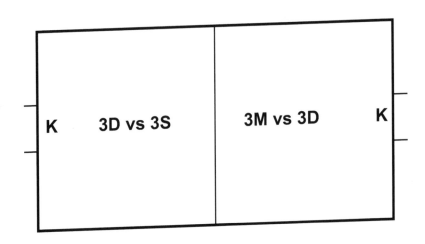

Diagram #101: Typical phase play exercise.
Phase play demands that everyone stays in their own half. Here one might be trying to have middies connect to strikers. Again, hundreds of possibilities according to the coach's purpose exist. Of course, one could move to a player joining his teammates on the other grid.

Certainly many forms of phase play foster possession, though this format is not elaborated upon a great deal since mobility is an emphasis throughout the text. Clearly the author believes that mobility as a result of combination play is attractive/effective football. Possession activities that allow players to get their hips facing many teammates and using the creases for possession seem very productive. In general if you want to develop defense through a possession activity simply provide a large grid which forces a high work rate, communication and all aspects of defense to be difficult. That simply relates to the fact that the team in possession wants to spread out a great deal making defending difficult. Defense wants compactness in order to pressure and/or double team the ball. A word of caution in regard to the amount of space used in possession activities. Don't become a tight space 'freak', because there are times when large spaces aid the purpose of our activity to a greater extent. Try to use the amount of space that relates to the purpose of the activity.

Because possession is a competitive activity, generally players put in a good effort that usually makes it a very worthwhile part of your practice. The literature which abounds with far too many patterns is often merely a disrespect of players, involves imitating professional teams that your personnel may have little in common with, and most of all involves too much standing and not enough ball contact in a game related environment. If players become competent in combination play, are encouraged to mobility with players filling in to maintain shape they will be doing far more of what the game demands at the moment, and this is generally far superior to drilled patterns. Do not misunderstand, there is a place for pattern play, but there is a much greater need for versatile combination play!

Certain possession is aided by avoiding long vertical balls, and by using diagonal balls that allow teammates to face each other by getting their hips to face teammates. One simple idea is inside/out, outside/ in focus. By adding abundant combination play to this we have essentially a whole tactical (philosophical) system of play. This concept has been elucidated through out the entire text.

Hopefully the activities on changing the point of attack, which have been clarified in this text, will help possession for your team.

Ultimately the level of football is determined by the speed of play. Teams that can control the ball, move quickly, change the point of attack, play third man-on rapidly will invariably experience success. All such attributes require quality one touch passing. However the demand in a possession activity of all passes being one touch can cause mindless behavior and numerous turnovers that is in direct conflict with possession. One excellent solution to the problem is to have teams play competitively with unrestricted play, but the first team to complete 10 one touch passes winds. Play several rounds. This speeds play without causing mindless passes of the ball.

Less accomplished teams can be rather successful by adding a neutral player or two. They can often be the central midfield player(s) who are often used to maintaining possession and providing quality service. One area that is sometimes neglected that causes poor possession is not the player with the ball, but poor support by teammates. One must attempt to firm up support so the player with ball does in fact have available receivers when only touching the ball once. Conceivably more possession is lost due to poor support as opposed to poor one touch passing.

In any case possession and speed of play must compliment one another, be developed simultaneously to have any real meaning to high level performance. This format of possession which allows two touch and even more in a competitive team game does that. It is such a pivotal possession activity because it fosters excellent decision making at the same time developing speed of play.

Naturally the amount of space will relate to the number of players and their ability, but on the first few occasions of this possession be generous with the amount of space until players become somewhat competent with the form of possession you are trying to accomplish. Another way to allow early success is to have available neutrals outside the grid, however one touch passes to neutrals do not count for the scoring of one touch passes.

So the coach can coach, do not keep score, demand players keep score by calling out the point awarded for the one touch passes. This method should be ingrained into players for all such scoring so as to free the coach up for coaching the activity as opposed to being score keeper! In coaching the activity be certain to indicate to players proper support as well as the appropriate passing technique that should be used for the given situation. Quality layoffs to facilitate some passes of longer distances to break pressure should also be encouraged.

Many very accomplished coaches incorporate a possession activity in nearly every single training session they conduct. Less experienced coaches who do possession in nearly every training session are thus in good company. Competitive games that simulate the actual game are seldom the wrong decision.

TACKLING/SHIELDING

Tackling can be practiced by placing three or four grids one on top of another that are about 5 yards square and players dribble through each grid and the defender in each grid tackles the ball and then lets the dribbler proceed to a shot on goal.

Shielding can be done in grids about 3x3 yds and two players battling for the ball, naturally using shielding to maintain possession in the small area. Be certain players emphasize shielding as opposing to dribbling the ball in the tight area. Generally this is played competitively by the coach blowing the whistle every 10 seconds and whoever has the ball at that time scores a point. Play to a score of who ever leads after 5 trials wins. Even if one player wins the first 3 rounds that pair continues to play the whole five rounds. After five rounds winners play winners and losers play losers. Key points are side on which gives distance from the defender, strength and in a game situations gives vision of teammates to the shielding player. Another exercise is for three players with locked hands to maintain possession of the ball against a defender outside trying to get the ball. This is also a good combat (body contact) exercise to help shy contact players to become accustomed to the contact that exists in soccer.

By simply playing 3v3 in an area of only 10x10 yds one can accomplish a great deal of shielding and tackling. One way is mere possession, another way is with opposite endlines as the goals, one endline per team, or even only a 5 yard wide goal for each team. By all means get to the playing stage because that best translates to the actual game and is a lot of fun for players!

11

Goalkeeping Technique/Activities

Goalkeeping development is likely the most neglected area of soccer, especially for younger age levels. Of course without an assistant coach or keeper coach it simply is the most neglected area of training. Additionally, many field players, and certainly coaches who were not soccer players, simply don't know much about goalkeeping. In accordance with the entire text the keeper must understand first, second and third attacker and defending responsibilities because she too at times fills every one of those roles.

Generally the **keeper warms-up** with the whole team doing the jogging, dribbling, passing/receiving, stretching and whatever the coach incorporates in the warm-up. This simply gets away from the all too common practice of separating the keeper from the team even before they all get a chance to work together. This also facilitates team building and communication skills.

An overview of keeper skills here involves warm-up movement, catching, dealing with crosses, breakaway strategies, special situations, all manner of distribution, communication, decision making, footwork, combat contact, safety and psychology (mental toughness). Combat contact is not vicious or unsportsmanlike, it is necessary to have the keeper become familiar with hitting the ground correctly as well as securing space for saves against other players, not just opponents, but teammates as well. Some of each of these provides an excellent warm-up for games. This should include ball gymnastics, footwork, multiple saves, diving, various kinds of catches, boxing, deflecting and many other detailed technical skills.

Too few coaches spend time in the warm-up where the team is working as a group of the whole in receiving/passing and the keeper calling for the ball. This can emphasize strong shots, ground or air balls, slow balls requiring the keeper to move quickly and strongly to the ball, distribution by the keeper and other technical skills while working with the team. Just a sample wrinkle could be that the players are roughly in their positions while moving, using the whole half of the field with 3 balls and playing combinations with the keeper calling for balls from close and far away. One should not lose this opportunity for true team building with the game as the focal point. It never gets better than that. Attending to the keeper's voice is important lesson to learn.

Of course the shortsided games, scrimmages, and regular games are the true test of the keeper's ability.

Some of the following will further continue the warm-up. Certainly ball gymnastics can logically follow, alone or in pairs, including: over and under, around each leg and figure eights on the ground and in the air, Maravitch catching between the legs while reversing hands, very hard bouncing and catching, air tossing/catching, some footwork with cones staggered in various locations as to cause shuffling, forward movement with explosive movement and back pedaling. To maintain interest, a save at the end of the cone arrangement is a good idea.

Once the general warm-up is completed the keeper will have further warm-up specific skills. Sometimes this should include field players depending on the coach's plan. For building out of the back, centerbacks and/or wingbacks would seem appropriate. For saving shots, strikers would be likely candidates.

Some jumping, bounding and other explosive movement over gates should be part of the late warm-up activities or part of the actual instruction related to the day's skill emphasis. Agility, coordination and plyometrics will all improve performance and prevent injuries.

Many keeper coaches appropriately include **footwork** as part of the keeper's warm-up. One exercise that is extremely game related and therefore more meaningful and more fun is to set 3 flags (cones, obstacle course markers) in a triangle configuration about 8 yards apart. With three servers the keeper is asked to go from one goal to the other making saves. First clockwise and then counter clockwise and finally the servers serve at random simply calling out 'ball coming'. This is functionally useful in terms of footwork, catching and on occasion even dives. This is very rigorous, demanding intermittent rest and stretching periods so as insure quality and avoid injury. When done rigorously this is also fitness training. The added benefit to this exercise is the field players get some shooting practice. It is best to make it somewhat game related by demanding the field players perform a preparatory touch before taking the shot since the quality of this touch often determines the quality of the shot. Be sure shots are kept well below the 8 foot height of the bar. The distance from the triangle is determined by the quality of the keeper and field players shooting. For age sixteen and above 15 to 20 yards should be about right. For Wayne Rooney maybe 50 yards is more appropriate. Life without humor is not life!

Few of us spend enough time in shooting and finishing exercises. While these exercises are an opportunity for the keeper, if the keeper is placed in an environment that represents a shooting gallery we are not performing her a service. Also useful in scrimmage activities is to defend an entire endline of the game, especially when the distance is more than 8 yards and less than 44 yards. Another good activity is to have two players passing the ball back and forth about 20 yards apart and 16 yards from the goal line and after a random number of passes take a shot. During the entire passing sequence the keeper is expected to be properly positioned, in line for saves and about 4 yards from the goal line.

For youth teams, if there is an assistant coach, older keeper or parent volunteer some of the previous mentioned activities could have catching being made at the end of some of the movements. If such a person is available, the reaction saves could be done by the helper in which a ball is held in each hand with arm fully extended a few inches higher than head height and one of the two balls is dropped and the keeper is expected to catch the ball before it hits the ground. Reaction movement can also be done with the keeper and the other keeper (or server) with a ball in their hands passing a third ball back and forth to each other using the contact with the ball for the passes. The pace and distance is determined by the level of the keeper(s). The agility ball is also excellent for improving quick reactions to the ball. An agility ball is simply a ball with all sorts of bumps on it and a server sends a ground ball to the keeper and when it makes sudden unsuspecting movements the keeper must quickly react and catch the ball.

Two-fisted punching passing (volleying) with a single touch between the keepers can be fun and definitely with help refine the technique.

This is in the warm-up, but obviously punching must be done in relation to the goal and finally with players (opponents and teammates) in the penalty area. Later on the keeper will learn single handed punching, but in order to develop the proper technique of leading the whole body with the hands the two fisted technique is taught and mastered first.

Also, multiple saves can be incorporated by the server sending a ground ball very slowly from about 18 yards out and the keeper is expected to come forward at pace and pick the ball up while the server sends another ball high in the air (10 to 15 feet) behind the keeper who must save the second ball as well. Generally we do not encourage backpedaling, but instead encourage the keeper to turn and run side–on with head turned and eyes always on the ball. Second attempts at a save are an imperative part of keeper training. Throughout all the activities demand that the keeper who has mishandled a ball go after the errant saves. Even if they have gone to the ground on the first save, demand they pursue the ball until it is safely secured, out-of-bounds, or in the back of the net. Actually a good training activity is to have the keeper go to the ground; then serve a second ball for a save so that they develop the skill of getting up quickly. Another variation is after the keeper has made a save and is on the ground is to have a second ball served that is also on the ground but requires the keeper to crawl (move) a yard or two without getting up. In any case, multiple saves is an important part of high level keeping.

The keeper can now be sitting on the ground facing the server and the ball is thrown to the extended hands to one side, then the keeper returns the ball to the server and another serve is made in rapid succession. In this exercise the emphasis is on the keeper coming forward with every save. This concept of forward movement is constant through all the saving/catching activities. Also the keeper is strongly encouraged to lead with the hands for virtually all saves. If another keeper and server are available one might want to do a few out-of-reach catches from a standing position in which the keeper deflects the ball over the bar to the other keeper.

As far as cushioning of firmly struck balls, the wrists should be cocked forward. While the fingers, gloves, arms, torso, and even the legs will provide some cushioning, none of these provides as much cushioning as the wrists cocked forward. While so much is made of the 'W' or 'O' catch, merely emphasizing to the keeper to keep their hands behind the ball may be simpler and a better concept. The medicine ball tossed, later on punted just above the head of the keeper demands that they are securing the ball correctly. If they do not get enough of their hands behind the ball it goes through and if done in front of the goal the result becomes extremely clear to them. This self-teaching of the keeper is worth much more than any coach can achieve by simply using words. In this way the keeper teaches herself.

There is a tendency for keepers to allow a ball to bounce and then secure it. This is dangerous because it allows an opponent time to contact the ball and score a goal. To rectify this problem, serve a hard ground bouncing ball about 1 to 3 yards in front of the keeper from various distances and have them make a save while the ball is on the rise. Once keepers gain confidence and experience with this training it is much more likely that in a game situation they will get to the ball as soon as possible and if the save can be made sooner by catching the ball on the rise, they will do so.

Once players have some basic skills, consider balls tossed straight up overhead and as the catch is made the knee closest to the server rises and body contact is made in order to alleviate the fears of contact. Somehow keepers seem to enjoy this exercise a great deal. Be absolutely certain that you are developing confidence in body contact and not hitting the keeper so as to cause them fear of contact. This unfortunately is one of those areas that demand the art (perceiving) of goalkeeping instruction.

To develop **speed of movement** of both the feet and hands, sometimes punting a small ball which travels very quickly from about 18 yards will help the keeper not only with reaction speed, but also vision! Small soccer balls about 6 inches in diameter work well for this activity.

The basket catch is a fundamental skill for all keepers. Balls struck with pace that are low enough for the keeper to catch and fall over and cover must become a conditioned response. Covering the ball does not mean falling on the ball as this would hurt or cause the ball to come loose. The knees must be on the ground enough so that there is a tiny space between the abdominal area and the ground so the ball is secure with the hands. Repetition will allow the keeper to perform this smoothly and safely. The head should be up somewhat to survey all the action and thus be able to protect oneself from collisions.

When the ball is low and to the side the keeper is sideways with one knee close to the ground with hands out in front and the ball is immediately in one continuous motion tucked into the abdominal area, often referred to as the 'bread basket'. All spaces between body parts must be smaller than the ball. Many items mentioned here are pictured at the end of this chapter.

The simplest way to deal with **breakaways** is to have 3 or 4 different style players go 1v1 with the keeper and have them develop the timing of when to leave the goal and make the save. Develop the instinct that the save is generally best initiated milliseconds after the player has touched the ball and the keeper knows where the ball is going! On various occasions use different players for this instruction while the rest of the team is working on possession training or other skills. As the attacker approaches, keepers should steer the player to a location that they know they can cover, guarding the near post. Also, keepers must be schooled in 2vK, 2v1, 1v2 and other variations such as 3v2. This develops the coordination between the keeper and defenders. The 3 on 2, 2 on 1 exercise in this text for field players is excellent for the keepers dealing with numbers down situations.

An important tactical point is studying the attacker's degree of control. Quick decision making is the same as a field player defending the 2v1: Eliminate the likelihood of a pass to the second attacker (delay without allowing the first attacker to shoot), then play 1v1 against the first attacker. From here, the progression is the same as those of field players, gradually add another attacker at less than full effort until the keeper has mastered the tactic. Then increase the effort to challenge the keeper's decision making, quickness, reach and technique. As always, it is best to work up to a smallsided game, using full size goals or the goal size for the age level in a small field grid.

Crosses can be dealt with by having two servers, one on each side of the field near the endline. The servers take a touch toward the endline and serve to one or two players inside the penalty area and outside the goal area box. Often it is a good idea to have one shooter at the near post area and one at the far post, but many variations of subsequent sessions is a good idea. Teasers, balls that require a rapid decision as to save calling "Keeper" or leave for field players by calling "Away", are extremely important. Include ground, lofted and driven balls so the keeper experiences all possible game situations. Have the shooter move not only toward the goal, but also across the face of the goal so the keeper must see the ball and the shooter and **always be in line with the ball as it crosses the face of the goal**. This is a critical skill, as many so-called accomplished keepers even at higher levels do not move across the face of the goal well as the ball moves across the face of the goal. In all of these active environments it is often best to ask a question rather than give a correction. This procedure helps in two ways; A) the keeper has to think about the answer B) the coach learns how the player is making the decision. In the latter instance, the coach may want to help the process of how the keeper makes decisions as opposed to the specific correction. A basic activity is to have wide players play various crosses to the keeper who saves and is required to deliver the ball to the server on the opposite side of the field. This simulates the game situation of **distributing to the weak side**, where players are often unmarked.

Properly falling (diving) to a roundoff position so as to cushion the fall generally is started from a kneeling position (with young keepers it may start from a sitting situation). The ball is gently rolled on the ground from approximately 8 feet away to the side so that the keeper must reach out with the hands and fall to make the catch. Gradually the services are more crisp and further out. The body should round off so as to contact the ground gently and sort of follow through and return to a vertical position. Every attempt is made to make the contact with the ground as soft as possible. Be certain the keeper is still leading with the hands and moving slightly forward. In many instances the ball is used to cushion the contact with the ground. Eventually with more mature players we move to the standing position. From the standing position the impact is greater and the ball is used regularly to cushion the fall. For avoiding deflections into the goal be certain that the ball is forward of rather than behind the player.

Finally, with able keepers, generally around 14 years of age (though this varies greatly) the keeper is expected to dive over a small obstacle such as a pillar or mat. For very high-level keepers the object to be dived over becomes wider and/or higher. At early stages this can be performed using a mat until the technique is perfected. The main concern here is that the keeper becomes competent with the fundamental catching, footwork, kicking, throwing, and basic skills of punching before starting on these advance skills that require greater confidence, courage, flexibility, strength and skill.

The security of the ball when on the ground can begin at an early age. **One hand should be firmly behind the ball and the other on top of the ball**. The instructor can gently strike the ball to get the player accustomed to what might be necessary for securing the ball in a game situation. The elbows should be forward to protect the head. Absolutely be certain that the player faces forward. While there is a remote chance of a collision to the frontal part of the body this is enormously safer than a straight on strike to the spinal area. Unfortunately the instinct of young players is to roll away from the opponents, leaving the spine exposed. This tendency must be obliterated through instruction and repetition.

Foot movement can be developed by two people each 12 to 15 yards straight out from the goal post with one serving a soft ground ball straight at the post with the keeper saving and returning an air ball to the server. Just as the keeper has released the ball and made a **shuffle step** or two to the other post the other server releases a slow ground ball toward the other post. Teaching proper basic foot skills such as shuffling while using the ball is economical and the transfer of learning to the actual is immediate. Quick, moderate sized steps, feet never touching each other, and balls of the feet balance are the main coaching points. Good footwork is characterized by quiet sound.

A simple **distribution** activity is having two players both wide at any desired distance and the keeper merely delivers a ball that is rolled, overhead thrown, half volleyed, or punted, depending on the distance required. Goal kicks must also be practiced. Goal kicks should be to outside midfield players. While players able to send balls 50 yards or more often go up the middle this does not seem wise as offensive players are out numbered there, the opponents are facing the ball and central defenders are often chosen because of their size/strength and ability to head/clear balls well.

Keeper wars is a great activity because it is game related, competitive and just plain fun. Unfortunately this generally requires two goals facing each other about 25 yards apart. With a single keeper a field player can be the opponent for the keeper. Various options include: Overhead throwing; rolling, dead ball shots; hand saves only; punting; friendly 15 foot high lofted service that must be headed; 1v1 no line of restriction; left (weak) foot use only; after every attempt at the other keeper's goal the player must run and touch a cone about 3 yards away from her goal line; each keeper is 12 yards from goal and the other attempts to chip at goal (can use an excellent field player chipper); punching only; or half volleys only. There is no limit to the possibilities. These games should end with unrestricted play.

Reading the game: If a power defender steps up for the penalty kick do you think he going to take a finesse shot? Maybe you, the keeper, ought to stay put as he is likely going to try to over power you. If the team's schemer steps up for the PK maybe you ought to guess as she is likely going to place the ball near one of the posts. There is plenty of information: A PK taker far from the ball is likely going to attempt a power shot, a severe angle taker is going to have difficulty with power so maybe wait just until they begin to strike the ball and see what direction the non-kicking leg is facing toward. 'Herky-jerky' approach probably indicates a placement/feinting type of shot. High speed of approach likely means a power shot. Last post looked at may be the location of where the ball is going. Being set on balls of feet, hands well spread to make the goal appear small, and a low crouch to spring from and encourage an upper 90 shot that always has the chance of going over the top might help. With a nervous type player, usually seen in the facial expression and body stiffness, it might be that you want a confident smile indicating you are going to save the attempt.

Certainly on breakaways finesse and power shooters may differ. Maybe you have no concern for the power player chipping you so you can come off the line a bit earlier. All of these events must be practiced in training sessions before they occur. Of course, mental visualization the day of or before the match, but especially the evening before will all help. The coach must point out all these finer points to the keeper. Naturally scouting reports information should not be disregarded.

Positioning is vitally important and the historical rope connected to the two posts and having the keeper see how to reduce the size of the goal is still a useful technique. Changing the length of the rope will have the keeper see how the area available to the shooter is reduced. Moving the rope sideways will show the amount of goal that exists from various angles. Naturally, positioning instruction during scrimmages and shortsided games will help. Never forget, 'Catching them being good' in the words of Tony DiCicco, is even more powerful than correction. If the keeper is well positioned, point out why you thought he was well positioned. This may help the keeper to assume good positioning in the future. In terms of how far off the line the keeper should go, in a very general way they mirror the ball. When the ball is in close proximity to the goal, the keeper must be close to the goal line, but when it is at midfield they are more likely around the penalty spot, and when is it is in the far final third the keeper is likely around the 18 yard line. This varies considerably with the age, and more specifically according to the keeper's ability to get to where he needs to be when the situation changes drastically and rapidly.

Another defensive situation that calls for excellent communication is the offside trap. Although this is frequently orchestrated by the freeback or centerback, keepers have additional input, especially when the trap is close to the goal. Keepers can see all players, and generally have time to assess the opponent's attack. Thus, if keepers want to remove the trap, they communicate this to the defenders. Such moment-to-moment adjustments involve the direction of final defender(s) and the keeper. The decision to trap or remove the trap for the entire game or half, however, usually comes from the coach.

Dealing with **special situations** is always economical because all you have to do is have someone take the direct kicks, indirects, corners, big throw-ins and penalty kicks with the keeper in goal. It naturally allows you to train for set plays while the keeper defends them. Be certain to prescribe the number of players and location of walls so that it is virtually automatic for the team to be ready very quickly when opponents have specialty situations. Once each of the various situations is taught, which is best done one at a time on a given day, then a scrimmage in which the coach calls for all the various special situations is in order. Call both as they occur and randomly for adequate repetition. Since the day before a game is invariably a light day this is a perfect time for such an activity.

Distribution: Conceivably the lowest level of goalkeeping in many quarters from the youth to the professional level could lie in this domain. While the techniques in this area are reasonably straightforward, the decision-making is often disappointing, and this could be a polite way of describing the state of this skill. Most often when there is abundant opportunity for secure possession the ball is mindlessly punted up the field without even having an intended receiver. Some insist on getting one extra foot of distance by encroaching the 18 yard line at the risk of a handball and give up 10-20 yards of accuracy! This is not a good trade off. In any case, teaching the keeper the decision making of when to punt the ball long and when to distribute to teammates needs to be worked on a great deal. Variety with purpose in this area is important. If the opponent moves way up with high pressure the long punt is likely the best choice because their numbers for receiving are reduced. Also, no one wants to risk giving the opponent the ball near his or her own goal area. On the other hand if one is up in the score and there is safety in distributing the ball to ones own team, usually the defenders, by all means use that option. If the keeper is not instructed as to the why of these decisions, it may be that they will establish bad habits, which are difficult to correct later on.

Punting is invariably inferior for the same reason for the novice and intermediate level player because the self service of the ball is thrown instead of merely dropping it to their feet. The delivery to the foot is often inferior because players use a single hand for the self-service. While this technique may work well for professionals and mature players who have repeated the punt tens of thousands of times, for younger players it is absolutely best to start the self-service with two hands. Later on they can move to the use of the one handed self-service. Poor kicks are mostly a result of poor self-service, while accurate punts are a result of quality self-service. This fact is clear after thousands of observations of young, intermediate and mature players. Occasionally one sees a poor strike of the punt by a mature or even high-level player also caused by poor self-service (pro's are nearly always excluded from this problem). A low follow through is required for best results. After having picked up the target the keeper should see his foot striking the ball. Side on kicking can be an option for the totally competent player who has mastered the straight on skill. This option is best suited to professionals, although even their accuracy often leaves much to be desired. Technically throwing the ball for self service instead of dropping the ball can often be corrected with a single 20 minute session of punts against a wall or net. I have done this with results that totally changed the keeper's ability to punt in a single session. It often just requires very targeted instruction. Regarding the various techniques, correct repetition in training (non-game situations) is vital. The **rolling ball** should be released with finger-tips well spread apart, low to the ground and follow through is of critical importance. The follow through requires both the arm, body and step-ping of the feet in order to achieve quality over significant distances. Quality means proper pace, excellent directional location and topspin on the ball. A bouncing ball is clearly inferior service for the underhand distribution throw.

For the **overhand throw**, extension of the arm high overhead as much possible is desired in the early stages of instruction. This avoids sidespin which is difficult to receive and far less accurate. For young keepers the first portion of this is to learn how to cradle the ball in the hand and us-ing the forearm for another point of contact in order to secure the ball safely. Sometimes pointing the non-throwing hand to the target as part of the motion helps to perfect the correct technique and help with ac-curacy. Again the follow through seems to be the number one fault.

Goal kicks problems start with lack of rhythm in approaching the ball, which is often caused by too much speed and distance from the ball and poor stride length. A moderate pace and distance approach to the ball works best. Again, after having chosen a specific location the keeper should see the ball when he strikes it. Often there is inadequate empha-sis regarding striking by having the knee over the ball. This is impera-tive for striking low line drives, but keepers usually want some lift so in this case the extent of the knee over the ball is not as critical as a striker trying to score a low ball on goal. Landing on the kicking foot is often shared with players by coaches and clinicians, but the reason is seldom shared. Landing on the kicking foot keeps all the power exerted moving to the target, fosters a good follow through and avoids the circular mo-tion that causes a loss of power.

For **clearances** of balls on the ground sent to the keeper by teammates (back passes), some very specific training is in order. Generally there is good competence of clearing balls with the dominant leg; right side (keeper perspective) with a right footed player or left side with a left footed player. The difficulty comes when one has to clear a ball on the left side with left leg for a right footed player or vice versa. In some cases the ball must be cleared wide to the left and making such an attempt with the right foot is dangerous as this can cause an own goal. In order to avoid this incorrect behavior one merely needs to provide many repetitions of clearing a ball somewhat left up field. Some repetitions of sending the ball out-of-bounds are also necessary as there are times when opponents are in front of the keeper. The advantage of a keeper who is reasonably competent as a field player generally will develop a high level of competence sooner than players who started keeping permanently at too young an age. Delaying full time keeping until age 12-14 is probably a better idea. This same weak foot development is necessary for collections by keepers when they decide to dribble or control the ball for pass completion to the left side. After the initial control of the ball away from the goal either leg usage is acceptable. Balls sent to the keeper by field players are usually given a hand signal and voice command to send the ball wide of the goal. These must be ground balls, usually with the inside of the foot push pass.

In summary one begins to know some of the technical details that allow for quality distribution. Quality technical details clearly elucidated here still are no substitution for abundant repetition. Revisiting all of these topics is necessary. Teaching it once and not returning to the topic is inadequate. Even professionals review the simple fundamentals daily. In fact, warm-ups are attempts to maintain existing skills before the trainer goes into the instructional phase of the session. Yes, precursors to the topic are done in the warm-up, but these are skills the players already possess. Be certain that instruction is not dominated by talk, but instead by brief demonstration and/or instruction and the majority of time is spent on DOING!

Get Set Position: Get set position is very important. Even if you are not in the ideal location, be certain that you are ready to move up or down, left or right to make the save. The get set position is weight on balls of feet, knees slightly bent and feet shoulder width apart. Shoulders are in front of feet, hands loaded to front and side, elbows slightly bent. Head is still, with eyes straight to the ball using focused vision to begin the catch. In the most basic terms, it is a position of balance.

If a keeper is moving, astute shooters by instinct or conscious decision will direct the ball to the location from which the keeper is moving, which will nearly guarantee no save will be made. By the time the keeper stops and changes direction the celebration of the goal is already taking place. In more direct clarification the get set position is akin to a loaded spring ready to be released. It is a time saver for the next required movement. It puts the body, eyes and mind in a state to be able to respond with the minimum amount of time and in the realm of goal keeping often milliseconds can make the difference of completing a successful save versus a goal being scored. Unfortunately the results of many meaningful games are determined by a single goal. As with all skills it must be rehearsed in practice, become habitual in nature, or else it will fail in the high pressure situations of a game.

Strength with Ball: Simply place the ball on the ground and do push-ups having both hands on the ball using the 'W' hand position on the ball. Try to focus not so much on the 'W' hand position but on having the hands close enough together so that they always have a great deal of their hands behind the ball as opposed to on the side of the ball. Now simply propel the body into the air and again 'catch', re-contact the ball using the proper hand positioning. The coach is more concerned with the proper hand positioning than the height the player has risen from the ball. After the technique is perfected there can be a bit of concern for gaining height, which is a strength developer. Just a couple of inches are adequate for this exercise.

Either standing, sitting, or on the ground, have both keepers firmly grab the ball and attempt to wrestle the ball away from each other. Use all three positions for a variety over many sessions.

Safety: The emphasis of moving forward for proper saving of the ball is also a major safety feature for avoiding collision with the goal posts. It also assures that deflections will be away from the goal. Again the side-on position should be maintained so as not to expose the spine to any charge.

Keeping the head up so as to keep the spinal chord in a non-vertical position is critical beyond any emphasis that could be placed upon it. This reduces the chances of death or becoming a paraplegic to an enormous extent. The human body can withstand substantial blows from almost any angle, but when the spinal column is straight and hit directly in a straight line there is no place for the impact to go, and thus dangerous spinal breaks become extremely more likely. This emphasis on this is placed because there is some ill-conceived notion that after the save the keeper wants to lower his head and deliver a blow to the opponent.

Unfortunately this is not a theoretical declaration, but this has been done with the results being serious injury, death or putting one in a wheel chair. All of these events have actually occurred. Upon forward dive saves keep the head up!

Of course proper warm-up, injury prevention exercises and a proper fitness program will greatly reduce the loss of players for games. For females a very simple knee injury program that is feasible for all teams because it does not consume huge amounts of time is detailed here. Some knee injury programs are unrealistic due to the time demands. Olympic trainers shared this program with me and I used it with what I believe were positive results. Merely include backwards running in the warm-up, maybe with some turns, especially jab steps, and also include bounding from both legs. Also single leg jumps in which the player attempts to have one foot land on the ground and move to a 90 degree knee angle and maintain balance for about five seconds is useful. These three exercises were considered pivotal to female Olympians for the prevention of knee injuries. All three included in the warm-up only consume about 5 minutes, which makes them extremely realistic. A total distance of 100 yards is realistic for the backwards running, about 10 bounding running jumps with each leg should suffice and about 6 single leg jumps with each leg is about right. The backwards running could be five twenty yard backwards runs with returning to the start line with twenty yard forward runs. The employment of this program did not have an adequate sample to draw any scientific results, but I had very few knee injuries using this program for many years, so it seemed to be effective.

Agility, Coordination, Explosiveness, Jumping, Fitness: These areas must be dealt with by all keepers and their coaches. Certainly jumping over gates, practicing touching the cross bar and stretching to achieve significant range of motion must all be performed. While ballistic stretching has been discouraged for many years, static stretching having replaced it, and now the order of the day is dynamic stretching and plyometrics. In simplified terms these are stretches with movement. Movement that simulates the particular sport one is training for becomes sport specific and is the most desirable. Yet on the counter balance core work (abdominal strength etc.) is a necessity for all sports. The weight room and their trainers have taken on many of these responsibilities by incorporating medicine balls, stretch bands, wobble pillows and dozens of other training tools in addition to traditional weights. More common in the outdoors are ladders, rings, gates, pull kites, bungee belts, coaching sticks for jumping and movement changes of direction, and dozens of other training tools.

Clearly this whole realm is for enhancing strength, flexibility and injury prevention. Unfortunately this domain can be as damaging as it can be helpful in the hands of the uniformed. Yet lay instructors can generally safely use simple activities with ladders, rings, and obstacle course markers.

Actually very much can be done in terms of strength with personal body weight on the field by minimally trained personnel. Whenever possible consider using the ball at the end of a given movement. Some of the pictures in this section give insights into how to do this. In any case there is no intention here of elaborating on this domain to any great extent because there are many excellent sources for this data. The expertise in this area has increased enormously and is certainly beyond the scope of this book.

Foot saves are reasonably well established with players who were adequately trained as field players. For those who entered the ranks of goalkeeper prematurely simply serve many balls to the youngster that would best be 'saved' by using the feet. Obviously working in the goal area is best for this training. Special emphasis must be given to the non-dominant foot, as this will present the biggest problem to the keeper.

Boxing technique was mentioned as a warm-up activity, but this is only subsequent to boxing instruction which can be as simple as having the keeper start in the goal area and serving balls that demand the keeper reach a good deal and clear the ball. This is best done with a crowded box of players because that is when the skill is often needed in game situations. Logistically the need for more players is a problem because of the time pressure factors of training. In any case, if possible have at least two or three players for the keeper to contend with when doing this training. **Deflecting balls** over the cross bar or around the posts should also be practiced so as to gain proficiency in this area as it is also called for on occasion during the game. This can be done with two keepers and two servers, each pair on opposite sides of a flat faced goal. This allows many trials in a short period of time.

Diagram #102: Simply repeat the procedure by deflecting the ball back and forth from foot services.

Any technique which a keeper has that is very effective, but possibly not textbook correct, should be left alone as there are nearly always several skills needing attention. This is a general rule of all coaching. Sometimes tweaking a player who is very effective with a given technique is just not smart. Example: I had an All American player who was a great striker of the ball; she could hit knuckle balls that were a nightmare for keepers, could chip even when moving at pace, bent balls well for direct kicks and passes. In short, she was an excellent ball striker. Yet instead of landing on the kicking foot she raised her leg, often landing on the non-kicking foot after striking the ball. Now, mind you, I am not talking about something that resembled an American Football punt, but the leg followed through about a foot off the ground. Why would I demand landing on the kicking foot? It would make no sense. So, if it is effective forget about the textbook technique. In summary, there is always a bit of latitude for individual style.

Communication: The keeper has the opportunity to view the whole field so it is natural for him to become a key part of communication to his teammates. Simply calling "Away" or "Keeper" must become habitual. Therefore it is constantly used in training.

Whenever possible try to end all movements with a save. Too often there is too much training done away from the goal and without the ball. Even footwork obstacle courses can end with a save. Not only is it more fun but it also is much more game related. The more the keeper

189

can see the exercises relating to successful goalkeeping the more likely he is to give a quality effort, which is so important to eventually having a keeper who is confident and competent.

As in all training, the game is the best teacher. Weaknesses observed in games must be addressed as well as maintaining a long range developmental plan to insure the keeper's progress. A final word is that the notion that keepers must be irrational (I think the word most often used is crazy) is a total falsehood. Keepers might need more cognitive competence than any player, though I admit that the courage required of good keepers may well be greater than what is required of field players. This is not to say that the courage of going up for a 50/50 head ball does not require the courage of a lion. Whether we are enamored or not by the courage required for a good player, it is a fact of life that the game demands both physical and mental courage. The mental aspects might actually be more demanding than anything. In particular the keeper generally needs better focusing skills than any player on the field since he often may be idle for long period of time, especially in lopsided games. As coaches we must demand focused concentration in training sessions so that proper habits for games are established. Let us not confuse seriousness with solemnity. There is room for humor and fun, it just has to be appropriate to the situation, time and place.

Working Alone: Personal individual practice is very important because the visualizations created by the individual are more powerful than those offered by another person. Use of a wall, handball court or a pitch back will all help to get numerous repetitions in a short period of time. Deliver a huge variety of balls to the wall to avoid boredom and be prepared for all game possibilities. Facing the wall and having a friend (coach, parent, sibling) provide service to the wall can help build reaction speed for reaction saves. The live medicine ball is also excellent for developing strength and sureness of catching skills. Even a fence or flat faced goal behind the keeper when there is a server will eliminate waste of time and greatly increase numerous repetitions, which is so necessary for developing muscle memory.

Many players, especially goalkeepers, keep a journal in order to foster their playing development. This is an excellent idea because it facilitates more focused training. All games are also recorded with emphasis on positive elements of performance as well as areas to be improved. Once the player has recorded positive aspects of performance and areas of improvement, the next step is a specific plan for improving the areas that they feel are deficient, and also activities that build upon present strengths. If the player feels that it would beneficial for the coach to view the journal and comment this can be a part of the journal. Probably the most productive communication of the keeper and coach would be a face to face conversation. If the coach is too negative, by all means do not involve them in your journal. Journals can include a seasonal plan of major goals with specific activities and clearly described activities to meet weekly goals for each session.

The mere writing fosters thinking of ways to improve. By all means include visualization, relaxation, focus and other activities in your journal. Research has proven that when these activities are done just before going to sleep, the results are much stronger because it remains with you all night. This makes the visualization much more powerful. For years many great athletes have done this. Self improvement activities are always more powerful than those imposed by others (coaches, parents, trainers, etc.). Ownership of one's growth is always the mark of anyone with significant accomplishments. It's easy to put it off, so it is important to get your journal started NOW! Procrastination is the road to mediocrity. Excellence is characterized by action. Getting started is the hardest part. Once you start you'll see significant progress and that will make it fun. You'll never want to quit once you start, and best of all, it is an extremely useful life skill.

Posting your goals in addition to planned activities are of great value. Room bulletin board, loose leaf covers, the refrigerator, iPhone, iPad, personal mirror, school locker and any place that you encounter often throughout the day are all possibilities.

COACHES SHOULD FEEL FREE TO PHOTOCOPY THIS SECTION OF THE BOOK TO BE GIVEN TO PLAYERS FOR THEIR USE. COPYRIGHT LAWS ONLY PERTAIN TO SALE OF ANOTHER INDIVIDUAL'S WORK, BUT INDIVIDUAL USE AND TEACHING PURPOSES ARE NOT FORBIDDEN.

While the size of keepers has increased dramatically, the techniques have remained relatively constant. Maybe the one change is that strikers (shooters) score a great percentage of goals with low ground balls since this seems to be the most difficult location to make saves, especially with the advent of the taller keepers. Many maintain that the women still have some difficulty with high balls due to their smaller size and their jumping ability is generally considerably less than a male. However, this too is changing somewhat.

Ready Stance: Weight on balls of feet, knees slightly bent, and feet shoulder width apart. Shoulders are in front of feet, hands loaded to front and side, and elbows slightly bent. Head still, with eyes straight-forward to begin the catch.

When players are near Calvin prefers to raise his hands for additional facial protection.

Nick's coach feels that the compromised hands position allows the best protection for both low and high shots.

Clearly there is always some room for minor variations of technique. What is not variable is knees bent to be ready for explosive movement.

Note hands are well behind the ball; fingers as well as the thumbs; a quiet catch is emphasized, always attempting to catch the top half of the ball. A weighted medicine ball hand or foot served above the head helps to perfect this technique.

Sideways catch of low ball: Note space between legs is not large enough for ball to go through, and player is ready to pop up to make a quick distribution. Knee should be a few inches off the ground (less than ball diameter).

The ball is already saved and Megan is already moving to a stand-up position for increased visibility.

Abdominal area securing of the ball.

Note that the ball is lower toward the abdominal area and the head is up higher for greater visibility

Accuracy Throwing: In this case the overhand throw toward the small goal target attempts to improve accuracy. Early stages must emphasize very much over the top to avoid side spin which causes difficulty for the receiver.

Two hand bounce catch: Usually warm-up activity. Keeper stands with feet facing one direction and bounces the ball and catches ball being certain two hands are well behind the ball and body, arms, hands all cushion the catch. Four locations are used while covering 360 degrees. This is excellent for abdominal flexibility.

Air Ball Development: Knee up nearest attacker to insure a safe catch. This begins to develop catching skills when pressured by an opponent. The knee lift is a must to attain maximum height in catching. This keeper could be leaning forward to a greater extent, which means starting the catch from further back.

Ball gymnastics in pairs: Circular handling, figure eights in pairs, over/under, bounces etc. encourage flexibility and firm grip handling.

Solo work: Throwing against the wall using many different angles, bounces, distances and speeds simply provides many catching repetitions of a variety of ball catches to improve handling.

Here a partner is serving balls off the wall which develops quick reaction for reaction saves.

Securing the ball on the ground so as to avoid a goal being scored and at the same time protecting the facial area. Of critical importance is that the keeper face the charge as to never expose the spinal area to a potential charge.

Note the body forward angle of the body for the save! Angled forward for all saves for safety of never colliding with the goal post and equally important so that all deflections are away from the goal. Novice keepers constantly want to dive backwards because it gives a millisecond more time, but the trade off is absolutely incorrect. Creating the angle of deflection away from the goal and the safety issue far out weight the millisecond of extra time gained for the save.

Both keepers have a ball in their hands and by hitting a third ball the are constantly reinforcing the muscle memory of leading with both hands. The additional benefit is that quick reaction is also being developed.

Right after a collapse dive forward the ball is secured by knees on the ground and ball under body. The concern here is not to have the keeper fall hard on the ball causing it to come out of the secure position. Hands and arms are securing the ball.

Here Calvin is showing a lead up activity that he uses with young keepers to get use to hitting the ground and not using their hands because the ball is in the hands. Two keepers facing each other shuffle and fall to the ground holding hands and developing a round-off shape to avoid severe ground contact.

197

The keeper is making the decision to save or call away for crosses with the reality of striker attempting to score. Here tracking the ball across the goal is critical and often not performed well by reasonably developed keepers. Of course the communication of "Keeper" or "Away" is constantly demanded. There are two severs on each side (one not seen) and all distribution is to the weak side.

Here the two keepers are wrestling with the ball to gain strength and have a little extra motivation by competing against one another for the ball. The fun adds to the effort of developing strength.

Multiple Saves: The keeper is moving quickly forward to save the slow ground ball, which he will distribute back to the server.

Now there is an immediate high ball thrown high behind him toward the goal and you see him saving the second ball. The emphasis on this skill must focus on the keeper keeping his eyes on the ball and running side-on (not back pedaling) with head turned so as to see the ball and all players.

Keeper Wars is great fun and outstanding training fully explained in the text. It looks like Megan burned Nick here; he seems a bit unhappy about this attempted save.

Sweet revenge for Nick; it looks like Megan didn't get off the line enough to close the angle to the goal. Win some, lose some, Sport at its best!

Here the keeper is avoiding a direct collision, as opposed to putting the head down and causing a direct hit of the attacker. Head up avoids the straight spine greatly aiding safety as indicated in the text.

Here the coach is simply dealing with reaction saves, improving reaction speed, by randomly dropping one of the two balls and the keeper is required to catch the ball before it hits the ground. For more accomplished keepers the balls are held lower. This keeper saved the ball so quickly that the hands should be lowered to increase the challenge.

Many arrangements are possible to train footwork, here the emphasis is on shuffling. A save is made after the keeper moves through the obstacle course. That increases motivation and makes it more game related.

This a straight on forward save, which ends in a dive smothering the ball for protection.

A small 6 inch ball is served from 18 yards to speed up reaction time as the small ball moves faster than a standard sized ball. Sometimes this is done with a tennis ball served off of a tennis racket. The added benefit is the perfecting of visual skills as well.

Note the hands forward and the wrists cocked forward for saves above the head. This insures the save and the wrists cocked forward provide excellent cushioning of power shots. In the picture on the right, the keeper is using incorrect technique, less cushioning and also the remote possibility of breaking the wrists.

The ball was deflected over the bar. Not shown due to a late taken photo shot the keeper was well over two feet off the ground when this deflection was made.

This photo was taken after a diving roundoff save and in one continuous rocking motion the keeper is getting up using the lower leg to propel her to an upright stance. This is far more important when the save has not been made and the keeper must be ready to go get the ball or deal with a rebound shot.

The picture on the left shows the correct position for anyone near the goal. The picture on the right shows incorrect positioning when near the goal. In the second shot any powerful hit ball on the side of the head away from the goal can cause a collision with the post. This is bigger problem for field players that do not have the same hand reaction speed as goalkeepers.

Megan displays a significant follow through allowing her punts to go well beyond the midfield. *(Photo by JD Hysler)*

On this goal kick she displays excellent use of the hands to aid balance. The ankle is fully locked down and the knee over the ball allowing the ball to be driven as opposed merely lofted.
(Photo by JD Hysler)

The bouncing ball is being cleared at the top of the penalty area instead of allowing it to reach near the goal.
(Photo by JD Hysler)

Note the two hand self service delivery for maximum accuracy. Too often we see poor punts because the hand self-service is poor due to the use of one hand. Most poor punts by players prior to the professional level is due to poor self-service.
(Photo by JD Hysler)

This deflection is well over the bar. Actually the keeper was even higher than shown when the ball was deflected. *(Photo by JD Hysler)*

Here the coming out early to deny the shot as opposed to having to make a save in the goal area is clearly shown. The courage required is considerable and is attained by very conscious coaching which builds confidence step by step to reach this level of confidence. *(Photo by JD Hysler)*

While tactical work performance can be in the range of 65% of proper performance, technique requires about 90% correct performance; otherwise we are merely reinforcing incorrect technique. Invariably there is a lead up activity; a simpler activity if the first intended one is marginal. While there are always individual nuances, the technique must be basically practiced correctly. If necessary leave an activity for a future date so that you have the time to create a good lead up for what you are trying to achieve. Instructional level as opposed to frustration level is always best. Independent level, that which the player can already do well is done briefly for maintenance (especially in warm-up), but moves on to challenge (instructional) level in order to foster maximum growth.

Some routines are necessary so that when the coach is not there, or the keeper wants to workout on their own, they can. At the same time variety, especially the extending a skill to a further level is absolutely necessary.

Things are simplified if there is a keeper coach, but in the absence of such personnel have the keeper come to practice earlier or stay later, which ever is best for all concerned. Certainly separate sessions during the season or even in the off-season is another way of achieving higher level performance. Maybe a teammate or older more experienced player will volunteer to help.

Just don't expect quality keeping to result without quality instruction. Clinics and camps can greatly assist development.

The Keeper War Game provides outstanding motivation and is a great skill developer. There are many varieties so that nearly any skill the coach wants to develop can be used in this extremely functional activity.

One of the worst alternatives is to do nothing. Don't expect good keeping unless it is trained for. For those coaches who have an adequate keeper with little or no training, just remember this is a great disservice to the players true potential.

12

Special Situations

Free kicks and corner kicks account for a significant percentage of goals. Therefore they should be practiced from both offensive and defensive standpoints. These areas are often overly incorrectly addressed in youth soccer, which should focus more on basic technical skills and the run of play. In this chapter, there is no intention to fully treat all aspects of this topic; we will merely present a few basic principles and deal with what might be a best approach and the more common errors and misconceptions.

While regular instruction in restarts is necessary for mature teams, these sessions should be for short periods of time, fifteen minutes or less. Any longer instructional period for these rather sedentary activities becomes counterproductive. The time to teach special situations is between two rigorous activities, such as shortsided work and scrimmaging. A few minutes at nearly every session is far better than an entire session devoted to special situations.

Since attacking instruction precedes defending instruction, it is important to follow this model in relation to special situations. There are no new skills needed here; therefore the emphasis is on tactics. Like the rest of the game, special situation tactics adjust according to the third of the field.

Timed movement is most important element of special situations. Players should not waste time and energy jockeying, jostling and jawing. Instead they must be focused on when the teammate will strike the ball, and at that time get free and get to the position they have determined to be the most productive when the ball arrives. Some of these decisions such as the location of where to be will have already been made when the coach prepared the team for that particular special situation.

Movement simply means that the player is never where they want to be until when the ball arrives. All players should be in a location other than where they want to be so that can get to their desired location when the ball arrives moving at pace. These movements can be direct runs, checking to or away, or away and to the desired location. Arms should be out making space, but not throwing elbows or similar unsportsmanlike behavior. The last thing a team wants is to score a goal and have it recalled due to a foul. This movement is critical because the snail-moving player will easily beat the stationary speed demon. Thus, timed movement is the key to being free at the appropriate time.

A suggestion to defenders is to anticipate where you think the offensive player will go, thinking of dangerous vital areas. Not allowing the offensive player to bump you off balance before he goes to where they want to be will also help. While it is instinctual behavior, players should be reminded to lean forward and be on the balls of their feet the instant before the ball arrives.

Another important behavior is if it is an air ball and the offensive player is going for the header, as a defender you must go up with him! Even if he wins the ball and you have caused him the slightest misdirection it may be all that is needed to avoid the scoring of a goal.

For some reason these very critical elements of special situations seem to never get discussed or taught. Yet, without these more basic elements nearly all well conceived special situations will fail.

All the unwarranted nonsense that one often sees when the kicker isn't even ready to kick the ball cause distractions from the basic, most important elements for achieving success with special situations. It goes without mention that many games are determined by the effectiveness of attacking and defending special situations.

Let us suppose that our team is awarded the ball in our own defending third. Since a free kick does not present an immediate scoring opportunity at this distance, the opponents will not use a wall; instead, they will mark players and/or space to begin defending while they are in transition from attack to defense. The tactical advantage will go to which ever team makes the most rapid transition. If we can put the ball into play very quickly, perhaps we can penetrate before they reorganize. A long pass may take several lax defenders out of the play. Therefore, our practice session works on quick organization and counterattack. This is not always used, but we must be capable of the quick special play.

The opponent may use one man to encroach upon the ball in order to delay the free kick. Though this is contrary to the spirit of the game, it happens all too frequently at every level. At any rate, the encroachment forces a decision: whether to call for ten yards, thereby submitting to the delay, or whether to put the ball into play quickly, which means passing around the encroacher, which immediately puts him out of the play!

Because of coaching or poor modeling, most young players are apt to call for ten yards. But this may not always be the wisest choice. The defense is counting on the referee's intervention; therefore, they may not be concentrating on a quick transition. A quick diagonal pass that beats the encroacher may be a powerful weapon against this tactic.

This decision should be made by a team captain, someone appointed by the coach to handle such cases. Coaches should teach the other players not to immediately call for ten yards at every opportunity. This only plays into the hands of the defense. In the defending third, anyone can take the kick, but it makes most sense for a defender to do so, in order to have as many strikers and midfielders in forward positions to receive a pass. Also, other receivers need to provide support in many locations.

Free kicks at midfield can be treated similarly, but perhaps with more intensity and quickness. One pass can put a team in scoring range. The team with the better organization and discipline will win the advantage. To train players for quick transition, the coach must clarify their responsibilities: At the whistle, they must anticipate and react. (The whistle means "GO!"). The player nearest the ball retrieves it, and, if necessary, throws it to the player nearest the location of the restart, who has already chosen a target player or space. A stopwatch can be used to time the transition, and motivate players to move quickly. The forward diagonal pass is usually more effective than a straight forward pass. Forwards should look to get behind the defense. Midfielders can offer support.

In the attacking third, free kicks will have to deal with a wall of a varying number of defenders. This wall almost never allows the full ten yards, even when repositioned by the referee. But even younger players can chip the ball over the wall to an oncoming teammate for a quick shot. Older players may be able to shoot around the wall with a banana kick. Or they may have enough accuracy to put the ball through a hole in the wall. Many defenses are terribly disorganized in wall settings, and do not even respond to the screams of their keeper to move left or right. This lack of organization can be exploited by a properly trained team.

If the defense is well-organized, it may be better to play the ball over or around the wall. Many teams devise set plays for both direct and indirect kicks in the attacking third. These plays are only as good as the techniques of the individual players. The key is to keep it simple, and go with your strengths and do what the situation demands! If you have a player who can curl the ball around a wall, use him. If your team has a strong header of the ball, get another player to serve the ball to him.

Service across the goalmouth to the 'back door' is generally very effective. This is because the keeper must cover her near post. Even if the keeper moves well to the back post a ball directed at the near post forces the keeper to stop and return to the near post. By this time the goal may have already been scored.

The way to open up space in these restarts is to fill in space vacated by a marked player who brings the defender with him. The essential attacking areas are, as always, near post, far post, and center near the top of the goal area box. However, the offsides rule may restrict these possibilities. Therefore, a direct kick on goal may still be the best weapon. Be certain someone is ready to finish poorly handled balls.

An assessment of the opposing keeper is especially valuable in these plays. How far can the keeper reach? Can he move left as well as right? Is the keeper's vision blocked? Does he come off the line readily? This knowledge will help a team to plan a successful strategy on free kicks. The simplest and most basic tactic is to train hard to get the ball on goal as this facilitates many possibilities. It may go straight in, a possible hand ball, a deflection, be mishandled and allow a follow up shot or may result in a corner kick. Over the top of the goal immediately gives the other team the ball and has no chance of scoring. This is senseless and unnecessary. Avoiding over the top requires vigilant, consistent coaching demands.

Now let us examine these free kicks from a defensive standpoint. We have already seen how organization, discipline, and quickness play a major role in any defensive situation. Another important aspect of defending against free kicks is thorough knowledge of the rules, coupled

212

with a high regard for sportsmanship. The professional foul has no place in soccer, especially in the youth game. If coaches insist on clean sportsman like play and refuse to condone intentional fouls, teams will give up fewer direct kicks. Though perhaps obvious, this concept is too often ignored. Young players should be instilled with the spirit of fair and clean play. Therefore, coaches should spend at least as much some time emphasizing the difference between assertive, hard play and cheap shots at opponents. This involves going to the ball courageously and having your arms out to protect yourself and make space for winning the ball. It also means never throwing elbows or kicking at the opponent instead of the ball.

That said, it is recognized that all teams will give up free kicks. Excessive delay by any defender must be discouraged not only for the sake of sportsmanship, but also because a well-coached opponent will exploit this momentary let-down with a quick attack. The mental disposition is extremely important here. Stopping delivery of a quality ball should be accompanied by still maintaining the concept that all areas have some coverage. Also, there must always be a mind set of winning the ball since this assures a team of the opponents not scoring immediately. This important concept seems to be constantly ignored.

Corner Kicks

Corner kicks present an excellent scoring opportunity. For offense, sometimes the best choice is a single play with one or two options. The opponents think they know what is coming, but something different occurs. Be certain to go to the ball while moving before it arrives. This means that one's starting position is about five plus yards further away from the desired location. Moving players can get to many more balls and go higher for headers. Moving players will always beat stationary players to the ball even if the other player is faster and stronger. Balls over ones head usually belong to a teammate behind you. Arms must be out to make space for your ball contact. When possible head the ball down as the keeper is invariably upright trying to cover the area just under the cross bar. As an offensive attacker always attempt to have a body angle facing the goal. This means starting further from the goal than the desired final position.

Defensive corners involve one major coaching decision: man to man marking or zone marking? At one time, zones were more common, but in the modern game most teams play man marking on corner kicks. One advantage is the ability to create favorable physical match-ups: tall vs tall, quick vs quick, etc. Go up with your opponent even if he is going to win the ball so he does not obtain a power header on the ball. Body angle should be facing away from the goal so that all contact with the ball directs the ball safely away from goal. MOVEMENT WITH MARK IS CRITICAL.

Practice against picks, especially those that verge on being illegal obstructions (moving picks), is a necessity. In fact, players must be coached to defend against illegal plays because these are not always noticed by the officials. The mind set must be, win the ball. During training we often have everyone, offense and defense, run around the goal on every corner service that hits the ground. Regular heading practice of 5-10 minutes is an even better way to avoid heading refusals.

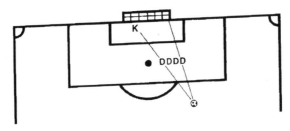

Diagram #103: Keepers also need to see the ball.

The number of players in a wall for direct and indirect kicks should generally follow the guidelines illustrated in the diagram below.

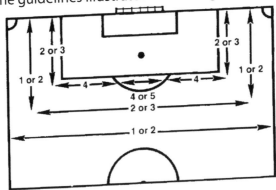

Diagram #104: These are guidelines. The individual keeper (or wall builder) may call for more people in the wall, esp. against dangerous free kick specialist. Walls can only be manned after all players are marked.

Who sets the wall? On most youth teams, it is the keeper. But since the keeper has a great deal to attend to in these situations, such as making sure that all attackers are marked, or being ready for a quick shot, someone else may set the wall. Often it is a striker or flank player, who has less defensive responsibility. Communication between the keeper and the field players is vital. Frequently the centerbacks are the most talented in this regard.

This training must be fully developed, and is best taught by merely setting up in front of the goal, using two groups (a defense and an offense). Through repeated trials, the coach can teach the rules, check for flaws, and assess individual strengths, such as air control, courage, power, and jumping ability. These assets can be used to gain an advantage.
The coach should stress the importance of adequate numbers and correct locations so that defenders can follow the rule of going forward, especially near the far post and central goal area. This requires a minimum of two players, but generally more are required. With enough players in the shaded area of the diagram below, all players can feel comfortable about going forward with conviction.

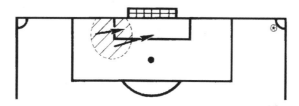

Diagram #105: Since forward movement is essential, some players should be well beyond the back post as the corner kick is taken.

Winning the ball depends upon maintaining vision and moving forward with a good power jump. A coaching tip here is to remind players to concentrate on the ball. Defensive headers are aimed higher on the head, the intention being to clear the ball as high, far, and wide as possible. Midfielders and forwards should be trained to anticipate these clearances.

The reason for two or more defenders at the far post is to maintain coverage if one of them must vacate the area to track down an attacker. This will allow for defense against the flick-ons to the far post. Another defender is needed to defend against flick-ons to the central area or near post. This defender covers the center of the goal to approximately six yards out. Merely developing an awareness of this danger area in the defensive unit will help to deal with this potent offensive tactic.

During these practices, the keeper must repeatedly decide whether to leave the line to cover the cross, or remain in goal. To perfect the keeper's technique, corner kicks can first be delivered without the pressure of receivers; then other attackers can be introduced to work up to match conditions. A major part of this session is communication. The keeper makes his intentions known with conviction and authority: "Keeper!" or "Away!" "Away" means a field player will send the ball away. Once the decision is made and announced, the keeper must follow through without hesitation.

Like corner kicks, the penalty kick requires special training. For the kicker, it is important to practice under as realistic conditions as possible. The coach can set the stage by creating a hypothetical scenario: "The score is 1-1 with four minutes to go in a championship game. You are brought down in the penalty area and will take the kick. If you make it, practice is over. If not, everyone does two laps with a ball." In a real game, the coach should do just the opposite with the penalty kicker; that is, take the pressure off by expressing confidence in the outcome: "Don't worry about the kick! I know we'll achieve all of our goals anyway." Anything positive will help.

Kickers need to practice placing the ball towards the corners of the net; keepers will have difficulty reaching these areas. Accuracy is more important than power. The kicker should pick a spot (the back bar of the goal is frequently excellent). Approach the ball a slight angle, definitely not a severe one, with rhythmical steps, moderate controlled speed, check both posts before the kick, but see your foot striking the ball. Moderate starting distance, not super close and not very far away, somewhere around 4 or 5 yards should serve a penalty kicker well. Once committed to a location, generally speaking it is not a good idea to change your mind. Train for "worm burners", removing all chances for sending the ball over the top of the cross bar. Also, keepers cannot jump down, mostly they have to depend on gravity which is slower than propelling upward.

There should be a complete follow-through right to the intended location. Psychological games of poor sportsmanship between the kicker and the keeper have no place in soccer. Neither keeper nor penalty shooter should get caught up in them. It is more likely that such poor behavior will backfire by causing a loss of focus. In any case, it does nothing positive for the game.

This is just as important from the keeper's standpoint. The keeper, however, is not really at a psychological disadvantage: Everyone expects the kicker to score, so all the pressure is really on the kicker.

Fortunately, there are clues to help the keeper anticipate the direction of the penalty kick. Players who approach the ball with speed and significant distance usually use power to score. In this case the keeper may want to stay centrally. Kicker's visual survey (frequently the last looked at location is the kickers preference), prior knowledge of the kicker's style, better foot, or favorite target and where the foot meets the ball all can help the keeper. A conscious attentiveness to the players during the game also gives clues: power players are likely to use power, finesse players will generally use placement. Maybe staying centrally for power players is best and guessing for placement players. The keeper can consider all this information, but it is where and how the kicker's foot finally meets the ball that tells the most. This ultimate piece of information allows very little time for the keeper to react; nevertheless, proper training can help the keeper improve reaction speed and build confidence. Again, knowledge of the rules and experience is the best prevention of penalty kicks; defenders must be very aware of the type of contact permitted in the game.

Awareness of the rules and basic principles of soccer and player roles is also critical to the most common restart: the throw-in. Coaches should not overlook throw-in violations in practice. Young players should practice the proper technique until it becomes automatic. The long throw-in to the goal mouth is a great weapon. To increase distance and accuracy, training with the "bounceable" medicine ball is very helpful.

The tactical awareness of throw-ins derives from quickness and the principles of player roles in soccer. With the whistle signaling out-of-bounds, there is often a mental let-down. The team that maintains concentration and hustle gains the edge. This frequently results from fitness, but focus is also huge.

The thrower is the first attacker, who needs support from a second attacker and mobility from at least one third attacker. The receiver should stay 3 or 4 yards away from the touchline, since the ball going out of bounds from your teammate is a throw-in for the opponent. The throw-in can arc over the wing's head or bounce beside his feet, to be met at speed. The wing may also need to check in, then out. A defender usually offers deep support, in the event that the other receivers are marked. In the defending third, the keeper can move to the edge of the penalty area to control a throw-in. Again, the first law of offense (spread out) and the first law of defense (compactness) are in full force.

Having completed the throw, the thrower should move on to the field of play to offer support. The receiver may be shielding the ball from a defender, and need to return it to the thrower. Another option for the thrower when the receiver is marked and facing the thrower is to toss the ball to the receiver's head for a quick return pass to the thrower's feet. A simple hand signal from the receiver sets this play without being seen by the defender.

Defending against throw-ins is aided by sustained concentration, quick transition, knowledge of the thrower's distance, and anticipation. The thrower usually tries for the wing first, since that is potentially the most penetrating move. Double coverage of that wing may be helpful. A defender given the responsibility of marking the thrower can minimize the effectiveness of a quick return pass. A coordinated team defensive effort might force the throw-in back towards the thrower's goal. Defending a long throw-in from deep in one's defending third is essentially the same as defending against a corner kick. As always, numerical superiority around the ball is half the battle.

In the attacking third, attempt an immediate cross either directly from the throw-in or a layoff. Seldom do numerous passes on the flank gain anything, and frequently the ball is lost without even having a chance at goal. The early cross can be effective because the attacking team may have equal numbers, or even numbers up, on the weak side. Slots should be filled in anticipation of immediate service. Be certain on corner kicks that the starting position of all players is 4-5 yards back from where they want to contact the ball. MOVEMENT for losing a defender and attaining a high jump for heading the ball is imperative! For specific plays for all restart situations there are several complete books devoted strictly to special situations plays. See "The Complete Book of Soccer Restart Plays" by Bonfanti and Pereni.

218

It should be clear that the principles of player roles on attack and defense hold true for special situations like free kicks and throw-ins. The team that gains the advantage is the team that maintains its concentration after the whistle blows, organizes quickly and correctly. Restarts are a contest of time. The attack tries to penetrate, support, and mobilize faster than the defense can pressure, cover, and balance. While most young teams are conditioned to stop and rest at the sound of the whistle, superior teams learn that the whistle means "GO!". If a team is to be successful it must implement the rapid transitions during practice.

13

Team Tactics Coaching

The first area of confusion is the use of the word tactics. There are individual tactics (decisions), small group tactics especially combinations, support, cover, etc., and there are team tactics. Unfortunately experts often assume that the listener, reader, understands which ones of these are being referred to. And with other experts they frequently do understand, but with lay audiences they frequently mix all three together and this greatly confuses communication regarding tactics. This leads to the erroneous statement that there are no tactics without technique, which if stated there are no quality team tactics without individuals with technique would be somewhat accurate. But there are always tactics; even a 7 year old playing 1v1 must decide to speed dribble, make a move, attempt to beat his opponent, shield, shoot or whatever.

Coaches and fans love discussions of team arrangements and tactics, but these discussions are not productive for teams with poor technique (dribbling, passing/receiving, etc.). Players who cannot perform tactics well and execute 1-2's, takeovers, overlaps, do not spread the offense, etc. will not result in a good successful team. Until players have the skill and understanding to execute technique in game situations, understand the principles of player roles and small group tactics, such discussions are meaningless. Players under twelve require more emphasis on technique and small group tactics, which are best taught using shortsided games. Too often, teams fail to develop players and do not achieve long range results when they bypass these necessary developmental stages. But once the players on a team are ready for this step, team tactics present a whole new challenge for the coach. High school athletes are able to benefit from team tactical instruction. This chapter will introduce the major areas of team tactics coaching: Team arrangements, player positions, low versus high pressure, guidelines for teaching tactics, and applying tactics to common situations such as the offside trap are discussed.

To begin, it is important to distinguish a team arrangement from team tactics. While there is some relationship between the two, team tactics go far beyond team arrangement (systems). Significant team tactics include finishing activities, changes of field, methods to maintaining possession, use of width and depth in attack, rapid transition, use of long and short passes, exploiting an opponent's weakness, and so forth.

The choice of a team arrangement, however, can be the starting point for team tactics, as certain formations lend themselves to particular tactics. No single team arrangement is always best. Any arrangement must depend upon the personnel of a given team. The competition, age, field, and many other factors also affect the adaptations used for a certain match. A coach must be somewhat open minded to variations best suited to the team's personnel. Sensible adjustment and emphasis of a basic system is wiser for a given opponent than trying a whole new system.

The basic criteria in choosing a formation are to exploit a team's own strengths and minimize its weaknesses. This is admittedly difficult, and calls for thorough knowledge of each player. While there are certain advantages to each arrangement, usually the basic arrangement is maintained and merely adjusted to contend with the opponent. For example, a team may withdraw its left midfielder or wing to mark the opposition right midfielder because he is that team's creator (schemer). The team formation adapts in order to mark, thus reducing that opposing player's effectiveness.

Due to its balance in numbers over the field, and its simplicity, the 4-3-3 is a good basic system to use as a teaching model. All systems have their own merit. Width somewhere, either in the front, middle or defense is a necessity. While most would prefer to have width in the midfield because it is easiest for the midfield to offer lots of help on offense and defense, many choose the 4-4-2, but it is somewhat complex for inexperienced teams. The concepts for the strikers is somewhat complicated and detailed in the two man front, however at the higher levels this is the most common system at the present time. The 4-5-1 is becoming more common but it is only appropriate for high level teams. Also, 4-2-3-1 and 4-2-1-3 are gaining popularity.

With this or any system, the constant objective is to maintain four man width in the third of the field where the ball is. Also, front and rear support are a great asset. It is nearly impossible to have proper ball support

222

and some mobility without at least four players in the general area of the ball. On defense, in the defensive third it is difficult to put pressure on the ball, delay, cover, and balance and stay compact with fewer than four defenders, especially if the attack involves three players up top. The 4-3-3 encourages fluid movement, and easily adds an extra player in the midfield by a front runner moving back. In addition, a defender can step up to midfield very easily. A further advantage of the 4-3-3 involves the development of wing play, thereby facilitating crosses and spreading the defense. With two wings, the attack is more apt to use the entire width of the field. This is critical to high level play. Also, midfielders and backs are encouraged to fill the attacking lanes opened up by the wings who stay wide on offense. Any and all systems can be excellent---the 4-3-3 is ONLY favored here as a teaching model.

However, learning to apply the same principles of play to different thirds of the field does change somewhat. For example, the principle of pressure on the ball varies greatly from one third of the field to another. A player with the ball in his defending third should consider any player within five yards as pressure, while a player in the attacking third may not consider a very close marker as pressure. The safety/risk ratio is the basic principle in these examples. Two or three strikers must become accustomed to the risk of dealing with at least four or more opponents.

While the differences among systems of play are sometimes exaggerated, all share many common elements. The constant need for four defenders when defending in their own half of the field is kind of an axiom of all systems. In short, all systems need some mobility and players covering for one another on defense and offering support to the ball on offense. Thus, again the basic principles of penetration, support and mobility and pressure, cover and balance on defense are virtually always in affect. Players who understand these basics of the game can meet all the various demands of the game of soccer in both shortsided play and the eleven aside game.

There is no intent of a full discussion of systems, obviously the 4-4-2 lends help to the midfield and requires midfielders to take a bigger role on offense in order to have adequate numbers in the attack. The 4-5-1 simply requires that to an even greater extent. The 3-5-2 is for teams with an abundance of very able midfielders who can play in tight spaces and of course have three very able defenders.

In any case young players need to spend most of their time with the ball. Young players need to experience many positions before they settle into one position. Thus functional training, training for a given position, is left for experienced players competent with the ball. Certainly high school age level players should be ready for functional training. In fact, one of the most fundamental tenets of sports psychology and team building is that the player clearly understand his role in the team!

The basic possession tactical exercises are important and common for all levels. There are virtually hundreds of variations for possession games such 2, 3, or 4 teams; neutrals on or off the field; target players out of the grid; 1, 2, 3 or unlimited touches; demand for some sort of combination; the list is endless. Good practice seldom lacks a possession exercise related to the topic of the day. A simple suggestion might be considered in this regard. If numbers permit consider two or more groups for these exercises so as to have more ball touches, thereby assuring more technical development as you teach a given tactic. The chapter on possession covers all these options quite well.

Possibly the final position a player sets into is more of a mentality than physical attributes or skills. No coach wants weak players, slow players, poorly skilled players, or any other low level attribute anywhere on the field. But probably a risk taking defender is a bigger problem. Strikers who will not take chances are of little help to a team. If a striker misses one shot and stops shooting he certainly isn't a valuable striker. Of course central middies are sort of a hybrid of both attributes and often can work in tight traffic. Wingers who cannot serve a ball would not seem like a sensible choice either. Therefore some considerations to skills must be given. These areas are laden with very varying opinions of where a player is best suited to play. In the end all these choices must be made by the coach. In any case, watching players in 5 v 5 and similar environments, gives the coach the best ideas for placing players. If in shortsided games a player regularly stays back one would be best to consider this player for defense. It certainly is a better guide than asking the player, and infinitely better than the parent's opinion. If the youngster constantly goes up front, demands the ball and scores goals occasionally, one might consider that mentality as someone who might be a good striker for your team. This is not to say that a players motivation for given location is of no use, but tendencies in shortsided games might provide a better alternative. Unfortunately in today's society the coach must frequently also 'sell' the position assigned to the player.

In relation to zones and man-to-man defenses there virtually is no team that plays 100% of either. All teams play a combination of both man-to-man and zone. Generally teams that mark up in their own third or half of the field would be called man-to-man teams, while teams that maintain their shape and start marking somewhere near their penalty area would be called zonal defenses. In rare instances, a team could be a bit more extreme, but this is rare.

Regarding high and low pressure is similar in that hardly any team in the world would pressure a team for the entire field for the entire game. The fitness requirement is likely impossible. For brief periods of time or down in score with only minutes left in the game teams often play full pressure defense for the length of the pitch. Generally teams that defend over the midfield line, close to three quarters of the field are considered high pressure teams. In any case high pressure is much more common at the present time than any time in the last four or five decades.

A unique form of pressure used by Barcelona is to high pressure for five seconds after the ball is lost and then return to a more traditional defensive pressure somewhere near or just above the midfield line. Thus, they are never in total high pressure or low pressure for an entire match, but play both traditionally and high pressure for brief periods of time throughout the match.

Low pressure teams generally choose somewhere close to midfield line as the place where they apply strong pressure. In any case the major point of confusion here is that teams that play low pressure do so everywhere all the time. However, teams that play low pressure must play very high pressure in their half or third of the field. This is absolutely necessary since any team that allows opponents into its half of the field that often is going to have to do some serious quality defending, as any laxity can cause quality service into their penalty area possibly resulting in a goal.

The one obvious advantage of low pressure is that there are very many players defending, and the ball is often in front of many players. Low pressure teams often do so because it permits many opportunities for quick counter attacks, as there is often considerable space behind the opposing defense. With extremely fast or highly skilled dribbling attackers this tactic can be very effective. Especially if there are players who can deliver quality service rapidly.

Transition is a case of no choice. All teams that are successful must be able to move quickly from offense to defense and from defense to offense. Teams that are weak in transition are invariably weak teams. In order to develop this the coach must demand it in practice in virtually every activity or the likelihood of a team having good transition is improbable. Obvious implications are open up (be open for whoever won the ball), spread out so as to keep the defense from being very compact. Moving from offense to defense means instant pressure on the ball at your line of defense, also cover and balance. Incidentally every team should be reminded at every game what the line of defense is for that particular game. This is a coach's decision and should always be clear to all players on the team, though this seldom seems to be the case. The exception is if a team never changes the line of defensive pressure, then there is no need to define the line of defense for every game.

The next area that is often overlooked is changing of rhythms of play. This is one of the most sophisticated elements of team tactics. The best way to develop this is in scrimmages with any numbers available to the coach. The scrimmage game has one team play possession with an eye on very safe attacks to score, while the other team attempts to score immediately. Obviously the fast attack team must use long balls more often, seek every opportunity to go forward and score. It must take greater risks. The restriction by the coach can be they must take a shot within 10 seconds (or whatever time the coach thinks appropriate) or within ten touches under penalty of losing possession. The low pressure team may need many changes in point of attack, use abundant layoffs, use their keeper as necessary and all the measures that slow down the game such as slowly taken throw-ins, goal kicks, etc. Obviously the playing fast team does the opposite. THE KEY IS EVERY SIX (OR WHATEVER) MINUTES THE TEAMS CHANGE ROLES. So in thirty six minutes each team will have played the slow and fast rhythm at least 3 times. No matter what the warm-up to this session it also demands alternating slow and fast activities. If possession precedes the scrimmage it also has the two teams reversing roles. For instance, one playing strict possession and the other hitting a target player outside the grid with three passes or less.

A good coaching tactic is starting the scrimmage with a specific score for each team. If the coach wants the red team to play high pressure he might indicate that the red team score is 0 and the blue team has 2 goals and the time left in the match is 15 minutes. For the low pressure the coach might indicate that the team is ahead by 2 goals and wants to play slow, possess the ball a great deal, not take many risks in going forward, use the keeper or what have you. Some coaches prefer to keep the foot on the accelerator at all times because their team seems to lose focus when they play low pressure. Essentially there are no right answers; the coach must decide what is best for his/her specific team. In any case, starting a scrimmage with a specific score and amount of time remaining in the match is a valuable team training concept. In due time simply give the score and time remaining and see what decisions the captains and team make. Did they make a good decision? Do you want to compliment their decisions or tweak it a bit? When coaching reaches this level it really get to be great fun!

All in all, changes in rhythms are the mark of high level successful teams that can play well to any given game score. Many authorities would likely indicate that Brazil, if not the finest at changing rhythms, is certainly one of the best.

After each special situation has been detailed, probably about 15 minutes for each, early in the season, the team is ready for more development. In other words the coach can now just run a scrimmage and in addition to naturally occurring special situations, the coach calls additional ones he wants to rehearse. A few reminders of specific detailed improvements can be offered, and then play again. More than one stoppage every three minutes will not achieve its goal as players will often lose all sense of the game environment that the scrimmage was meant to initiate.

Regarding the offside trap, it is much easier to teach how to beat it than to teach the coordination necessary for it to be effective. If you are thinking you have had great success with it, it may only be a result of the naïve level of the competition not knowing how to beat it. An overlapping player, a speed dribble, and diagonal service can all be devastating in beating the trap. Services not in line with the keeper are important as the ball often simply goes to the keeper. To avoid this strikers should not stay in line with the keeper to receive service. Having one striker constantly on the weak side so he can see the ball, defense and other striker will be devastating. Having strikers learn how to run the line, going east/west instead of straight forward and then cutting behind the defense can really wreck a trap since the player moving can be slower than the defender and still beat him regularly. The moving player invariably beats a stationary player. This is especially true if the defender is moving forward. Running the line first and foremost allows the striker to see the defenders' line of trapping.

Teaching players how to chip effectively is also a great help to successfully beating the offside trap as the ball will not drift to the keeper and the striker can run on to it with room to shoot. Furthermore, beating the trap is more constructive and allows the defending team to become truly competent of defending as a team! Also, defending teams will now have the real challenge of learning to perform the offsides trap against high level offensive tactics.

Most of all team tactics sessions must still embody many ball touches, little talk and many activities that embody the tactic being taught. A quick review of the desired behavior, pattern, possibly a few moments of shadow play and then play, play, play. Players learn by seeing and DOING. After a minute or two of talking, attention wanes enormously.

14

Shortsided League Games and Indoor Training

Bear in mind that the suggestions made in this chapter apply to all levels of teams, though much is focused on developmental players. The increases in technical development and the demand for fitness in short-sided play is increased a great deal for **all levels of players**. In addition, running a training session of a mini tournament of three or four aside lends great motivation to the practice session.

Shortsided play both games and training has great merit for every age level due to the increased ball contact and simplicity of learning the various roles of first, second and third attackers and defenders. With the addition of intelligent inducements, often referred to as restrictions, the shortsided game becomes critically efficient and useful.

Anyone who has seen a full field game among beginning players under the age of twelve can bear witness to the chaos which results. Even inexperienced adults find themselves on the field with twenty-one other players experience a great deal of confusion. Does it have to be this way? The answer is no! The fact that high level adult soccer uses eleven players on a hundred yard pitch does not mean that this arrangement is also best for inexperienced players under twelve years of age. Coaches and program directors should also consider the fact that no country in the world recommends 11 aside for players under twelve! We have already proven the benefits of shortsided games as part of practice sessions. This chapter will present a strong case for shortsided league games and indoor training that hasten the technical and tactical development of players.

This is especially true for young players because they do not strike the ball far and accurately enough to contribute positively to a full field game.

Shortsided league play is preferred to 11 v 11 games for many reasons. Players can only improve through abundant practice with the ball. In a 90 minute professional match, each player actually has contact with the ball for less than two minutes. Young inexperienced players do not possess the ball as well, and have shorter games; therefore, they get very little ball experience in full-sided games. Consequently, they have less involvement, and less fun. This leads to less running off the ball (less support), probably the fundamental element of developing quality soccer at any age. Six aside matches essentially provide twice as much ball experience as full-sided games. Many adult league also use the reduced numbers, particularly co-ed and over 50 (sometimes 60 or some such age) age level leagues. Of course with indoors eleven aside is virtually impossible. Obviously 3 or 4 aside double the ball contact once again. Therefore, 3 aside has about four times as much ball contact, tactical decisions and necessity of movement for transitions as 11 aside.

Shortsided games present better opportunities to be open to receive a pass. Therefore, players tend to go to open space with the realization that they may get the ball. Passing becomes more frequent and purposeful. Increased support raises the level of play above the chaotic bee swarm. This opens the possibility for better use of space and increased vision, which lays the foundation for short passing. Altogether, 6v6 offers appropriate roles, space, skill, power, and time to implement a game that truly resembles soccer.

Skill development is thus enhanced by shortsided games much more than by fullsided games. One technical example is a major aspect of dribbling; namely, feinting. In its early stages, feinting must work in order for players to want to develop it. In the bee swarm, feinting is meaningless, for there are players immediately nearby in every direction! In shortsided games there is space to allow an attacker to beat an opponent with a feint.

Another example is tackling. In 11 v 11 with non-developed players, tackling is of little use. If a player makes a clean skillful tackle, the ball will probably go to another player in the pack. Young players then begin to substitute kicking away at each other for proper tackling. Technique gives way to mindless blasting away at the ball.

What about scoring? Generally, the number of goals scored relates more to the number of people defending a goal rather than the number attacking. Smaller sides allow for more (and possibly better) goals, which multiplies the fun and excitement for young players. Smallsided games are free to use keepers or not. Obviously, with keepers, larger goals are used. In game situations when three aside is played in competitive games it is usually played without keepers and using small goals.

Positional play is greatly reduced in shortsided games. This allows players to develop all-around soccer skills rather than only one aspect of the game. This eliminates the misplaced emphasis on functional training with very young players that are learning the game. With players moving around more freely, the games begin to resemble quality soccer. Everyone must mark at times, and help each other. Teamwork advances rapidly. There is far less standing around. Player mobility, an all important skill, is learned simply by playing.

In shortsided games, the principles governing first, second, and third attackers and defenders come clearly into play. This is the very foundation of tactical awareness. With this understanding, defenders will tend to compact and attackers will spread out, intelligently applying the primary tactic of higher levels of the game. Once this is established, transitions from attack to defense, and vice versa, become simpler, quicker, and more efficient. Three aside is an excellent format for teaching defensive cover, an extremely important skill.

There are even administrative advantages to shortsided leagues. Two six aside games can be played simultaneously on a full soccer field. In fact, the full soccer field with goals is no longer necessary. This eases scheduling problems, and frees up field space, which is at a premium in many areas. A single referee can maintain better control with fewer players and less space. The need for experienced referees is decreased, and more people might become referees since the job becomes easier and less intimidating on the smaller field. Furthermore players would be allowed to let the game become their teacher.

The case for six aside league games could be further supported, citing nearly every aspect of the game. In many countries, shortsided league games serve as the transition from street soccer to full-sided matches, which can occur somewhere around the age of eleven. In America, where street soccer has not yet taken hold, the need for six aside is even more pressing. Sound development of the game depends upon shortsided programs. In adult leagues it reduces fitness demands and simply is more fun.

Maintaining skills during the winter, at least in northern climates, requires indoor training. These programs are generally six aside, not by design, but rather by the space limitations of typical gymnasiums and indoor centers. Nevertheless, they offer most of the advantages of an outdoor six aside experience, including conditioning, technical development, decision making, and tactical awareness.

There are some great advantages to training indoors. The surface is smooth, dry, and level. The ball rolls and bounces more predictably and precisely on a gym floor. Wind, rain, and darkness are not a problem. The change of pace indoors can be stimulating and refreshing. Skill can play a greater role than aggression or power, if we promote it.

In addition to these advantages, there are of course some differences. While not necessarily disadvantages, they may change the nature of the game. The outdoor game calls for sophisticated pacing, whereas the frequent substitutions of the indoor game encourage all-out effort for short periods of time. This can be used as interval training, a very good conditioner for the outdoor game. In terms of tactics, the long ball is virtually eliminated; intermediate and short passes, 1-2 movements, exchanges, and combinational play become the tactical choices. The emphasis is on the greatest possible accuracy and precision.

Also the demand to change roles quickly and completely is greater in the indoor game. Defenders must be able to strike and shoot. When they do, the need for a striker to move into a defensive role is imperative. In short, the indoor experience is excellent for development of `total soccer' and the all important aspects of transition.

We must not overlook the value of the indoor game for shooting. The reduced height and width of the goal calls for greater accuracy and consideration of angles. While the low ball that is not on goal frequently rebounds to permit another opportunity, the high shot is wasted. Indoor players soon learn that keeping the ball down is a good idea. Even so, the chip shot is still an indoor weapon, as it can be used to keep the keeper from coming out too much to deny shots.

Indoor training presents an excellent opportunity to improve individual techniques. Frequently, during the season the need for tactical development and team coordination leaves little time for players to build individual technique. Advanced dribbling training can be a focus of these indoor workouts. Stepovers, chops, sole rolls, lifts, and power drives can be done in order to beat a single opponent. Special attention should be given to feints, shields, and 1v1 activities.

Much of the appeal of indoor training stems from indoor tournaments and professional indoor leagues. This creates enthusiasm and offers models for young players to emulate. There are two distinct sets of indoor rules, however, each bear discussion because they affect player development. A look at the MISL (Major Indoor Soccer League) will give us some background. During the 1970's, when the MISL was in its infancy, the indoor experience was essentially soccer played indoors, very fast in pace, with exciting displays of individual skills and spectacular keeper saves. With the wide use of rebounds off the walls, the action was virtually non-stop. Players depended greatly upon fitness and technical skill. With the ball and players moving and changing directions at such speed, tactical organization was low on the scale of importance. This is quite typical of any game at an early stage in its development.

Much has changed since those early years. Through the middle 80's even the least successful team in the MISL began to show definite signs of advanced tactics in both defense and attack. Definite styles of attack have evolved and clear organization now exists for man up situations that occur spontaneously. Crisp ground passing has increased enormously. Most importantly, there is less use of the boards, and when the boards are used, there is more purpose than previously exhibited.

This brief history points out the direction of the indoor game's development. Although fans, especially the uninitiated, may enjoy the non-stop action of the ball bouncing off the boards, research indicates the less the boards are used, the higher the level of soccer. Many seasons finds the league champion used the boards the least of any team in the league.

This realization gives rise to another type of game, which is known as 'mini-soccer', or Futsal which uses a low bounce ball. Mini-soccer does not use the walls; there is an out-of-bounds. Many coaches find that mini-soccer is a great variation of the out door game. Because this game can be played in unsophisticated facilities, its use as a training method is growing. But the major reason for recommending this form is that it demands and develops playing the ball with control and purpose at all times.

One proponent of the mini version, Anson Dorrance of the University of North Carolina, agrees: "There is no question that mini-soccer is technically the superior form of indoor soccer. Use of walls encourages sloppy technique. When you have a sideline to negotiate, you have to be precise in where you pass the ball, how you take it down the court, and how you beat opponents in tight spaces."

The final plus for the mini-soccer version is that it is an international game, thereby inviting additional experiences. One might add that FIFA has taken a look closely at both forms of indoor soccer and adopted the Futsal version. Indeed there is room for both varieties, especially in terms of player development. As a result they have created the five aside game which is a combination of the two games. It has no walls, but it uses a live "fuzz ball". While all are valid, the deciding factors should be the facility, age and ability of the players. With older players, however, using the walls may hinder their technical and tactical development. Certainly the wall is not an evil in itself; the misuse or overuse of it, however, does present a problem.

The single drawback of Futsal is the dead ball has a tendency to reduce quality collection skill. Experience teaches that a week or two with the regular ball when the outdoor season begins generally takes care of the problem.

For reasonably skilled athletes playing with walls, then, it is wise to limit the use of the walls only for getting the ball to an intended receiver at a specific location or for 'wall passes.' Blind use of the boards only hinders player development in terms of intention when releasing the ball. This misuse could become a major setback for young players, who need a great deal of time and quality coaching to develop constructive passing/receiving ball habits.

All three games contribute to rapid and close collecting, 1-2 movements, quick thinking, and quick, accurate shooting. All teach a great deal about rapid transitions and require players to attack and defend more urgently. Strikers must defend more and defenders must attack more. This develops complete players.

In summation, the quantity of ball contact in shortsided games greatly facilitates technical development of players. There are literally hundreds of restrictions that can be used in training to also further the tactical development of players of all ages.

15

Pedagogical Soccer Coaching Techniques

While this listing contains common methods of coaching soccer, there are also several that have never been in print before as they were created by the author. This is especially true for some of the methods that apply to ages 5-12 as there was a lack of adequate knowledge in this area due to the advent in previous times in which young players played street soccer and so there was little need to perfect some of the very basic skills. Certainly that era of self-generated individual technical development is almost gone in the whole world, though Africa still maintains a bastion of 'street' soccer.

Of course in the last decade a great deal has been to advance knowledge, curriculum and other aspects for youth levels. To my knowledge there is no source that specifically focuses on methods of instruction for soccer. This is not, nor does it pretend to be a research academic endeavor, but instead totally focuses on practical methods garnered from experience. Hopefully you will find several that will assist your coaching development.

A quick run through of what is presented may serve you best, and at a later date you might refer back to this document for something that seems relevant to a topic you are planning on doing for your team. Many are incorporated in the text with the corollary activity, neither the text nor this sort of reminder list totally duplicate each other.

A few concepts are sure to come through if you follow some of what is presented here. Number one transitions for your team will improve. The number of ball touches will greatly increase. The competitive (games emphasis) will raise the level of motivation for your team. In the end you will find coaching more fun, which is bound to spill over to your players.

Certainly some of the items are very mundane, yet a novice coach might find those very items very useful. Due to the fact that the array of methods covers an extremely wide range of items I was unable to create categories to assist you in just choosing what you think might be relevant to your coaching. You can overcome that drawback by skimming through and just spending extra times with the items you find most relevant. The bold face print attempts to categorize the essence of the method and that should help you proceed economically.

1. When defenders are replaced by the player who lost the ball, **do not permit stoppage time.** While this amounts to free passes as the defender picks up the vest, technical skills are still being developed. Play is continuous, without any stop. Also, do not allow the player to hand the vest to the next defender, make her pick it up which eliminates wasted time (reduced repetition) and even adds a bit of flexibility to the exercise. It's no wonder that so many teams are so poor on transition, quick counter attack and not quickly getting on defense when the ball is lost. Teams get in trouble when opponents use quick throw-ins and direct kicks. All training activities must not allow needless stoppages that are nothing more than opportunities for losing focus and creating bad habits. Doing a counter attack or quick defensive recovery exercise will never compensate for constant bad training habits of allowing unnecessary stoppages to transitions in training activities.

2. Along these lines, depending on the specific scrimmage exercise, place a vest about 15 to 30 yards from the goals. Whatever the restriction is for the exercise it is not to be followed if the ball is won in front of the vest. Usually a maximum of 7 (less for advanced teams) touches is permitted before a shot is taken. Passes are included in the number of touches. So in actuality we do quick counter attack everyday while spending zero extra time on quick counter attack. That's economical training at its best! This of course simultaneously trains the defense for quick recovery. The added benefit of this **non-delay on transition situations in training** increases focus, adds ball touches to the session and increases fitness. This eliminates the waste of time of running to nowhere without the benefit of ball touches. Line drills automatically create these bad transition habits. With rare exceptions the line drill must only be used for a minute or two to clarify the tactics with the appropriate techniques. Then immediately, though gradually, go to some sort of live action, continuous motion, defensive pressure, game activity and the like! If the team that lost the ball does not abide by the no shot rule (because they exceeded the number of touches), that team has to touch a goal post while the new

possession team free passes, if the whole team does not touch the goal post before 10 passes (no double passes), they must all touch the opposite goal post from the one they touched the first time.

3. Passing grids for U-6 and U-8 simply generally don't work except for very brief periods of time to introduce a pattern or whatever; they **must have a competitive game**, even if it is as simple as 5 v 1 or similar.

4. A **group of the whole**, starting with everyone with a ball and progress to dozens of other options is necessary from U-6 to U-12 and often beyond that. Later pairs and threes become more common as peers and team become more the nature of the child (players).

5. Whenever possible **coaching position** should be where you can see all groups. This often means arranging the pairs or groups in a way that allows visual access by the coach for the activity. Use of sidelines often alleviates this problem.

6. The coach always has the sun, wind and rain in his face; **players are always in the most comfortable position**, location or whatever.

7. Great clinicians and coaches ANSWER QUESTIONS BY **SHOWING THE ANSWER** THROUGH USE OF THE APPROPRIATE ACTIVITY. GRANTED THIS REQUIRES ENORMOUS EXPERIENCE, ABILITY TO THINK ON YOUR FEET AND TO HAVE A HUGE REPERTOIRE OF ACTIVITIES. In any case I assure you that when dealing with both players and other coaches this technique engenders far greater attention than verbal responses.

8. **Avoid games of elimination and have games of INCLUSION.** When someone is eliminated be sure they have soccer activity to do, such as juggling, ball touches (basic, toe taps, etc.), fitness activities, passing receiving/activities or anything that assures they are not disengaged. Naturally the exception is if they are watching to learn from the activity.

9. **Written plans are best**, but you should know what you have written without looking at it constantly. The written format does just the opposite of what its opponents say. Opponents claim it is rigid or restricting, but in fact it does just the opposite as it allows the coach to move on to the next activity easily when things are not going well. Of course the option to just have the players play with an inducement or even completely free play is always a good option.

10. 75% plus of every session must be competitive and/or is a game. **All sessions should end with free play**, as this is what will be done in

actual matches. The idea of playing all the time with an inducement is taking a great idea and abusing it by over doing it.

11. Good sessions for youth players approach about 1000 ball touches. **Technique is acquired more than taught**---any player who has touched the ball a few hundred thousand times will invariably exceed the youngster who had great instruction but less than half the touches of the youngster with many more ball touches. In warm-up older groups progress to pairs, three's for third man-on concepts and even fours for developing anticipation in such activities as sequence passing. Consider combination play as an integral part of warm-up activities.

12. **BASIC BASICS ARE:** These are the elements that you don't do progressions for, but instead you enforce these elements all the time. **A)** Go to the ball in everything **B)** Not striking a dead ball; everything is done starting with a preparatory touch, except in dead ball situations **C)** Goal side defending **D)** Demand opening up on offense and compacting on defense (pressuring the ball rapidly!) **E)** If you use hand service give exact instructions such as two handed under hand delivery or whatever (older groups should use simple punts! **F)** Demand eye contact in huddle or stoppages, not to be abrasive, but so you know the reaction (receptivity of the players) **G)** Head up to develop vision for; choosing best option, team play, affects looking long but develops habit of playing open man, and much more **H)** Support and Cover (progressions are done for this), but also requires frequent reminders.

13. To start an activity, once players know what to do, just **toss the ball up** in the air near opposing players: This is especially true for shortsided games and scrimmages. In this way you get their attention immediately with no time wasted.

14. Any activity you plan on only doing **once, seriously consider not doing it at all**. The first time you spend so much time teaching the activity and not accomplishing much learning of soccer or having much repetition that there is probably something more productive that you could do. Better to have repertoire of 15-20 activities and do those regularly. Naturally on each occasion try to stretch it further. Demand higher expectation, add a wrinkle to it, reduce the space, even out the numbers or even numbers down, emphasize a different technique or tactic; in short see if players can perfect it to a greater extent.

15. Use the word **INDUCEMENTS** instead of restrictions: Its not just a word game, its an entirely different view; it's positive instead of negative; it's actually the correct word! Therefore think inducements for your shortsided games instead of restrictions.

16. You can give out verbal points for things well done but never pay off because you really are looking for **intrinsic (internal) satisfaction (rewards)** more than extrinsic rewards! I have seen this done by great teachers and adopted it myself; and it works even though you never payoff. If questioned by a child deal with them individually after practice, as they are usually very bright and will understand your explanation. Joey, "It is only a way of me saying you did well." Of course if you prefer tangible rewards, stars, dollar store items, healthy snacks feel free to so, though I do not prefer this method myself.

17. Be sure to have **two or more coaches**. Those that can't find one, usually don't want one. For low levels they may need a band aide and when you lose the group for the one, you may never regain attention. For older ones among the things needed are functional training, keeper instruction, multiple groups, individualized instruction, etc. In youth programs with 12 teams I noticed that the better performing groups had more than one coach irrespective of the level of experience of the coach.

18. Have no fear of throwing in an unrelated activity, often this is shooting, as it has been clearly shown in research that the unrelated item causes INCREASED LEARNING. This is formally called **Contextual Interference** and is researched proven beyond controversy.

19. **Immediate awards** are proven much more powerful than delayed rewards, especially for young players.

20. **Sandwich Approach** is better than saying, "Well done!" "Marie you did well to get to that ball, next time for a short pass use the inside of the foot push pass, and you complete many more passes." Positive opening, correction, how it benefits the player.

21. **Get to practice and games early.** You'll know what your facing that day. Exam day, feminine needs, something that you wanted to discuss with an individual, receive parent communication, illnesses, field preparation, whatever. It gives a chance to make a sensible decision and/or change in your plans.

22. Have **two parents come to half time talks** so they can tell all the others what we are trying to do and this does away with parents

yelling things that conflict with your game plans. Two is good because they can't report their own version. Basically it is a way of disciplining non-supporting parents, having monitors, and for the supportive people they know what the team is trying to do. Clearly this works GREAT!

23. Of course your example from the sideline (coaches and parents) **must allow players to think**, learn from mistakes, coach each other and truly enjoy the game without constant commentary from the coach. 90% of it is not anything the players don't already know. Lynn knows she should have gone outside instead of kicking it to the keeper. Your comment is only aggravating Lynn. Teachers don't go around giving all the answers to the test questions during the test! Does that make it clear? Research is positively clear that if I figure it out myself vs you telling me it is remembered better and longer.

24. **Relays are almost always pairs** instead of two teams. This causes more fitness and more ball touches when ball is involved, and less non-sense that occurs in a line causing boredom and admonishments.

25. **Two or more groups are needed** as often players are standing around for no apparent reason. **Stations** are sometimes effective in having maximum participation. Muscle memory requires many repetitions. It is not what the teacher teaches; it's all about what the learner learns!

26. Telling exactly what the activity is at all times is not a good idea. Sometimes the **guided discovery method** is the best. During the discovery period the coach can refine the diagnosis. Example: We are going to perfect the technical aspects of the wall pass. The plan focuses on the accelerated run, but during the discovery period the coach observes that the all necessary eye contact communication is missing, so instruction starts there instead of starting with the accelerated run aspect! In all cases DO WHAT IS APPROPRIATE TO YOUR GOALS, THE ABSOLUTES OF DO X ALL THE TIME ALWAYS SEEM TO HAVE IMPORTANT EXCEPTIONS.

27. **Summarizing** at the end of a session has been proven to increase learning. This is especially true when the players formulate the summary. It's is okay for the coach once the players have formulated the summary to refine it so that it really gets at the essence of the session. Generally players will get the essence when the session was very good, but none of us has a very good session every time we have a training session.

28. **Use a name** when the suggestion is to an individual. Do not use a name when an item relates to the whole group. Generally **for individual correction we do not provide a stoppage**, but for whole group situations we do a stoppage.

29. **Stoppage procedure: A)** "Freeze" **B)** Walk through of the correction **C)** Optional: Do stoppage correction at speed **D)** Do the stoppage at game speed, clearly indicating when we return to live play by identifying which touch by a given player puts us to live mode; "On Anne's second touch we are playing live." Anne could be the first, second or third person to touch the ball.

30. Never ask players to play at 50% or 20% or 80%. You don't know what you are asking for and the players certainly don't know what you expect. Besides, you are teaching a BAD HABIT by encouraging players to play less than 100%. Much better choices are: crab defender, hands on head, hands behind back, hands on knees, hands on ankles, no body contact or whatever all depending on how much pressure you want. Now you are forcing the defender to use his legs as all good defending first depends on legs, which is a good thing. You also have allowed your offensive success to occur. Everyone is now benefiting from the environment instead of having one group learn and the other obtain a bad habit! Generally we adjust the numbers, have restricted space or provide the amount of space to obtain the degree of pressure desired.

31. Try to set up an environment that allows for all or most of the activities with **a minimum of time consuming changes**. Example: the 6 goals shown are first used for 1v1 to any goal, then 1v1 to a particular goal, then 2v2 to any goal, then 2v2 to a particular goal, the same progression for 3v3 or even 4v4 and then teams go to any goal and then teams go only to the central goal. Maybe you'll have to lengthen the field for the full scrimmage, but you used the same environment economically. Of course it is not always this simple, sometimes you'll set up two different environments in two different locations.

32. For a team of 16 you might want to have 4 **vests of** 4 **different colors**, and one set of 8 for full team possession or scrimmage activities. Dream world would be 8 blue, 6 red, 6 yellow and 4 orange. This would provide for 2, 3, or even 4 teams. Modern culture no longer permits shirts and skins. You could also have one group as Rainbow (meaning no vests) or require white or gray t-shirts for all training. This would reduce the number of vests needed.

33. There are several ways to **facilitate numbers up** to force the team in possession to work quickly. When using cone goals, place a ball on each cone and when one gets knocked off with a shot, the shooting player has to retrieve his ball and play begins immediately with the ball knocked off the cone. With full size goals, simply have a supply of balls in the goal to restart with while the shooter retrieve his errant shot. These rules provide the numbers up and learning to play quickly, urgently and use numbers up effectively. Other ideas: last player to pass ball can go to a knee, errant passer must touch a cone on the side of the field, out of bounds ball must be retrieved by the offending player. You see there are many ways to create the temporary numbers you desire for the purpose you have in mind.

34. For very young age levels: To develop team play and get the superstar to pass, but not discourage him (in fact raise his level) place a midfield line that demands the ball be passed over that line before a shot is taken, but the passer can continue to receive a return wall pass or overlap and still get the ball back or be the scorer. Now instead of discouraging the youngster we have raised his level by having learned to **PASS AND MOVE**. I have a whole paper of over 20 such methods to encourage team play, break up the bee swarm; have teams open up on offense, while never discouraging good skillful play such as team shape instead of rigid positions!

35. Frequently **multiple teams** of three, four teams or even pairs can be best choice. Don't get stuck with the two teams option---use the format that best suits your purpose. Two simultaneous short sided scrimmages are a must on occasion.

36. With intelligent demands sequence passing can foster the all important **anticipation** that every coach struggles to develop. Example: Demand that every player who gets the ball will be able to see (will be facing) the next number of the sequence group. Simultaneously demand much direct crossing from one side of the group to the other. Avoid 'wagon train' circular movement.

37. **Do not allow stoppages**. When doing 4v2 while the new defender is grabbing the vest on the ground encourage at least 2 or more passes during that time. Do that kind of thing in EVERYTHING YOU DO. All the stoppages in training translate to poor transition in the game---habits are very resilient behaviors. This is among the many reasons why lines are dangerous, and yet the literature has almost nothing by line drills line setups in the great preponderance of

publications including even the supposedly highest level soccer publications. So whenever you find a continuation motions exercise be quick to consider it among your primary activities. Of course competitive games are the best.

38. An excellent pedagogical technique is to have the two teams that are about to scrimmage doing the training concept **with their own ball in the same area** of the scrimmage which will follow. This is live, real, the other team in the area provides token defense and cements the concept of the day. Once you see both groups effectively doing the activity you can go to the full competition with a single ball.

39. You'll find that anytime you have outside neutrals (players standing outside the grid) in hundreds of situations it becomes much more game like if after they have been played to they **exchange places with active players of the exercise**. This results in much better transfer of learning to the actual game, which is a critical element to players applying and enjoying an exercise. Anything that forces players to be active thinkers will aid application to matches.

40. There are hundreds of exercises that can be vastly improved by requiring players to move from **one grid to another** (move from one area to another) as opposed to staying in the same place. Example: Once players are competent in 4v2 do the exercise without grid cones. Every time the ball goes out of control to a distant location the entire group moves continuing the 4v2. When the four players in possession cheat by maintaining an unfair distance to each other, simply take the worst offender and have her be a defender. This should allow this much more game realistic approach to become habitually appropriate. Side by side grid change activities also can demand MOVEMENT FROM ONE GRID TO ANOTHER.

41. Fixing the insanity of failing Cubillas, the Peruvian soccer superstar, at our American licensing courses probably occurred from a lack of knowledge of how much South American training is done. The technique is so simple and effective. You just begin to play and the coach simply sticks to one major point that he is trying to get across. It's the **pinnacle of the play method**. Example: The coach wants the outside backs to get forward on offense, so every opportunity that looks like it would have been a good idea he reminds the player who could have done so to do it. This is often done without a stoppage, but sometimes with a stoppage. I have witnessed this exact activity by a Peruvian coach of a men's team that I would train occasionally. Anson Dorrance used the exact same topic and method with his

University of North Carolina team in a spring season training session in which I participated. Wendy Gebauer used me as a cone---very humbling.

42. There are probably legitimately about 50 distinct exercises for the multiple gate activity. There are numerous ways to score. I often have **multiple winners**; more than one individual, pair or team winning. Example: First one going through all gates wins, but also the player who has her head up and avoided collisions gets a point. Always try to see them doing things well. Tony DiCicco says, "Catch them being good."

43. My friend Mark Nicole, EUFA A License, does something usually frowned upon, but it works great with the young players. No matter what he is coaching, he always finds ways to **be very positive**. If the youngster beat the defender he compliments that, if the defender stripped the ball from the attacker he compliments that. Compliment whoever did well.

44. **Keeping Pedagogy**: Do almost all of the training in relation to a goal and focus on crosses, breakaways, special situations and distribution in game simulated situations. Actual crosses, various players from different angles with varied numbers from zero on up to having defending should all be dealt with. Likewise for distribution and special situations. There simply is too much training done that does not simulate game situations and therefore is not as economical as it can be.

45. While there may be an infinite number of training environments and activities, one method that is very useful and seldom ever seen is **training of pairs**, and thus it is listed here. Some coaches assign the pairs and ask the pair what they think would be the most useful concept to work on and then allocate a period of time for that to be done. One of the coaches may help pairs that need someone or have another pair be the 'bodies' necessary for a given pair to achieve their objective and then the pairs reverse roles.

46. **Four aside games with four goals** is a pedagogical method, an activity, a game and many other things, but it is so fundamental to training all teams that it is mentioned here as a pedagogical method. It has dozens of various wrinkles depending upon the objective of the coach. Two simple examples are: The Dutch often use it for teaching change in point of attack using the discovery method instead of direct instruction. Ajax uses it for functional

246

training employing the diamond configuration.

47. For **training players in 1 vs 1**, there are almost an infinite number of possibilities. It is mentioned here as a reminder that it must be done frequently and competitively often!

48. Always consider the **fundamental level** such as doing it with a still ball, add slow movement, add speed, add token defense, or full defense and finally perform it in a game. The game level is generally having numbers up that allows the skill to be done successfully by adjusting the space and number of players on each team. For defensive topics, numbers down is often employed. Many ways to facilitate this have been enumerated in prior items in this pedagogical guide.

49. **Define cheering** to deal with problem parents. Calling out to players with the ball is coaching, not cheering, and is not to be done by parents. Calling out a player's name fits into the same category. Coaching is not the spectator's role.

Hopefully by just reading these pedagogical techniques you will find yourself being more cognizant in the use of a specific method of doing a given skill. You need not memorize any of this, once you know there are many ways to make happen what you want to teach you find yourself using more advanced methods in detail. More than likely the pedagogies that you will recall are the ones suited to your personal style of coaching.

This synopsis of coaching techniques is included even though most of these strategies were clarified throughout the book in conjunction with the appropriate activity. This is just a sort of reminder list for your convenience.

16

Warm Up, Stretching, Cool Down

One of the most abused terms in many team sports is the word warm-up. Certainly among players there is the confusion, or at least a lack of clarity in knowing the difference, between warm-up and stretching. Warm-up is positively needed to prepare for rigorous exercise, while stretching is controversial. There is no verification for static stretching, although most informed coaches believe in dynamic stretching. Post rigorous exercise seems to show stretching for extending the range of motion (increasing performance) and injury prevention as useful.

There is no definitive research to indicate the amount of time necessary for physical and mental warm-up, but most informed sources would give a figure of at least 15 to 40 minutes depending on temperature, weather and other factors. For training, 15 minutes is more common since many coaches will not follow the warm-up with the most rigorous exercise of the day. For games, 40 minutes is more common because players are expected to perform at full capacity when the whistle blows.

Many teams do not warm-up adequately as indicated by Doc Counsilman of Cortland and Indiana University who revolutionized the entire topic. He was the swim coach for Indiana University when in the 1964 Olympics the Indiana swimmers on Team USA scored more points than all the other countries combined, including the USA non-Indiana University entrants. This was only one of his monumental accomplishments, which he claimed was due to a proper warm-up, which included two miles of swimming before any competition or practice session. Prior to Doc Counsilman there was a fear by most that too much energy devoted to warm-up would drain the athlete and decrease performance.

In any case there is definite evidence that proper warm-up, MOVEMENT that results in sweating, increased heart beat and breathing is necessary. There is little denigration of stretching, but the problem remains that many confuse stretching with proper warm-up. Many still use the practice of static stretching which after a very rigorous warm-up and used intermittently with much movement may even be helpful. What is definitely known is that extensive stretching in terms of range of motion and time period will definitely reduce power in the subsequent activity. The main issue here is that extensive warm-up is necessary, while pre-game and pre-training extensive stretching is to be discouraged. Most research leans heavily toward extensive stretching in the warm down which follows rigorous exercise.

While mentioned frequently and throughout this text continuous hydration with possible added emphasis in the 24 hours prior to rigorous exercise is extremely important. The best time to review the game plan is well before the match. Players are more cognitive (less emotional) at that time than moments before the match. Furthermore, we do not want a long sedentary period of time after the warm-up and the beginning of the match. Often the National Anthem and player introductions are already a bit more time than desired between warm-up and play. Note that the word review was used in regard to the game plan, as the plan should have been clearly explained prior to match time. Normally the day before is best. This allows for input, questions, and more thorough explanation. It might be that the coach wants to do a walk-through of some of the more important points for maximum clarity.

The following in no way is prescriptive, and a version for training could be about 15 minutes. With young players all warm-up and fitness can easily and best be done with the ball. For older groups many prefer a light jog to start the warm-up. Some use a very light stretching for social (team building) and mental preparation for easing into more rigorous exercise. Dribbling individually is a good idea, with many coaches moving to pairs or even three's. Juggling for a couple of minutes is not a bad idea, though some prefer this be done in three's with two touches, which means control the ball and pass, which has an enormous amount of game relatedness, as opposed to individual 'circus' juggling. Heading, due to the courage component, needs constant refreshment, not only for technical needs, but also for being certain there are no refusals during matches. A smallsided game with technical/tactical restrictions is used for training. For games an unrestricted smallsided game, or even more likely a possession activity is appropriate. Possession insures that the decision making process (the mind) as well as the body is tuned up for the match.

A simple keeper warm-up should simulate everything done in a game. Among the many activities: some ball gymnastics, goal to goal shuffle saves, diving from knees to standing, rolling throws, overhead throws, punts (into a net or receiver at midfield on touchline), goal kicks, basket catches, receiving a variety (air, ground, line drives) of firmly struck balls, and some simulated contact with tossed balls. Crosses, special situations and breakaways are taken care of in the shooting exercise fully explained below.

In many cases at the youth and high school level a half field is not available well in advance and thus all of the above can be accomplished in small areas. For the shooting, crossing, and special situations the following on the big field can be accomplished with the goal keeper in goal. The original version was seen at the University of Central Florida coached by Amanda Cromwell and later modified. Many will also modify this exercise to their purposes. Long ball striking near the midfield by defenders is one useful common activity practiced by many coaches. Corners kicks could easily be inserted into the basic shooting activity.

The following diagram basically clarifies the entire shooting activity for the whole team.

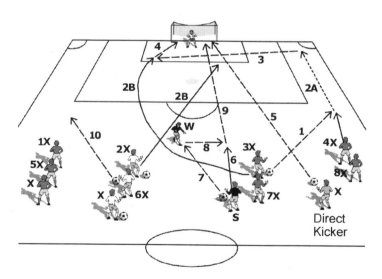

Diagram 106: Showing a full team warm-up shooting drill that incorporates wing service, shooting, direct kicks by the player that takes directs, and one touch shots off the wall pass by strikers.

As with all line drills keep the exercise moving quickly. The next person should start the next movement when the previous player served the ball, not after the shot was taken. Be certain everyone who goes in a line who should have a ball, has one. NO ONE SHOULD HIT A DEAD BALL EXCEPT THE DIRECT KICKER ASSIGNED PLAYER; EVERYONE ELSE ALWAYS TAKES A PREPARATORY TOUCH EXCEPT FOR ONE TOUCH SHOTS! Note where the balls are located to start the exercise.

Step 1: With the team arranged as in the diagram 3X passes a ball to space for 4X who dribbles goal line and serves a cross. 2X, having left his ball, crisscrosses 3X and they occupy the near and far post as shown. Note the bent run by 3X. Movement Numbers 1, 2, 3 & 4 in the diagram.

Step 2: The direct kick taker attempts a shot: Emphasis is on goal, and definitely not over the top. After 4 or 5 rounds (shots) from the location shown, the direct kick player moves to a similar location on the left side. If more than one person takes direct kicks, after one has completed about 8 shots (4R + 4L) the other player takes his turn. Number 5 in the diagram.

Step 3: Next, the striker takes a couple of dribbles, makes eye contact with the wall passer (W) and takes the return pass for a one or two touch shot. If ball is set up nicely, one touch shot, if the wall passer gives a poor ball or even an intentional air ball a preparatory touch is taken. In short the striker does what was called for---no unnecessary touches! The wall passer moves to the ball. Numbers 6, 7, 8 & 9 in the diagram.

Step 4: 6X passes a ball for the next player 1X who dribbles goal line and serves as was done on the right side in situation #1 in the diagram. Number 10 in the diagram initiates the movement.

Step 5: The entire procedure is repeated from right to left.

This should be done in a practice session before it is used in a game. We never want to overload players with new information on game days. The second or third time this is done it moves along quickly and easily. This is definitely a line exercise that requires that everyone stay focused and communicates with one another. There should never be more than two strikers in the striking line. Strikers must go to all lines, be servers, crisscross for shots and play wall pass shots from distance.

Personally I would never consider playing a game without having some kind of actual playing such as a possession game. We always want to warm-up the mind, decision making, as well as the body before a match. The shooting activity really is a whole lot simpler than appears in the diagram above.

The concept to keep in mind is that the warm-up touches on what will be done in the game. A clear definitive sign of an adequate warm-up is increased breathing, increased heart rate and sweating.

After the game a proper warm-down in the neighborhood of 10 minutes is generally adequate. Significant stretching should occur at this time.

Game discussions are best for the next session when players can be more attentive, emotions and fatigue are not interfering with the analysis. Often the next sessions will have components in them that relate to the match, so this is very appropriate. Also brief discussion with assistants and captains can have taken place so that the discussion is more comprehensive and has more support. Obviously, items that conflict or interfere with the plans of the head coach are eliminated, reduced in emphasis or simply explained as items that other team members thought significant, but will not be reflected in the teams training session at this time. Note how truthful this is, and yet avoids developing hidden or hurt feelings. It shows respect for others opinions, but forthrightly indicates that this will not be the direction of our present training.

Meals should be consumed right after vigorous training or games. Replenishment for the depletion is far more beneficial when consumed soon after the strenuous exercise. Within the hour as opposed to even two hours after has been found to be very significant! If this is near impossible consider quality energy bars or fruit to bridge the time between the vigorous session and a proper meal. This becomes even more crucial with inappropriate tournament schedules that are common in the United States.

Though not yet documented this may even be a bit more crucial with females due to proneness for iron deficiency, their calcium needs and the female triad considerations.

17

Continuing Growth in Developing Soccer In the United States

While good coaches develop their players as people and athletes, they also develop themselves as role models and teachers. Each season they seek to improve their craft. While continuing to observe matches, attend clinics and licensing courses, read articles, mentor others and get mentored, watch videos, they also learn from their own meditation. Though this description may depict a professional coach, it also applies to the part-time volunteer coach who seeks excellence. Each year, the youth coach may get to only a few college or pro games, or clinics, or read only one book. But making a child's soccer experience a positive one requires knowledge as well as passion. The coach who shows his studiousness in regard to the game provides a better model.

While guidance from informed sources is important, the personal reflections of the coach should not be underestimated. Such consideration allows the coach to solve specific problems, which often relate to communication and motivation. Frequently, the coach knows the player, the family, the community, and the program better than anyone else. No soccer `expert' knows the particular group as well as the assigned coach does. Combining the coach's own contemplation with outside resources creates a role model that will be respected and remembered for a lifetime. If this could be turned into a formula for the successful youth coach, it might look like this:

Knowledge of Children + Caring + Soccer Knowledge = Competent Coach
(developmental stages)   (love)   (technique, tactics,   (positive lifetime physiology, psychology)   memories)

The role model image is the single most important feature. Respect, character, morality, manners, controlled language, even appropriate attire all contribute to a quality role model. A clear set of values and an approach to discipline, while unique to each individual, are also essential. The quest for improvement is easily sensed and appreciated by players. They need to know that we all continue to learn, and must learn, in order to grow.

Again, the criteria for excellence have little to do with wins and losses. A commitment to fun, participation, and emotional and athletic development reflect a coach who feels that both the players and the game are important. With this attitude, the coach will not only grow in the activity, but also derive greater enjoyment. This provides a role model whose behavior conveys the message: "It's hard work, but it's worth doing!"

To deal with the work load, coaches need assistants to handle the various duties, such as communication, information, equipment, meetings, transportation, and special training sessions. Parental involvement alleviates problems and helps build for success. Administrative ability also allows the coach to concentrate on coaching, a prerequisite for the success of a team or program.

These enlightened approaches are beginning to make inroads virtually everywhere in American youth soccer. More coaches are becoming sensitive to a child's needs; more coaches are becoming aware of how we learn; more coaches with playing experience are bringing more knowledge to their teams. The National Youth Sports Coaches Association is training and licensing thousands of coaches every year. The United States Soccer Federation and the National Soccer Coaches Association of America have both created new advanced courses that focus on youth soccer. More parents are sharing their children's enthusiasm for the great game. The game continues to grow, change, and become more competitive. The game of ethnics is now American. At this moment, we are an emerging soccer nation! The success of the 1994 FIFA World Cup in the US, the world dominance of our National Women's Team and the impressive showing in FIFA World Cup 2002 by the National Men's Team are indicators of positive development.

A World Cup trophy, only a dream now, will one day come. Due to our large population, cultural and climatic variety, wealth, nutrition, number of players, history of accomplishments, and most of all, our great athletes, success is inevitable when we become a true mature soccer nation.

Still, the pessimists fear the extinction of soccer. The fact remains, however, that the NFL, MLB, and the NBA took well over fifty years to establish themselves, and only after repeated failures. Others decry low scores, ignoring the fact that today's young players will patronize a game that they love and understand. The informed appreciate the entire game, seeing goals as a bonus for creative passing and dribbling. They understand goal mouth chaos, great collections, powerful shots, athletic saves, accurate heading, third man-on combinations, turning from pressure, etc. In the meantime, our better college teams can serve as models as well as MLS and WPA is giving youngsters hope of a career in playing professionally, and we are actually exporting players to other countries. But a professional league is only one aspect of developing the sport. The game will advance when it can draw from a large pool from all classes of American society, some likely to come from less affluent economic classes. As the great game reaches further into the inner city, mental toughness will reach new levels. The player for whom there seems to be no alternative to success plays on against seemingly impossible odds. Affluent America's form of street soccer, backyard soccer, will also contribute. With millions of boys and girls playing soccer in the cities, suburbs, and countryside, the talent pool deepens. The growing number of leagues and youth tournaments will bring players from every social strata together on the soccer field.

Of course, we may be several decades away from this point, but we must first realize where we want to go if we are to get there. It is not too much to say that we want to go where baseball, football, basketball and hockey are; where boys and girls play their games in streets and backyards long before they join organized teams; where kids flock to professional games and read about their heroes in every issue of Sports Illustrated, newspapers, the internet, etc.

This is not to say that we want to replace any of these sports. Such a notion is absurd. Apple pie has not disappeared, even after hundreds of additions to the American diet. Pizza, tacos, strudel, hamburgers and hot dogs coexist, as will soccer and other sports. Any attempt to suppress the game will only make it stronger. The United States will likely be a five major team sport nation instead of four. History bears this out: once we were a one sport nation, then two, then three and possibly someday it could be six.

But how do we get there? We can begin by looking at other countries, then adapting this information to our unique situation. The entire body of experts recognizes 'independent'(so called 'street' soccer) playing, visible heroes, a strong positively unified national organization for players, quality officiating, and capable sports medicine as the key elements of soccer success in any country, including the United States. The need for more informed coaches continues to be vital. But along with this, we need to step up the promotion of the game in the inner city, for there is little major network exposure and far too little cooperation with nearby suburban programs. Television provides visible heroes that give young urban athletes the inspiration to excel; suburban leagues give them the opportunity to play on good fields with decent equipment and organized coaching. The athletic ability of the urban athlete could then combine with the organizational ability of the suburban program. Of course, there is a need for a strong national body to organize the various sections, ages, and levels of the game. The USSF has proven itself capable of winning the trust of the soccer world and FIFA by landing the responsibility of the World Cup. This event has showcased our talent for organization and promotion; if we can do this for the whole world, we can certainly do it for our own country. With the most sophisticated communication, information and media networks in the world, we certainly should be able to promote our sport. Quality officiating, which can only evolve from more experience and selection than is now possible, will be a natural consequence of soccer's growth in the next few decades. Officials who have played the game bring a wealth of knowledge and experience, which can only improve their performance and everyone's enjoyment of the game.

Also, training and sports medicine for soccer must reach the same advanced levels that it has in other American sports. At present it is only average, but as more sports medicine personnel deal with soccer training and injuries, the level of understanding will naturally improve. The increasing knowledge of the specifics of soccer will lead to a better understanding of the special stresses that the game puts on the player. Our outstanding equipment for general fitness and athletics will help bring training methods to state-of-the-art.

One aspect of training that Americans can not afford to ignore deals with the unlimited substitution permitted in most American soccer. At the youth level, this helps to develop the bench and often results in victories. Even when this is not the case, all must play. The coaches who lament their lack of bench strength are usually the ones who have not developed their substitutes. Even the notion of a sub or second string is antithetical to youth sports; everyone should get to be a starter some of the time. Furthermore, players should be allowed to play full uninterrupted halves instead of being shuffled in and out of games.

But free substitution at the advanced level may cause some problems. It tempts a team to play constant high pressure; this creates players who are mentally impoverished to play a whole match. A quality midfielder who is not replaced develops a keen sense of pacing, while those who are substituted invariably lack this important skill. Those players with Olympic, professional, or world class ability must learn to play whole games in order to pace themselves properly for high level tactics, skills, and the varied rhythms of the game.

Lastly, there must be an evolution in soccer coaching, particularly at the youth lower levels. As players become coaches, there will be a natural elevation to a higher stage of development. Player coaches develop thinking, especially in the area of purposeful passing, which is difficult to achieve without player experience. The most important coaching advance will have to be in the understanding of player development. Presently, most soccer coaches know what elements of the game to teach, some know how to teach these elements, but few know when to teach these various elements. Proper development depends upon the right step at the right time, based upon sound principles of physical and emotional growth. This book is an attempt to elucidate these steps. This development of players in America most emphatically begins with young players' introduction to the sport. The emphasis is on fun, ball control, and attacking skills; technique and tactics are developed simultaneously. With this background, the child's first league experience should be shortsided, stressing player roles in attack as the foundation for small group tactics. Then by age eleven or twelve, these players would be more capable of the full-field game, continually increasing technical and decision-making skills, as well as introducing player roles in defense. At age thirteen and beyond, As players mature functional training could begin to help players build on their strengths and minimize their weaknesses at particular positions.

Within this framework, there is still room for a variety of coaching techniques and styles. Soccer has the great advantage of drawing from a worldwide body of knowledge. We can learn a great deal from information, systems, styles, and coaches of countries with forty fifty or more years of high level international experience with accompanying professional leagues. On the other hand, to ignore these sources is to reinvent the wheel. Also, it is perverse to profess a body of knowledge gathered from only one source, whether it be one expert or one nation. Generally, by copying one nation, coaches are limiting growth. Even recently migrated coaches must learn from countries other than their own. Because our climate, culture, fields, player mentality and attributes, and coaching are somewhat different, the answer is not to copy Italy, Argentina, Germany, England, Holland, or any other single nation. We need people who are truly international in their knowledge.

This could be an American or a foreigner. In any case, it must be someone who is willing both to study the world game and to recognize our total cultural milieu, our physicality, mentality, disposition, problem-solving, values, and creativity. We do not need foreigners trying to implant their country's system in the United States; nor do we need Americans who are ignorant of the world game. Only from this global view, which is another way of saying from this philosophy, can we maximize our success.

All successful soccer powers learn from each other. Therefore, we must understand all the various systems and styles. Only then can we build an original system based upon our own players, and therefore best suited for us. The most successful team styles seem to evolve from the uniqueness of the players and coaches.

With that in mind, can we describe how the American system might evolve? While somewhat speculative, it is worth considering. First of all, it is probable that our system will be very versatile. With our literacy, intellect, and temperament, our players will master a well-rounded repertoire of soccer skills and tactics. As grass roots soccer spreads, there will be no deficiency in individual skill. Add to this our extreme coachability, admired by many visiting coaches from all over the world, and we have the markings of extraordinarily versatile teams.

Our diverse climates and ethnic backgrounds also affect a variety of styles. And our athletes play many sports in which tempo changes are common, like basketball, football, hockey, and tennis. Thus they will be able to change speed and play both high and low pressure. Our leaning will be toward high pressure because of our moderately cool climate, quantity of athletes, their collective temperament, and physical attributes. Transition is very sophisticated and will require some time to develop, as will changes of rhythm.

Due to American football and culture, there will be some tendency to be quite physical. This must be used constructively, not at the expense of skills and tactics. The emphasis must be on honest courage for 50/50 balls as opposed to playing the man. Our size, strength, and speed will enable us to exploit the air ball.

The abundant use of hands in other sports should carry over into soccer. The throw-in will be a major weapon of penetration, not just a way to get the ball back into play. Of course, there are also implications for keepers. Americans' excellent hand strength and coordination, combined with our great size and courage, has already helped produce world class keepers who are playing in the highest levels in the world. Our large population would seem to assure uniform strength in all positions, with great depth on the bench. While enormous geography tends to limit us, our affluence will help to overcome this. Our lack of proximity to any country except Mexico and Canada hampers much international experience, but our wealth permits long trips. American players as young as ten years are traveling all over the globe for soccer experience. However, at the same time our high level international experience with players in Europe is escalating rapidly.

Overall, contending teams from America will be fast, versatile, tending toward high pressure, excellent at one touch passing, able to control and exploit the air game, and anchored by excellent keepers. Eventually, we will develop coaching techniques which rank with the most advanced in the world.

This book has been an attempt to introduce some of these techniques. It stresses fun, participation, and development over winning. It focuses on integrating technical and tactical development as the necessary foundation for functional training. It supports a bias toward smallsided games. It clarifies and applies the principles of player roles to all aspects of the game. It emphasizes attack over defense, decision-making over drill, and developing players over collecting trophies. And it elucidates what to teach, as well as how and when to teach. While not a complete guide, this book does represent a complete approach, where knowledge and love of the player combine with knowledge and love of the great game of soccer.

All responses are welcomed and I hope this book has inspired many to learn even more about The Great Game.

Appendix I
The Prepared Coach

This appendix item focuses on equipment and how to use it. The philosophical preparation of the coach has been discussed in previous chapters. The actual business of coaching also entails a mental plan, which includes a long range plan for a season or even a few years, a short range plan which could involve a single session, and perhaps even an intermediate plan for a week or two. While the long range plan may be more general, the daily plan enumerates specific activities to achieve a specific goal.

Therefore, for each practice session, a clearly defined written plan is almost imperative. For a single session it may be just a 3x5 card, as long as each activity is clear in the coach's mind. A Soccer Practice Planner is recommended, as it organizes a whole season according to sound principles of player development and effective practice. In this practice planner, a coach can keep attendance records, a seasonal team plan, individual objectives and progress, and daily practice plans. Recording what has been covered and what still needs instruction is just as important as planning for a given session.

Once a coach has a plan and a safe playing area, it is time to obtain the necessary equipment. The tools of the soccer trade are relatively inexpensive, but there is the usual range of quality and price.

Ironically enough, one of the most important ingredients for a safe and effective practice or game is practically free, yet often neglected: WATER! Studies show that a player can lose as much as two liters of water per hour. Such a rapid fluid loss can reduce the blood volume to the muscles which need it most. The result can be loss of drive and concentration, often cramps in healthy athletes are rarely caused by low levels of potassium, salt, calcium, or magnesium.

The amount of salt that they lose during a regular match should cause no harmful effects, such as cramps; but dehydration can. If dehydration is allowed to occur, neither salt tablets, oranges, nor bananas will eliminate or prevent cramps. Children on balanced diets should have ample electrolytes, minerals, and vitamins to make it through soccer games, only needing water.

Players must replace their fluids. The fluid should not have high concentrations of sugar or salt. Concentrations of 2.5% or less are fine. There should also be water available during the game when a player needs to quickly replace fluids. The water should be cool, and players should be encouraged to drink it even before they feel thirsty. The sensation of thirst can come along after the actual need for fluids. Allow plenty of water breaks, especially during hot weather. After matches electrolytes can be valuable for rapid recovery.

The coach or assistant should have several balls for practice, but in many cases with youth teams, it is best to require players to bring their own ball. This ensures that each player has a ball, encourages touches of the ball before and after the training session, and allows for a warm-up if the coach is detained. It also means they might touch the ball on their own. And it removes a burden for the coach who has other items to carry. The coach should have several balls for those players who have forgotten, or came from a place other than home.

These soccer balls carried by the coach should be the same as those used in matches. At least on their home ground, players should be using a ball which they used in shortsided or scrimmage activity during training sessions. There are situations where balls are given special treatment for specific reasons. For example, they may be under inflated for heading activities, or over inflated to simulate a match which will be played on hard ground. A pump and needle are therefore necessary.

The prepared coach also has an adequate medical kit, including a first aid guide. Other necessities include large gauze, ointments, and tape. Coldpacks are not as good as ice, but should be included for occasions when ice is not available. The kit should at least suffice until a trainer, ambulance corps, paramedic, or physician can take over. All emergency contact numbers should be available, perhaps on the outside of the kit. Extra shoe laces can be kept in the kit. If eye glare is part of the kit, it should be used in a practice session to help the player safely adjust to it. Avoid introducing new elements at a time when there is match excitement.

For shortsided and scrimmage activities, scrimmage vests are needed to ensure clarity. Scrimmage vests allow many activities to go smoothly and avoid confusion. Besides, this simulates the actual game situation!

A whistle, while many prefer not to use one can help those whose voices do not carry well. Some sort of coaching board for explanations can also be included, but hopefully not over used. While I do virtually all my conditioning with the ball some may prefer other methods, therefore for older players fifteen and older who require conditioning work, a necessary tool is a stopwatch for taking pulse rates and timed activities are useful. Players should learn how to take their own pulse. After conditioning work, players should count their pulse for thirty seconds, then multiply by two for the actual rate. Fitness levels require a rate over 150, but for more mature players, serious fitness requires even higher heart rates. A good training session will get the heart beat to this range several times in a light session and possible ten to twelve times in sessions that emphasize fitness. Double check with a doctor and be positive to know the medical histories of your players. Be extremely assertive in gathering this information from parents as many do not like to share this data for various reasons. One way to have them come forward consistently is to have them realize that you are save harmless because you solicited the data and they withheld it! Mention that if they care to share data in private this is certainly acceptable.

Some type of markers are needed; they may be cones, disks, corner flags (or obstacle course markers). These can be used to lay out grids, small fields, goals, and obstacle courses. Of course, these areas would ideally be lined out with a field marker, but portable markers allow more flexibility. For dribbling and accurate passing practice, obstacle course markers are very useful. They can also serve as small goals. Though they may stick out of an equipment bag somewhat, their lightness and versatility make them a very functional tool.

A single container or equipment bag allows the parent volunteer to quickly prepare for practice, thus making the job easier, more efficient, and more fun. On game days, an extra game shirt of each color is in order. As virtually all play requires shin guards for every player, extra guards become necessary. Home games require corner flags, nets, net fasteners, pegs, and team benches. A scorebook should be kept beginning about the time players reach the age of fifteen.

If one is predisposed in this direction, it can begin much earlier, but careful use should be made of it. It should not be used as a discussion piece. While a scorebook can reveal much information to help in choosing and designing training activities, it is not usually helpful to share all of this information directly with the players.

Since shooting should be part of every practice, goals are necessary. Practice goals should be the same size as match goals. These should be down-sized for players under twelve. Attackers should practice shooting at goals with nets. The time spent putting the nets up and taking them down is made up by not having to retrieve so many shots.

For safety, enjoyment, economy and versatility, goals of all sizes must be portable; that is, able to be easily carried by two to four people. On fields with permanent goals, the goal mouth is invariably bare. Without turf, players' falls are more serious, keepers' dives are more dangerous, and play becomes unpredictable, causing more collisions and injuries. With unpredictable bounces, tactics and strategy break down. Chance replaces control and skill. Added to these safety and enjoyment factors, the economy of portable goals becomes obvious when consideration is given to the high financial and time cost of repairing turf. Injuries and lawsuits decrease when goals can be moved to safer areas. Portability not only allows for different size playing areas, but also for different goal configurations, such as sideways, back-to back, or diagonally, depending on the objective of the exercise.

Goal size is important! A full-size goal for younger players rewards bad shooting habits and technique, while punishing good keeping habits and technique! This is absurd. Goal size must be appropriate in terms of the field-size, the size and number of players, and whether or not there is a keeper. In any case having all the necessary equipment in ready and safe condition will greatly facilitate the success of your training sessions.

Appendix II
Giving Players Ownership of The Game

Don't be concerned if you do not like any of the suggestions for giving players ownership that are listed here. It is of no consequence, but if you want to truly foster the total growth of your players, be certain to find ways to give them ownership of their soccer and their lives! How you do it is not important, but that you do it is extremely important.

Ajax and other prominent clubs are turning very young players loose to find who the natural leaders are. One technique they use is to put the vests and balls on the field and have the coaches off in the distance to **observe which player(s) takes charge** of setting up a game. This is only one technique among hundreds. Maybe the most powerful ways to develop ownership of the game and leaders is during a session to **see who tries to lead others**. Another is for the coach not to pick the teams, but may **assign two captains** to choose the teams. When I do this I have a 3 second rule, if you don't name or point to someone in 3 seconds you lose your turn and your team has to play shortsided. It never happens because they get the idea that I am trying to get across. Maybe better still, just tell the **youngsters to make up two teams** without even assigning captains.

Sam Snow had eight year olds **set up the cones for the grids** for 3 v 1 activity. Within 15 minutes of the session it was unbelievable how much the players took over. I am not a big fan of the team **choosing its captain(s)**, but certainly this is a possibility.

Demanding that the cones get picked up, vests put away, goals moved or whatever **without assigning** any particular individual(s) is another way to foster player ownership of the game. Maybe you want to point out who didn't help while all the others worked. Maybe you want to ask the **question of that individual** why they think they should not help the others. Maybe you want to let it all go until a player gets upset with the culprit, and then let them solve the issue. Possibly doing all of these things is probably going too far. Maybe the coach is abrogating his responsibility by not at least taking care of some of these issues.

One coach at the end of the session does not say anything about equipment and simply declares "We're done". Walks to the area where play-

267

ers have their water and personal equipment and just waits for all the equipment to be picked up. If someone goes to the same place she simply asks, **"Where are you going?"**. Interesting enough they then start helping the others pick up the equipment. Sometimes less is more.

The point is, it would seem that all successful human activity demands a degree of discipline. The question is, can the coach find ways to develop discipline that the players **impose on themselves**.

I saw one youth coach ask the parent of a 10 year old boy to "Please put down his bag---Chris, please pick up and carry your own soccer bag." There was no fuss about it, the player complied and maybe he learned something. I'm not sure if he was disciplining the child or the parent. Probably he was doing both. In the case I saw it was done so simply and clearly that it appeared to get the job done without any hard feelings. In any case if players are to begin to assume responsibility for their game, these little details need to be attended to.

Another technique is the **fund raising** non-participant doesn't get any share of the funds raised? This can be done with or without warning so the child really gets the message of what team really means. Our team took extensive European trip that included the Dana Cup and our fundraising was handled in this manner. First of all, the trip was made as a cultural/soccer trip that encompassed London Theatre, our girls playing a no coached African boys team, a lecture on comparative education, a home stay in Germany, attendance to a men's professional match in Denmark, geology lectures by yours truly, a castle visitation, attendance to Lego Land and a few other experiences. For those who are thinking it was not a soccer trip I assure it was, we won the first six games in a row at the Dana Cup, although I can't say the competition was excellent, and lost in the semi-finals to Hjorring 3-0, the home club of the Dana Cup that had several national team players. The players' were 15 years old at the time and the players and parents still rave about the trip that took place 10 years ago! It had soccer, culture, education and fun!

Choice model is another method of empowering players to own their game. In this instance the coach has two good alternative productive activities in mind, verbalizes the choices to the team, and players choose one of the two alternatives. **Honoring players request** for a given activ-

268

ity is still another way to help youngsters take ownership of their soccer experience.

Before addressing the team the **assistant coaches and captains give me their input**. Their thoughts are given honest sincere consideration, but not all suggestions are shared with the team. Generally there is a great effort to keep all the data in one or two neat, simple and clear theme(s). Since there is often mention of those suggestions, and particularly good ones receive recognition, there are many worthwhile thoughts shared to the team. In a 10 minute half time: 2 minutes for input from captains and assistants while all get hydrated; 6 minutes talk with input from the whole team; and 2 minutes more of rest and players exchanging thoughts with each other. This is the goal, of course many variations occur, but there is never less than a minute on each end of the discussion of the plan for second half. Furthermore, we always are on the field on time for the game to proceed. I immediately mention that we were ready to play according to the referee's demands, and if the other team isn't ready that is noted to the official that we met their expectancy of being on the field on time! Things are much easier when there is a full 15 minute half time. We leave the "One for the Gipper" speeches for the Hollywood movies and try to stick to specific cognitive tactics that will help us win the game. Hopefully this empowers players to have data oriented suggestions as well.

Uniforms, practice gear and similar items, players are granted considerable leeway in terms of **choices**. Unfortunately, dollar amounts often require placing parameters on the choices that players can make, but in my experience this has never been a problem.

By not interfering with the officials calls, and encouraging captains to speak politely to the officials so that the teams concerns are duly noted also empowers players. This requires ongoing instruction, although it is surprising how able players become in this regard when empowered to do so.

At the earliest age that you can be successful in informing players of practice times and games, by all means do so. Too often responsibility parents are addressed instead of players. This is actually easier than one might think even for a 10 or 11 year old since game schedules are often handed out and on the internet. Also, practice times for most teams are regularly scheduled for certain days at a particular time. Absolutely practice apparel items should be the responsibility of the player at an early age. Regular lateness without a valid excuse should be dealt with some consternation as this impacts the other players development to benefit from the training. One technique is to have the player request to join in before stopping and explaining what he/she should do.

Instead of assigning corner kicks, penalty kicks see who comes forward to take on these responsibilities.

For the 3 or 4 aside tournament practices have the players make up the teams. Assign an allotted amount of time, roughly five minutes and give a warning once three minutes have elapsed so that the team can complete the task in a reasonable amount of time.

Pairs coaching discussed earlier in the text can have the players decide for themselves what skill they need to improve and who they are going to work with to accomplish the tasks. Sure there will be problems in the early stages of giving ownership, but that is mostly due to the fact that previously they were so spoon fed that it becomes part of their expectancies.

When coaching the high school varsity team Saturday practices were decided by the players. Occasionally Saturday was demanded. The time of Saturday practice if assigned by me allowed players to choose the time. Generally the only guide line might have been that it had to be in the morning. Still they were able to pick the time of the session giving them some ownership of the session.

If you plan to give some ownership of the team to players it needs to be clarified at the preseason meeting so that all concerned know what you are doing. Otherwise a degree of misunderstanding will take place; many will think you are a poor administrator if your program is not made clear to all concerned early on. Many helicopter parents do not understand the necessity of giving responsibility to players, especially those in their teens.

I am certain that many readers have used other techniques not mentioned here, but the concept is made clear by its title and the activities listed. Many would not do many of the items listed as it is not possible, makes them too uncomfortable or time constraints make it impossible. Also, some of the listed items are inappropriate for certain age levels. Therefore the entire domain is left for the judgment of the individual coach. There is no prescription that can be made, but it represents a general menu of some possibilities to be considered. Certainly, giving some ownership to players of their game will pay big dividends in the future of their soccer playing, and even have excellent transfer to their general life skills.

Bear in mind that taking ownership of your coaching is just as important as turning some ownership of the game to players. Sure we are all going to learn from as many sources as humanly possible, but in the end we must be consistent with our own personality, view of the game and view of our deepest purposes for coaching. Hopefully, somewhere in that ownership there is fun, sportsmanship, soccer development, hard work, etc. None of this precludes winning, but it does preclude winning at all costs! Interestingly enough as players get older the ownership given them will yield victories that never would have happened had they not been given ownership earlier in their playing careers.

It is also the mark of an accomplished coach who finds ways to empower assistants, including parent administrators for logistics and social events. Empowerment does not mean carte blanche assignment and then forgetting the item. Generally timely follow-up regarding assigned or assumed tasks is one of the many roles of a leader. Successful organizations still requires leadership, but dictatorship in a democratic society does not prepare young people or other adults for the roles to be played in this society. Checks and balances to insure that all details are attended to does not detract from empowerment. The job may not get done the way you wanted it to be done, but if it is done well, that's all that counts. Micro managing is not the sign of good leadership. Good leadership manages to have a smooth successful organization with all members of the 'team' getting their task done effectively regardless of their style.

At first it is time consuming, but after a season or two the time savings are enormous. Once the foundation is set players will step up to lead, 'sell' ideas to teammates and simply allow things to get done with much less backfire and discontentment.

Appendix III
Fun Soccer Games

Some coaches insert fun games into practice and pre-game routines that have nothing to do with improvement of soccer. Admittedly many are fun games, but there are so many fun games that improve soccer skills, that pure fun games unrelated to soccer are unnecessary. It merely is time wasted that could be better used to improve soccer, which is what the child signed up for. There are many such games, but this selection is sure to raise the level of motivation of your players while still accomplishing soccer skills.

Throw-catch is a game that instead of using the feet the players use their hands. This translates into soccer by increasing the speed of play, which often is its main purpose. Since the game allows players to physically tackle each other it also helps players reduce their fear of contact. It is also an excellent game for support because players simply want the ball. If by some chance, though this is very seldom problem a player intentionally holds the ball to get tackled, merely remove them from the game for a few minutes. If you feel it necessary to explain to them why they were removed by all means do so. Generally throw-catch is merely a possession game. Anytime the ball is out of the control of anyone, whoever gets it first, it is that teams ball.

A version that the rules remain the same but promotes heading is referred to as **throw-head-catch** which varies from a possession game to scoring across a goal line. The game progresses from throw to head to a teammate who catches the ball and when headed over the goal line to a teammate who catches the ball a goal is scored. Both of these games have been done with more than 50 teams of varying ages and never has it failed to provide enthusiasm to the players. As in the actual game of soccer promote long balls that break pressure effectively. Compliment both the user for their vision of seeing the far away player and the far away player's patience for getting free at a significant distance from the ball.

A third version is throw-catch but the ball is passed to a teammate by throwing the ball through one's own legs. This was seen as part of the warm-up for a Danish professional match. I guess the message is that even professional players need to enjoy the game in order to perform at their best. Should young players have less fun?

Safe areas tag generally has every player with a ball and dribbling. In the corners of the grid about 20 yards square, depending on the number of players and ability, there are four corner grids of 2 x 2 yards. Only one player can be in the square at any given moment so that when another player comes into the box the original occupant must leave. Have the "It" player carrying a vest, and when she/he tags someone throw down the vest so the "It" player must pick it up. No tagging back is generally required. Requires at least 8 players with four boxes. With less simply reduce the number of safe areas. With large groups have two players who are "It". Excellent for dribbling, vision, changes of direction, acceleration and most of all fun.

Moving goal(s) has many variations. Most common is two teams with neutral players carrying the moving goal. Scoring is simply shooting through the goal or more demanding passing to a teammate through the moving goal. With large numbers with two goals each team can have two players tending the moving goal. Obviously the teams score on the opposing team's goal. The goal is best made of a pool noodle with a rope threaded through it for safety reasons. Years ago it was played with a stick pole, but I consider that too dangerous in such an exciting game with an enormous amount of players moving in very varied directions. If the goal tenders do not keep the goal at FULL WIDTH simply award a point to the opposing team or with neutral goal tenders simply pick two new goal tenders.

Over-the-Net can be played as volley ball or tennis game that permits a single successive bounce. For high level players it generally is the volley ball version. With ages 8-14 it is often played as tennis with a total of 7 touches on one side of the net, only one successive bounce, and only two touches in succession by any given player. This can be played with 3v3 up to about 6v6 by simply allocation of more space. A very easy way to configure a field is to use yellow danger tape available from any hardware supplier and simply stick a big nail through the tape to attach it to the ground. With sneakers it could be done on a regular tennis court, but it is a much better game with a higher net available through many sources. Epic Sports has one that is adjustable for tennis or volleying. Possibly the most valuable skill acquisition is determining which body part to use for most effective control. This skill is critical in actual games as the choice of the most functional body part usage often determines the success of the ball collection.

Simply having an entire session of a **3v3 or 4v4 tournament**, which allows the ball and game to all of the teaching is hard to beat. It embodies many of the great benefits of street soccer that is so often touted as being a powerful teacher of the game as well as foster player creativity. Coach or player determined teams are both very effective. Have no concern for odd numbers as neutrals or even 4v3 or whatever takes care of the problem. Everyone must be playing as it is necessary to allow for rest time and hydration between games so that the level of play is the best that it can be. Winners, ties and losers compete against each other. Games of anywhere from 8 to 12 minutes are effective. Generally played without keepers and using goals of about 4' x 6'. If equipment is a problem one group can be on large goals with keepers or simply have a group on a single large goal and play half court game in which upon turnovers the ball must be taken out to 20 yards before the attack begins.

Viewager Heading is played on 3 x 6 yard grid with 2 players on each team. Teammates use underhand service and partner heads the ball below head height of the players defending the goal line. Defending team is standing on the goal line and may not use their hands to defend the goal line.

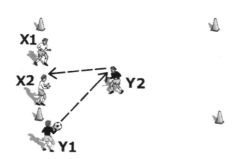

Y1 serves a hand service head ball to Y2 who attempts to head the ball past the two X players who are defending their goal line. After the shot anyone can retrieve the ball and it is their possession to set up a similar head ball shot. If X's got the ball then the Y players will defend the goal line on the right side of the diagram. If defenders have a hand ball then they must put an ear on the cone and have their body stretching across the goal line. The opposing team gets to shoot a head ball shot, but in order to score it must be below knee height. The benefit of this game is that no one seems to refuse or even shy away from heading the ball with power in order to score. You can tell it is a great game by the sound of communication and joyous laughter. Winners against winner with about 6 minute games. The first time the game is introduced play for at least 10 minutes so that they get the rules and rhythm of the game. The first time may require more than one coach to keep each group working successfully. It may be a good idea while other players are drinking to set up a demonstration group that gets their drinks at a later time. This technique of time usage is often effective! Technically coach proper forehead location, use of abdominal muscles and arms, eyes open before the ball is contacted and in time demand high line drive ball service requiring jumping by the heading player.

Hit the garbage can scrimmage provides variety for a game that simply is a lot of fun. Best with less than 11 players with a circle of cones around the garbage can that are about two yards away that constitutes a no goal keeping area. Provides many shooting opportunities that demand a degree of accuracy and rapid changes in point of attack. Generally played without a keeper.

Shooting Galore is a two touch shooting game mostly focused on ages 7- 11. Two obstacle course markers are placed about 3 yards apart as shown.

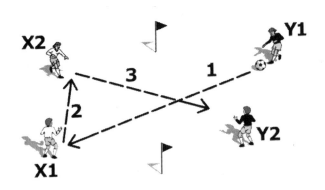

Y1 has just taken a shot, X1 has defended the shot and must one touch it to X2 for a one touch shot. The game is all about learning how to setup a teammate for a shot. Only 2 touches are permitted on each side and both players must touch the ball by either setting up the teammate of taking the shot. With younger players allow two touches for setting up the shot. Another version is to have one player immediately become a goal keeper after her teammate took a shot. When the shot is saved the ball is sent to teammate who can one touch shoot or return the ball to the saving keeper for a shot. No shots can be taken from closer than 8 yards which is marked on the ground with a vest. Play to games of 6 minutes each or a score of 10.

Relay races with the ball always seem to be favorite with players. Dribbling around a cone about 10 to 20 yards away is common. Avoid two teams and use pairs instead since that provides more ball contact and no waste of time.

Other exciting games are found in the "Shooting, Strictly Shooting" chapter of the book. Particularly Peter Duckworth Shooting, Goal Line Numbers Shooting, Gate Keeper, Kings and several others. Keeping interest up and somehow accomplishing the ultimate goal of getting players to touch the ball and play little games on their own requires these motivating games. In the words of Hubert Vogelsinger we must romance players to the game. Any coach who can get players to do things on their own and take ownership of their game has done an outstanding job which will accrue great benefits to the players' development.

Bibliography

Caruso, Andrew. **Soccer Coaching: Ages 5-12**. 1st ed. Reedswain, 1992. Print.

Caruso, Andrew. **The Great Game: Development and Tactics**. 1st ed. Reedswain, 1992. Print.

Caruso, Andrew. **Soccer's Dynamic Short Sided Games**. 1st ed. Reedswain, 1995. Print.

Caruso, Andrew. **Sports Psychology Basics**. 2nd ed. Reedswain, 2012. Print.

DiCicco, Tony, Colleen Hacker, and Charles Salzberg. **Catch Them Being Good: Everything You Need to Know to Successfully Coach Girls**. New York, NY: Viking, 2002. Print.

Dorrance, Anson. **Training Soccer Champions**. Cary, NC: JTC Sports, 1996. Print.

Michels, Rinus. **Teambuilding: The Road to Success**. 1st ed. Reedswain, 2001. Print.

Made in the USA
San Bernardino, CA
22 April 2018